TRIED BY WAR

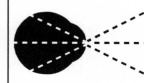

This Large Print Book carries the
Seal of Approval of N.A.V.H.

TRIED BY WAR

ABRAHAM LINCOLN AS COMMANDER IN CHIEF

JAMES M. MCPHERSON

THORNDIKE PRESS
A part of Gale, Cengage Learning

GALE
CENGAGE Learning™

Detroit • New York • San Francisco • New Haven, Conn • Waterville, Maine • London

Copyright © James M. McPherson, 2008. $32.00
Map by Jeffrey L. Ward.
Thorndike Press, a part of Gale, Cengage Learning.

LP
973.7
mcp

ALL RIGHTS RESERVED
Thorndike Press® Large Print Nonfiction.
The text of this Large Print edition is unabridged.
Other aspects of the book may vary from the original edition.
Set in 16 pt. Plantin.
Printed on permanent paper.

LIBRARY OF CONGRESS CATALOGING-IN-PUBLICATION DATA

McPherson, James M.
    Tried by war : Abraham Lincoln as commander in chief / by
James M. McPherson.
      p. cm.
    ISBN-13: 978-1-4104-1339-0 (hardcover : alk. paper : large
print)
    ISBN-10: 1-4104-1339-X (hardcover : alk. paper : large print)
    1. Lincoln, Abraham, 1809–1865—Military leadership.
2. United States—History—Civil War, 1861–1865. 3. United
States—Politics and government—1861–1865. 4. Executive
power—United States—History—19th century. 5. Presidents—
United States—Biography. 6. Large type books. I. Title.
E457.2.M478 2008b
973.7092—dc22
    [B]   2008045104

Published in 2009 by arrangement with The Penguin Press, a member
of Penguin Group (USA) Inc.

Printed in the United States of America
1 2 3 4 5 6 7 13 12 11 10 09

To Pat, for fifty years of
marriage and history

The insurgent leader . . . does not attempt to deceive us. He affords us no excuse to deceive ourselves. He can not voluntarily reaccept the Union; we can not voluntarily yield it. Between him and us the issue is distinct, simple, and inflexible. It is an issue which can only be tried by war and decided by victory.

— Lincoln's annual message
to Congress, December 6, 1864

CONTENTS

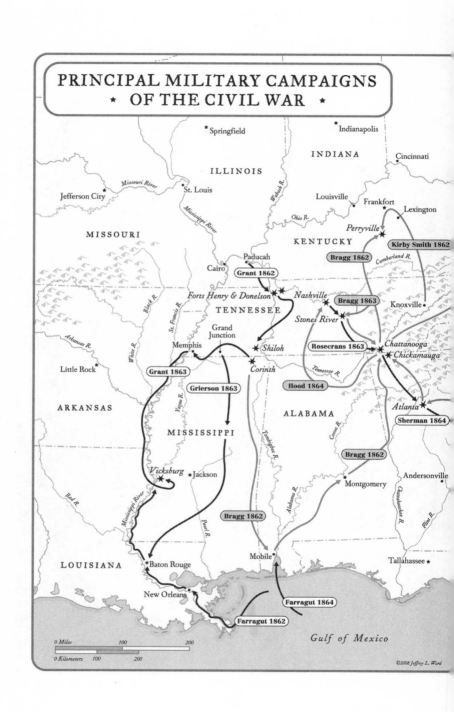

PRINCIPAL MILITARY CAMPAIGNS
★ OF THE CIVIL WAR ★

★ Springfield

★ Indianapolis

INDIANA

Cincinnati ★

ILLINOIS

Missouri River

Jefferson City ★

★ St. Louis

Louisville

Frankfort

Lexington

Mississippi River

MISSOURI

Ohio R.

Perryville

KENTUCKY

Kirby Smith 1862

Paducah

Cumberland R.

Bragg 1862

Cairo ★

Grant 1862

Forts Henry & Donelson ★★★

Nashville

Bragg 1863

Knoxville ★

TENNESSEE

Stones River

Black R.

Grand Junction

St. Francis R.

Arkansas R.

Memphis ★

★ Shiloh

Rosecrans 1863

Chattanooga
★ Chickamauga

White R.

Little Rock ★

Grant 1863

Corinth

Tennessee R.

Grierson 1863

Hood 1864

ARKANSAS

Yazoo R.

ALABAMA

Atlanta ★

MISSISSIPPI

Sherman 1864

Coosa R.

Bragg 1862

Andersonville ★

Vicksburg ★

★ Jackson

Chattahoochee R.

Montgomery

Red R.

Flint R.

Tombigbee R.

Alabama R.

Mississippi River

Bragg 1862

Tallahassee ★

LOUISIANA

★ Baton Rouge

Pearl R.

Mobile ★

New Orleans ★

Farragut 1864

Farragut 1862

Gulf of Mexico

| 0 Miles | 100 | 200 |
| 0 Kilometers | 100 | 200 |

©2008 Jeffrey L. Ward

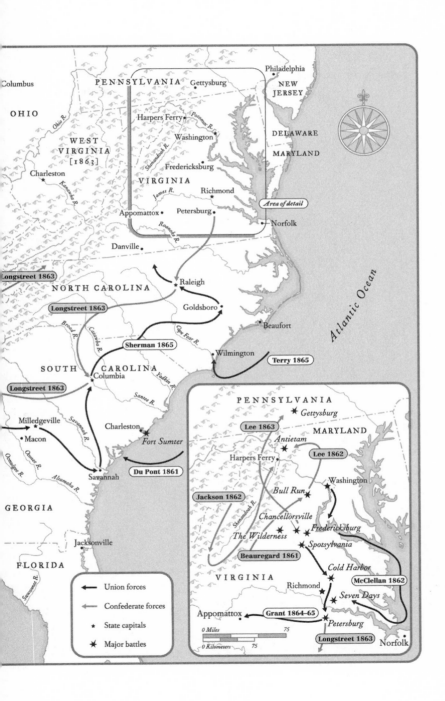

PREFACE

Abraham Lincoln was the only president in American history whose entire administration was bounded by war. On the day he took office the first document placed on his desk was a letter from Maj. Robert Anderson at Fort Sumter, informing him that the garrison there must be withdrawn or resupplied at the risk of war. Lincoln chose to take that risk. Four years later he was assassinated, five days after Gen. Robert E. Lee surrendered at Appomattox but while several Confederate armies were still in the field.

During those four years military matters required more of Lincoln's time and energy than anything else. He spent more time in the War Department telegraph office sending and receiving messages to and from his generals than anywhere else except the White House or his summer residence in the Soldiers' Home at the northern edge of

Washington. The president rarely left Washington except to visit the Army of the Potomac at the front, which he did eleven times for a total of forty-two days. Not only Lincoln's success or failure as president but also the very survival of the United States depended on how he performed his duties as commander in chief.

In the vast literature on our sixteenth president, however, the amount of attention devoted to his role as commander in chief is disproportionately far smaller than the actual percentage of time he spent on that task. On the 175th anniversary of Lincoln's birth in 1984, Gettysburg College hosted a conference on recent Lincoln scholarship. There were three sessions on psychobiography, two on the assassination, two on Lincoln's image in photographs and popular prints, and one each on his economic ideas, humor, Indian policy, and slavery. But there were no sessions on Lincoln as commander in chief — a remarkable irony, given the site of the conference. Of the seventeen collected essays on Lincoln published in 1987 by the late Don E. Fehrenbacher, one of the foremost Lincoln scholars of his time, not one dealt with the president as a military leader. In 1994 the historian Merrill Peterson published a splendid book on Lincoln's image in history and memory. There are chapters on Lincoln and the South, religion, politics, Reconstruction, civil rights, and several other themes, but no chapter on Lincoln and the army.[1]

Perhaps it is time to recognize the truth expressed by Lincoln himself in his second inaugural address, when the Civil War had been raging for almost four years: On "the progress of our arms . . . all else chiefly depends."[2] "All else" included many of the questions and developments that historians consider important: the fate of slavery; the definition of freedom; the destruction of the Old South's socio-economic system and the triumph of entrepreneurial free-labor capitalism as the national norm; a new definition of American nationalism; the origins of a new system of race relations; the very survival of the United States in a manner that laid the foundations for the nation's emergence as a world power.

It was the commander in chief who was held mainly responsible for "the progress of our arms" — or the lack thereof. This book offers a narrative and analysis of how — and how well — Lincoln met this challenge, which was unquestionably the chief challenge of his life and of the life of the nation.

NOTE ON QUOTATIONS

Original spellings and punctuation have been preserved in quotations without inserting the intrusive "[*sic*]."

INTRODUCTION

On July 27, 1848, a tall, rawboned Whig congressman from Illinois rose in the House of Representatives to challenge the Mexican War policies of President James K. Polk. An opponent of what he considered an unjust war, Abraham Lincoln mocked his own meager record as a militia captain who saw no action in the Black Hawk War of 1832. "By the way, Mr. Speaker, did you know I am a military hero?" said Lincoln. "Yes, sir . . . I fought, bled, and came away" after "charges upon the wild onions" and "a good many struggles with the musketoes."[1]

Lincoln might not have indulged his famous sense of humor in this fashion if he had known that thirteen years later he would become commander in chief of the U.S. Army in a war that turned out to be forty-seven times more lethal for American soldiers than the Mexican War. On his way to Washington in February 1861 as president-elect of a broken nation, Lincoln spoke in a far more serious manner. He looked back on another war, which had given birth to the nation that now seemed in danger of perishing from the earth. In a speech to the New Jersey legislature in Trenton, Lincoln recalled the story of George Washington and his tiny army, which crossed the ice-choked Delaware River in a driving sleet storm on Christmas night in 1776 to attack the Hessian garrison in Trenton. "There must have been something more than common that those men struggled for," said the president-elect. "Something even more than National Independence . . . something that held out a great promise to all the people of the world for all time to come. I am exceedingly anxious that the Union, the Constitution, and the liberties of the people shall be perpetuated in accordance with the original idea for which that struggle was made."[2]

Lincoln faced a steep learning curve as commander in chief in the war that began less than two months after that speech at Trenton. He was also painfully aware that his adversary, Jefferson Davis, was much better prepared for that daunting task. A graduate of the U.S. Military Academy at West Point, Davis had fought courageously as a colonel of a Mississippi regiment in the Mexican War and had served as an excellent secretary of war from 1853 to 1857 — while Lincoln's only military experience was his combat with mosquitoes in 1832. Lincoln possessed a keen analytical mind, however, and a fierce determination to master any subject to which he applied himself. This determination went back to his childhood. "Among my earliest recollections," Lincoln told an acquaintance in 1860, "I remember how, when a mere child, I used to get irritated when anybody talked to me in a way I could not understand." Lincoln recalled "going to my little bedroom, after hearing the neighbors talk of an evening with my father, and spending the night walking up and down, and trying to make out what was the exact meaning of some of their, to me, dark sayings. I could not sleep . . . when I got on such a hunt after an idea, until I had caught it. . . . This was a kind of passion with me, and it has stuck by me." Later in life Lincoln mastered Euclidean geometry on his own for mental exercise. As a largely self-taught lawyer, he honed this quality of mind. He was not a quick study but a thorough one. "I am never easy," he said, "when I am handling a thought, till I have bounded it North, and bounded it South, and bounded it East, and bounded it West."[3]

Several contemporaries testified to the slow but tenacious qualities of Lincoln's mind. The mercurial editor of the *New York Tribune,* Horace Greeley, noted that Lincoln's intellect worked "not quickly nor brilliantly, but exhaustively." Lincoln's law partner William Herndon sometimes expressed impatience with Lincoln's deliberate manner of researching or arguing a case. But Herndon conceded that his partner "not only went to the root of the question, but dug up the root, and separated and analyzed every fibre of it."[4] Lincoln also focused intently on the central issue in a legal case and refused to be distracted by secondary questions. Another fellow lawyer noted that Lincoln would concede nonessential points to an opponent in the courtroom, lulling him into a sense of complacency. But "by giving away six points and carrying the seventh he carried his case . . . the whole case hanging on the seventh. . . . Any man who took Lincoln for a simple-minded man would very soon wake up with his back in a ditch."[5]

As commander in chief Lincoln sought to master the intricacies of military strategy in the same way he had tried to penetrate the meaning of mysterious adult conversations when he was a boy. His private secretary John Hay, who lived in the White House, often heard the president walking back and forth in his bedroom at midnight as he digested books on military strategy. "He gave himself, night and day, to the study of the military situation," Hay later wrote. "He read a large number of strategical works. He pored over the reports from the various departments and districts of the field of war. He held long conferences with eminent generals and admirals, and astonished them by the extent of his special knowledge and the keen intelligence of his questions." Some of those generals, like Lincoln's courtroom adversaries, eventually found themselves on their backs in a ditch. By 1862 Lincoln's grasp of military strategy and operations was firm enough almost to justify the assertion of the historian T. Harry Williams: "Lincoln stands out as a great war president, probably the greatest in our history, and a great natural strategist, a better one than any of his generals."[6]

This encomium is misleading in one respect: Lincoln was not a "natural strategist." He worked hard to master this subject, just as he had done to become a lawyer. He had to learn the functions of commander in chief on the job. The Constitution and the course of American history before 1861 did not offer much guidance. Article II, Section 2, of the Constitution states simply: "The President shall be Commander in Chief of the Army and Navy of the United States, and of the Militia of the several States, when called into the actual Service of the United States." But the Constitution nowhere defines the powers of the president as commander in chief. In *Federalist No. 69,* Alexander Hamilton tried to reassure opponents of the Constitution, who feared executive tyranny, that the commander-in-chief power "would amount to nothing more than the supreme command and direction of the military forces, as first General and Admiral" of the nation.

Hamilton's phrase "supreme command and direction" seems quite forceful, but it lacks specificity. Nor did the precedents created by Presidents James Madison and James K. Polk in the War of 1812 and the Mexican War provide Lincoln with much guidance in a far greater conflict that combined the most dangerous aspects of an internal war and a war against another nation. In a case growing out of the Mexican War, the Supreme Court ruled that the president as commander in chief was authorized to employ the army and navy "in the manner he may deem most effectual to harass and conquer and subdue the enemy." But the Court did not define "most effectual" and seemed to limit the president's power by stating that it must be confined to "purely military matters."[7]

The vagueness of these definitions and precedents meant that Lincoln would have to establish most of the powers of commander in chief for himself. He proved to be a more hands-on commander in chief than any other president. He performed or oversaw five wartime functions in this capacity, in diminishing order of personal involvement: policy, national strategy, military strategy, operations, and tactics. Neither Lincoln nor anyone else defined these functions in a systematic way during the Civil War. If they had, their definitions might have looked something like the following: *Policy* refers to war aims — the political goals of the nation in time of war. *National strategy* refers to mobilization of the political, economic, diplomatic, and psychological as well as military resources of the nation to achieve these war aims. *Military strategy* concerns plans for the employment of armed forces to win the war and fulfill the goals of policy. *Operations* concerns the management and movements of armies in particular campaigns to carry out the purposes of military strategy. *Tactics* refers to the formations and handling of an army in actual battle.

As president and leader of his party as well as commander in chief, Lincoln was principally responsible for shaping and defining policy. From first to last that policy was preservation of the United States as one nation, indivisible, and as a republic based on majority rule. In May 1861 Lincoln explained that "the central idea pervading this struggle is the necessity that is upon us, of proving that popular government is not an absurdity. We must settle this question now, whether in a free government the majority have the right to break up the government whenever they choose." Secession "is the essence of anarchy," said Lincoln on another occasion, for if one state may secede at will, so may any other until there is no government and no nation.[8] In the Gettysburg Address, Lincoln offered his most eloquent statement of policy: The war was a test whether the nation conceived in 1776 "might live" or would "perish from the earth." The question of national sovereignty over a union of all the states was nonnegotiable. No compromise between a sovereign United States and a separately sovereign Confederate States was possible. This issue "is distinct, simple, and inflexible," said Lincoln in 1864. "It is an issue which can only be tried by war, and decided by victory."[9]

Lincoln's frequent statements of this policy were themselves distinct and inflexible. And policy was closely tied to national strategy. Indeed, in a *civil* war whose origins lay in a political conflict over the future of slavery and a political decision by certain states to secede, policy could never be separated from national strategy. The president shared with Congress and key cabinet members the tasks of raising, organizing, and sustaining an army and navy, preventing foreign intervention in the conflict, and maintaining public support for the war — all of which depended on the public's support of the purpose for which the war was fought. And neither policy nor national strategy could be separated from military strategy. Although Lincoln never read Carl von Clausewitz's famous treatise *On War* (*Vom Kriege*), his actions were a consummate expression of Clausewitz's central argument: "The political objective is the goal, war is the means of reaching it, and means can never be considered in isolation from their purpose. . . . Therefore, it is clear that war should never be thought of as *something autonomous* but always as an *instrument* of policy."[10]

Some professional army officers did in fact tend to think of war as "something autonomous" and deplored the intrusion of politics into military matters. Soon after he came to Washington as general-in-chief in August 1862, Maj. Gen. Henry W. Halleck began complaining (privately) about "political wire-pulling in military appointments. . . . I have done everything in my power here to separate military appointments and commands from politics, but really the task is hopeless." If the "incompetent and corrupt politicians," he told another general, "would only follow the example of their ancestors, enter a herd of swine, run down some steep bank and drown themselves in the sea, there would be some hope of saving the country."[11]

But Lincoln could never ignore the political context in which decisions about military strategy were made. Like French premier Georges Clemenceau a half century later, he knew that war was too important to be left to the generals. In a highly politicized and democratic society where the mobilization of a volunteer army was channeled through state governments, political considerations inevitably shaped the scope and timing of military strategy and even of operations. As leader of the party that controlled Congress and most state governments, Lincoln as commander in chief constantly had to juggle the complex interplay of policy, national strategy, and military strategy.

The slavery issue provides an example of this interplay. The goal of preserving the Union united the Northern people, including border-state Unionists. The issue of slavery and emancipation divided them. To maintain maximum support for the war, Lincoln initially insisted that it was a war solely for preservation of the Union and not a war against slavery. This policy required both a national and a military strategy of leaving slavery alone. But the slaves refused to cooperate. They confronted the administration with the problem of what to do with the thousands of "contrabands" who came within Union lines. As it became increasingly clear that slave labor sustained the Confederate economy and the logistics of Confederate armies, Northern opinion moved toward the idea of making it a war against slavery. By 1862 a national and military strategy that targeted enemy resources — including slavery — emerged as a key weapon in the Union arsenal. With the Emancipation Proclamation and the Republican commitment to a constitutional amendment to abolish slavery, the policy of a war for Union *and* freedom came into harmony with the national and military strategies of striking against the vital Confederate resource of slave labor. Lincoln's skillful management of this contentious process was a crucial part of his war leadership.

In the realm of military strategy and operations, Lincoln initially deferred to General-in-Chief Winfield Scott, a hero of the War of 1812 and the Mexican War. But Scott's advanced age, poor health, and lack of energy made it clear that he could not run this war. His successor, Gen. George B. McClellan, proved an even greater disappointment to Lincoln. Nor did Gens. Henry W. Halleck, Don Carlos Buell, John Pope, Ambrose E. Burnside, Joseph Hooker, or William S. Rosecrans measure up to initial expectations. Their shortcomings compelled Lincoln to become in effect his own general-in-chief as well as commander in chief during key campaigns. Lincoln sometimes even became involved in operations planning and offered astute suggestions to which his generals should perhaps have paid more heed.

Even after Ulysses S. Grant became general-in-chief in March 1864, Lincoln maintained a significant degree of strategic oversight — especially concerning events in the Shenandoah Valley during the late summer of 1864. The president did not become directly involved at the tactical level — though he was sorely tempted to do so when Gen. George G. Meade hesitated to attack Robert E. Lee 's Army of Northern Virginia, trapped with its back to the Potomac River after Gettysburg. At all levels of policy, strategy, and operations, however, Lincoln was a hands-on commander in chief who persisted through a terrible ordeal of defeats and disappointments to final triumph — and tragedy — at the end. Here is that story.

1
THE QUEST FOR A STRATEGY, 1861

From the moment of his election as president on November 6, 1860, Lincoln confronted issues of policy and strategy even though he would not take office for almost four months. The South Carolina legislature immediately called a convention to take the state out of the Union. Within six weeks six more legislatures in the lower South had done the same. Each convention voted by a substantial margin to secede. As they did so, their militias seized federal forts, arsenals, and other property. In February 1861, a month before Lincoln's inauguration, delegates from these seven states met in Montgomery, Alabama, to form a new nation they called the Confederate States of America. Lame-duck president James Buchanan maintained that secession was unconstitutional, but wrung his hands and said that he could not do anything about it. Spokesmen for the eight upper-South and border slave states still in the Union threatened also to go out if the government tried to "coerce" the seceded states.

Without power to do anything before he took office, Lincoln nevertheless began to explore what his options would be when he legally became commander in chief on March 4, 1861. "Ours should be a government of fraternity," he acknowledged in conversations with his private secretary John Nicolay in November and December 1860. "The necessity of keeping the Government together by force" was an "ugly point." Still, "the very existence of a general and national government implies the legal power, right, and duty of maintaining its own integrity." The president-elect insisted that "the right of a State to secede is not an open or debatable question. . . . It is the duty of a President to execute the laws and maintain the existing Government. He cannot entertain any proposition for dissolution or dismemberment."[1]

Lincoln never deviated from these principles. But the hard question was how to carry them into practice. In December he sent word to General-in-Chief Scott through congressmen and other leaders in Washington to be prepared to retake any forts seized by secessionist militia. When rumors reached Lincoln that President James Buchanan had ordered Maj. Robert Anderson, commander of the U.S. garrison at Fort Moultrie, on the shore of Charleston Bay, to evacuate the fort, the angry president-elect exclaimed: "If that is true, they ought to hang him!"[2] The rumor was not true, but several days later Anderson moved the garrison to Fort Sumter, situated on an artificial island in the bay and much more secure from attack than Fort Moultrie.

Meanwhile two powerful editorials appeared in the *Illinois Daily State Journal,* a Springfield newspaper that spoke for Lincoln — in fact, he may have written them. If South Carolina tried to resist the collection of customs revenue at its ports, "any resistance on her part will lead to war. . . . The laws of the United States must be executed. . . . Disunion by armed force is treason, and treason must be put down at all hazards. . . . If ten thousand armed men are necessary to execute the laws of Congress within a State," so be it.[3]

There was one problem with all of this tough talk: There were nowhere near ten thousand federal troops available. The garrison at Fort Sumter totaled about eighty soldiers. The whole U.S. Army numbered only sixteen thousand men, and most of them were scattered at frontier posts up to three thousand miles from Charleston. And Lincoln was acutely aware that a third of their officers were from the South, including a disproportionate number of high-ranking officers. As a loyal captain had informed Lincoln in October 1860, the secretary of war and the general-in-chief (Winfield Scott, who was, however, unquestionably loyal) were Virginians; every one of the chiefs of military bureaus in Washington was a Virginian or married to one; the colonels of four of the five cavalry and dragoon regiments were Southerners; and the commanders of three of the army's most important geographical departments were Virginians.[4] Virginia was still in the Union at the end of 1860, but its political leaders had made it clear that any hint of carrying out the kind of "coercion" that Lincoln and his associates were discussing would drive it into secession.

Lincoln was loath to take such threats seriously. He believed that an underlying Unionism remained strong in slave states — even those that had seceded. On his way to Washington in February 1861 he gave numerous short speeches. Their main thrust was an effort to calm passions in both North and South and to convince Southerners that he intended no threat to slavery in their states. But the president-elect kept alive the military option — to the clear approval of his audiences. At Indianapolis he asked the crowd: If the government "simply insists upon holding its own forts, or retaking those forts that belong to it, [cheers] or the enforcement of the laws of the United States in the collection of duties upon foreign importations, [renewed cheers] . . . would any or all of these things be coercion?" At Philadelphia and Harrisburg, Lincoln tried to assure those who deplored the prospect of war that "there will be no blood shed unless it be forced upon the Government. The Government will not use force unless force is used against it. . . . I shall endeavor to preserve the peace of this country so far as it can possibly be done, consistently with the maintenance of the institutions of the country."[5]

Those who noted the qualifying clauses in these sentences may not have been reassured. And their doubts would have been greater if they heard the following words in a second speech that Lincoln delivered in Harrisburg, to the General Assembly: "It is not with any pleasure that I contemplate the possibility that a necessity may arise in this country for the use of the military arm.

[Applause]." At the New Jersey capital in Trenton, after recalling the heroic sacrifices of soldiers in the Revolution, Lincoln hinted that another war might be necessary to save the nation to which they had given birth. "I shall do all that may be in my power to promote a peaceful settlement of all our difficulties," Lincoln said eleven days before his inauguration. "But it may be necessary to put the foot down firmly." The *New York Tribune* reporter who took down this speech interjected that "here the audience broke out in cheers so loud and long that for some moments it was impossible to hear Mr. L's voice." Lincoln was finally able to continue: "And if I do my duty, and do right, you will sustain me, will you not? [Loud cheers, and cries of "Yes," "Yes," "We will."]"[6]

While he was making these speeches, Lincoln had his forthcoming inaugural address very much on his mind. He knew that every word would be scrutinized as if with a microscope for clues to his intentions. He had written a draft in Springfield before departing for Washington. He showed it to Secretary of State–designate William H. Seward, whom Lincoln had edged out for the presidential nomination, and to Orville Browning, a close friend who would soon become a senator from Illinois. Both urged

Lincoln to modify one of the key sentences in his draft, which stated: "All the power at my disposal will be used to reclaim the property and places which have fallen; to hold, occupy and possess these, and all other property and places belonging to the government, and to collect the duties on imports; but beyond what may be necessary for these, there will be no invasion of any State." Believing that these bellicose words would drive the upper South into secession and ruin any hope of bringing out the supposed latent Unionism in Confederate states, Seward recommended striking out the whole sentence. Lincoln was unwilling to go that far, but he did adopt Browning's suggestion to delete the reference to *retaking* federal property and instead to say simply that the administration would "hold, occupy, and possess the property, and places belonging to the government."[7]

Many people in the South would have perceived this change as a distinction without a difference. On the day of Lincoln's inauguration the government held only Fort Sumter; Fort Pickens on an island off the port of Pensacola; and two minor forts in the Florida Keys. Fort Sumter had long since become the flash point of possible war. Confederate artillery ringed the bay with dozens of big guns ranged on the thick brick walls of the fort. To "hold, occupy and possess" Sumter and probably Pickens would require large reinforcements if the Confederate government decided to back demands for their surrender with force.

An uneasy truce had existed for almost two months at both Charleston and Pensacola as the Buchanan administration came to an end on March 4. But on Lincoln's first full day in office it became clear that the status quo could not last much longer. A letter from Major Anderson landed on the new president's desk informing him that the Sumter garrison would run out of provisions in a month or six weeks.[8] Lincoln had to make his first — and one of his most important — decisions as commander in chief. Would he keep his inaugural vow to "hold, occupy and possess" at the risk of starting a war that might drive the rest of the slave states into the Confederacy? Or would he heed the advice of the Southern Unionists, Northern conservatives, and his own secretary of state — who considered himself the "premier" of Lincoln's administration — and withdraw the troops to preserve the peace?

The withdrawal option was extremely distasteful to Lincoln — and to a majority of his party. Nevertheless he apparently explored the option, in return for a significant quid pro quo. The largest and most strategically situated slave state was Virginia. When Lincoln arrived in Washington, a Virginia convention was meeting in Richmond to decide whether to secede. The rest of the upper South would undoubtedly follow its example. In these circumstances Lincoln met with two Virginia delegates to a "Peace Convention" in Washington a week before his inauguration. According to his own recollection and those of others, he offered to withdraw the troops from Fort Sumter if the Richmond convention would dissolve without seceding. Several weeks later Lincoln reportedly repeated the offer to a delegate from the Richmond convention, saying that "a State for a fort is no bad business." The Virginians, however, said they had no power to make such a commitment, and the proposed deal — if there was one — fell through. Whether Lincoln made such a proposal, and would have carried it out, must remain forever moot.[9]

The question of a state for a fort apart, Lincoln seemed to have only two options: Pull out, or send in reinforcements and supplies to hold the fort. The countervailing pressures on the new president to do one or the other were so intense that he suffered sleepless nights, severe headaches, and one morning he keeled over in a faint as he tried to get out of bed.[10] During all this time Lincoln also had to cope with swarms of office seekers and patronage-hunting politicians who infested the White House day and night. Looking back in July on those weeks, Lincoln told Senator Orville Browning that "of all the trials I have had since I came here, none begin to compare with those I had between the inauguration and the fall of Fort Sumpter. They were so great that could I have anticipated them, I would not have believed it possible to survive them."[11]

Lincoln's trials began when he consulted General-in-Chief Scott about the bombshell letter from Major Anderson stating that he could not hold out for more than six weeks. Scott's advice depressed the president. "I now see no alternative but a surrender," wrote the general, because "we cannot send the third of the men in several months, necessary to give them relief. . . . Evacuation seems almost inevitable . . . if indeed the worn-out garrison be not assaulted and carried in the present week."[12] Lincoln was reluctant to accept this counsel. The next day John Hay, the president's second private secretary, whose opinions often reflected those of his boss, wrote an anonymous editorial in the *New York World* hinting that Lincoln would refuse to evacuate any of the forts still held by the U.S. Army.[13] The president convened his first cabinet meeting on March 9, at which General Scott reportedly said that it would require twenty-five thousand troops and six months or more of preparations to reinforce Fort Sumter. Lincoln asked Scott to put that estimate in writing, which he did.[14]

By this time Lincoln had begun to suspect that Scott's professional opinion was colored by his political convictions. Although loyal, Scott was after all a Virginian who deplored the possibility of fratricidal war in which his native state would become a battleground. He was willing to make large concessions to avert such a calamity. Scott was also influenced by Seward, who had been one of his advisers when the general ran for president (and lost) in 1852. Seward was working behind Lincoln's back leaking information to the press and assuring (through an intermediary) Confederate commissioners that Fort Sumter would soon be evacuated. On March 11 Scott went so far as to draft, on his own authority, an order to Major Anderson to "engage suitable water transportation, & peacefully evacuate Fort Sumter so long and gallantly held." Scott submitted the draft to Secretary of War Simon Cameron, who placed it in Lincoln's hands. The president's reaction was not recorded but can be imagined. Needless to say, the order was never issued.[15]

As the pressures for and against the evacuation of Fort Sumter continued to mount, Lincoln ordered the reinforcement of Fort Pickens so that if he ultimately decided to abandon Sumter, at least one contested symbol of national sovereignty would be maintained. This order miscarried and had to be sent again in April. But Sumter was a far more potent symbol; on its fate hinged the issues of Union or disunion, war or peace. On March 15 Lincoln asked his seven cabinet officers to submit written opinions on the question of evacuating or reinforcing Sumter. Five of them, led by Seward, recommended withdrawal in order to preserve the peace, calm passions, and provide time for Southern Unionism to reassert itself. Secretary of the Treasury Salmon P. Chase supported reinforcement if it would not provoke war — a rather fatuous recommendation under the circumstances. Only Postmaster General Montgomery Blair unequivocally opposed evacuation, because it would "convince the rebels that the administration lacks firmness and will." Instead of encouraging Southern Unionists it would discourage them, strengthen the hold of Confederates on Southern opinion, and cause foreign nations to recognize the Confederacy as a fait accompli. To give up the fort meant giving up the Union.[16]

Lincoln was inclined to think so too. But before deciding what to do, he drafted a memorandum summarizing the pros and cons of evacuating Sumter. In favor of withdrawal, wrote Lincoln in echo of General Scott, was the reality that "the Fort cannot now be reinforced without a large armament, involving of course a bloody conflict," while evacuation "would remove a source of irritation to the Southern people and deprive the secession movement of one of its most powerful stimulants" by "confound-[ing] . . . those enemies of the Union both at the North and the South who have relied on the cry of 'Coercion' as a means of keeping up the excitement against the Republican Party." On the other hand, evacuation would demoralize Lincoln's own party and concede the legitimacy of the Confederacy.[17]

It was this last consideration that was up-

45

permost in Lincoln's mind. He sought a formula that might maintain Sumter as a symbol of national sovereignty without provoking war. By the third week of March he thought he might have found such a formula. Montgomery Blair introduced the president to his brother-in-law Gustavus V. Fox, a Massachusetts businessman and a former naval officer. Fox proposed to run troops and supplies in to Sumter at night on chartered tugs while warships stood by to suppress Confederate artillery if it fired on the tugs. Lincoln was intrigued by the idea. He was also glad to talk with someone who offered a plan by which something *could* be done instead of telling him why it could *not.* But he continued to explore other options while he sent Fox to Charleston to confer with Anderson and sent two other emissaries to gauge opinion in South Carolina.

During the last week of March, Northern opinion seemed to harden against evacuation. So did Lincoln's. The break came on March 28. That day General Scott submitted a memorandum recommending that both Fort Sumter *and* Fort Pickens be evacuated, which would "instantly soothe and give confidence to the eight remaining slave-holding States, and render their cordial adherence to this Union perpetual." The president was angered, though perhaps not entirely surprised, by this new evidence that Scott's supposedly professional military advice was tinged with political considerations. He called Scott into his office and told him bluntly, according to Scott's secretary, that the administration "would be broken up" if he adopted any such policy and that "if General Scott could not carry out his views, some other person might."[18]

That evening the president and Mrs. Lincoln hosted their first state dinner for cabinet officers, foreign diplomats, and other dignitaries. Afterward Lincoln called the cabinet together to inform them of Scott's memorandum. "Blank amazement" registered on several faces as they realized that Scott was advising what amounted to an unconditional surrender. The next day the cabinet met officially at noon. This time all members except Seward and Secretary of the Interior Caleb Smith voted to reinforce Fort Sumter, and all of them voted to renew the stalled effort to reinforce Fort Pickens. Lincoln had already made up his mind to send both expeditions and would undoubtedly have gone ahead even without a cabinet vote. In a message to a special session of Congress three months later, he explained why. To "abandon that position, under the circumstances, would be utterly ruinous," said the president. "At home it would discourage the friends of the Union, embolden its adversaries, and go far to insure to the latter a recognition abroad; that in fact it would be our national destruction consummated."[19]

This decision put Seward in an extremely awkward position. Having assured Confederate commissioners as well as others that the garrison would be withdrawn, and still presuming to be "premier" of the administration, he made one last desperate bid to change Lincoln's mind. On April 1 he wrote a memorandum — which was no April Fools' joke — titled "Some thoughts for the President's consideration." The government had no firm policy, Seward declared, so he suggested one: Abandon Fort Sumter but reinforce Fort Pickens. This, he said mysteriously, would change the issue from slavery to Union. And to reunite the country, Seward suggested a confrontation with foreign nations that were interfering in the Western Hemisphere. Spain had sent troops to troubled Santo Domingo, while France and Britain were threatening to do the same in Mexico to force repayment of debts to their citizens. If such confrontations led to war, so much the better, for the South would return to help fight the foreign foe. "Whatever policy we adopt," wrote the secretary of state, "it must be somebody's business to pursue and direct it." He left no doubt whom he had in mind.[20]

Lincoln was astonished by the effrontery of this document and even more by its proposals. In a written reply he ignored Seward's bellicose recommendations to challenge foreign nations. He declared that the government *did* have a policy: to hold, occupy, and possess its property, including Fort Sumter. "I do not perceive how the reinforcement of Fort Sumpter would be done on a slavery, or party issue," wrote the president, "while that of Fort Pickens would be on a more national, or patriotic one." In any case, whatever policy was decided on and carried out, "I must do it."[21]

Lincoln apparently decided not to send Seward his reply but instead to convey its substance more tactfully in private conversation. Whatever the medium, Seward got the message. Thereafter he became a loyal supporter of the president's policies and a trusted adviser — but not before (perhaps inadvertently) throwing a small monkey wrench into the Fort Sumter enterprise. Because of Lincoln's endless preoccupation with patronage appointments as well as with the Sumter problem, Seward had taken charge of the project to reinforce Fort Pickens. For that purpose he had assigned the most powerful warship intended for the Sumter mission (USS *Powhatan*) to the Pickens expedition. The distracted president had signed orders to that effect without reading them carefully. When the mistake was discovered it proved too late to recall the *Powhatan.* In the end this mix-up made no difference to the outcome of the successful reinforcement of Pickens or the failure at Fort Sumter. But for Lincoln it was part of the steep learning curve he had to climb in his journey toward becoming an effective commander in chief.[22]

On the same chaotic and eventful day as the Seward memorandum and the *Powhatan* muddle (April 1), Lincoln also asserted his authority over General-in-Chief Scott by ordering him "to make short, comprehensive daily reports to me of what occurs in his Department, including movements by himself, and under his orders, and the receipt of intelligence."[23] The result of this instruction was to bring Scott on board for the reprovisioning of both Pickens and Sumter. The nature of the Sumter expedition had changed in a crucial way since

Gustavus Fox had first proposed it. A full-scale attempt to reinforce the fort, backed by warships that would have to shoot their way into Charleston Bay, would make the North the aggressor. It would unite the South, drive most of the remaining slave states into the Confederacy, divide the North, and fasten on Lincoln the onus of starting a war. Therefore he conceived a plan to separate the question of reinforcements from that of provisions. He would send in supplies only, while the warships stood by to go into action only if Confederate guns opened fire. And he would notify South Carolina's governor of his intentions. If the Confederates fired on unarmed tugs carrying provisions, they would stand convicted of attacking a "mission of humanity" bringing "food for hungry men."

It was a stroke of brilliance. In effect Lincoln flipped a coin with Confederate president Jefferson Davis, saying: "Heads I win; tails you lose." If the Confederates allowed the supplies to be landed, the status quo at Charleston would continue, peace would be preserved for at least a while, no more states would secede, and Seward's cherished policy of "voluntary reconstruction," whereby a cooling of passions would bring the presumed legions of Southern closet

Unionists out of the closet, might have a chance to go forward. But if Confederate guns opened fire, the responsibility for starting a war would rest on Jefferson Davis's shoulders.

On April 6 Lincoln sent a special messenger to Charleston with a dispatch notifying the governor (Lincoln did not officially recognize the existence of a legitimate Confederate government) "to expect an attempt will be made to supply Fort-Sumpter with provisions only; and that, if such attempt be not resisted, no effort to throw in men, arms, or ammunition will be made, without further notice, or in case of an attack upon the Fort."[24] Lincoln had plenty of reasons to expect the Confederates to attack. The envoys he had sent to Charleston a couple of weeks earlier had reported the bellicose mood they found there. On his way to Washington back in February, the president-elect had reviewed several companies of Pennsylvania militia in Harrisburg. Governor Andrew Curtin had said they would be ready whenever Lincoln needed them. On April 8, as the relief expedition to Fort Sumter prepared to leave New York, Lincoln informed Curtin: "I think the necessity of being *ready* increases. Look to it."[25]

The coin was in the air, and Lincoln expected to win whether it came up heads or tails. That same day, April 8, the Confederate secretary of war telegraphed Gen. Pierre G. T. Beauregard, commander of Confederate forces at Charleston: "Under no circumstances are you to allow provisions to be sent to Fort Sumter." Two days later came another telegram: "You will at once demand its evacuation, and if this is refused proceed . . . to reduce it."[26] Two more days after that, Confederate guns opened fire on the fort. For the second time in American history it was a shot heard around the world.

On April 13 the telegraph flashed news of the one-sided artillery duel at Charleston to the War Department and to newspaper offices in the North. Later that day Lincoln held a previously scheduled meeting with three delegates from the Virginia convention that had initially rejected disunion but remained in session "awaiting events." The president received them coldly and read a prepared statement condemning the "unprovoked assault" on Fort Sumter. Now that the Confederacy had commenced "actual war against the government," Lincoln told them that he intended not only to "possess, occupy, and hold" national property in the Confederate states but also "to repossess, if I can, like places which had been seized before the Government was devolved upon me."[27]

Here was the beginning of a military strategy consistent with Lincoln's policy of rejecting the legitimacy of secession and continuing to regard the Confederate states as part of the United States. When official word reached Washington on April 14 of Fort Sumter's surrender, the cabinet met in an emergency Sunday session and approved a proclamation drafted by Lincoln calling seventy-five thousand state militia into federal service for ninety days (the maximum allowed by law). Their purpose would be to suppress "combinations too powerful to be suppressed by the ordinary course of judicial proceedings." Their first task "will probably be to re-possess the forts, places, and property which have been seized from the Union."[28]

Lincoln's successful effort to place the onus of starting a war on the Confederacy paid off. The attack on Fort Sumter united a previously divided Northern people more than they would ever be united again. War fever swept the free states. Hundreds of American flags flew over rallies in cities and villages across the land. "The heather is on fire," wrote a Harvard professor who had been born during George Washington's presidency. "I never knew what a popular excitement can be. . . . The whole population, men, women, and children, seem to be in the streets with Union favors and flags." The "time before Sumter" seemed like another century to one New York woman. "It seems as if we never were alive till now; never had a country till now."[29]

Northern governors offered more regiments than their quotas under Lincoln's call for militia. About 90,000 men were eventually mobilized under this call. The government could scarcely arm and equip this number within ninety days. Although many people in the North (and in the South too, for that matter) believed the war would be over and won within that period, Lincoln did not share this optimism. The federalization of state militias was limited to ninety days under the Militia Act of 1795, which was still in effect. Recognizing that more troops for a longer term would be needed, Lincoln on May 3 issued a call for 43,034 three-year volunteers. And for good measure he also increased the size of the regular army by 22,714 men and of the navy by 18,000. The president enacted these measures by executive order, in apparent violation of the Constitution, which grants Congress exclusive authority to "raise and support armies" and to "provide and maintain a navy" (Article I, Section 7).[30]

These were among several executive actions by Lincoln that he justified under his constitutional mandate as commander in chief. Another such action was his proclamation of a blockade of Confederate ports on April 19.[31] A blockade is an act of war, and the Constitution gives only Congress the power to declare war. But Congress was not in session and would not convene (in a special session called by Lincoln) until July 4, nearly three months after the war began. This delay was not the result of Lincoln's desire to prosecute the war without congressional interference, as several historians have suggested. Rather, it was a consequence of the electoral calendar at that time. Most states held congressional elections in the fall of even-numbered years, as today. But Congress itself did not meet in its first regular session until December of the following year, thirteen months later. Hence several states held their congressional elections in the spring of odd-numbered years. In 1861 seven states remaining in the Union held their congressional elections from March to June. Thus the special session could not meet until all representatives had been elected.

Lincoln's message to that special session explained the executive actions he had taken — including an order to the treasury to advance two million dollars to three private citizens in New York to purchase arms and vessels. This order contravened Article I, Section 9, of the Constitution, which stipulates that "no Money shall be drawn from the Treasury, but in Consequence of Appropriations made by Law." The president pointed out that his oath of office required him to "preserve, protect, and defend" the Constitution. This duty overrode any specific constitutional constraints on executive action. The attack on Fort Sumter left him with no choice "but to call out the war power of the Government; and so to resist force, employed for its destruction, by force, for its preservation." In the first draft of his message Lincoln had written "military power" but changed it to "war power" in the final draft. He also used those words elsewhere in the message — he had employed his "war power" as commander in chief to avoid surrendering "the existence of the government."[32]

The Constitution makes no mention of war power; Lincoln seems to have invented both the phrase and its application.[33] "It became necessary," the president insisted, "for me to choose whether, using only the existing means, agencies, and processes which Congress had provided, I should let the government fall at once into ruin, or whether, availing myself of the broader powers conferred by the Constitution in cases of insurrection, I would make an effort to save it with all its blessings for the present age and for posterity." Lincoln believed that "by these and other similar measures taken in that crisis, some of which were without any authority of law, the government was saved from overthrow."[34]

Congress seemed to agree. By an overwhelming majority it passed a law that "approved and in all respects legalized and made valid . . . all the acts, proclamations, and orders of the President of the United States respecting the army and the navy . . . as if they had been done under the express authority of the Congress."[35] Some uncertainty remained, however, about the legality of Lincoln's declaration of blockade. Merchants whose ships and cargo were captured challenged it in court. They argued that because only Congress can declare war, the blockade was illegal before Congress in July 1861 affirmed the existence of hostilities.

By a five-to-four margin in 1863 the Supreme Court ruled that a state of war can exist without a formal declaration. The president has a duty to resist force with force; therefore the blockade and related war powers exercised by Lincoln were within his authority as commander in chief.[36] (Lincoln had appointed three of the five justices in the majority.)

Lincoln's April 15 call for militia had requisitioned a quota from each state, including the eight slave states still in the Union. Six of their governors replied with defiant refusals. "Tennessee will not furnish a single man for the purpose of coercion," declared its governor, "but fifty thousand if necessary for the defense of our rights and those of our Southern brothers." From Richmond came a telegram stating that since Lincoln had "chosen to inaugurate civil war," Virginia would join its sister states of the South. The governors of North Carolina, Arkansas, and Kentucky sent similar replies, while the prosecession governor of Missouri told Lincoln that "your requisition is illegal, unconstitutional, revolutionary, inhuman, diabolical. . . . Not one man will the State of Missouri furnish to carry on any such unholy crusade."[37]

Northern governors, by contrast, responded with enthusiasm. Massachusetts was the first state out of the gate. "Dispatch received," Governor John Andrew wired the War Department on April 15. "By what route shall we send?"[38] Two Massachusetts regiments were on their way by April 17. Two days later a mob attacked several companies of the Sixth Massachusetts as they transferred from one railroad station to another in Baltimore. The soldiers fired back. When the smoke cleared, four soldiers and twelve Baltimoreans lay dead and many more wounded — on the eighty-sixth anniversary of the clash between Minutemen and Redcoats at Lexington and Concord.

This affray blew the lid off emotions in Baltimore. Although later events would show that a majority of Maryland whites were Unionists, secession fever seemed to sweep through the city for several days. The governor (a lukewarm Unionist) and mayor (a suspected secessionist) sanctioned the cutting of telegraph wires and the burning of railroad bridges to prevent any more Northern troops from coming through Baltimore. They also sent a delegation to Lincoln, who acquiesced in a plan for troops to detrain and march around the city but refused the governor's demand that they avoid Maryland altogether. The United

States capital was surrounded by Maryland and Virginia, whose convention had voted to secede on April 17. Lincoln's first priority, he said, was to defend Washington. To do that he had to bring troops through Maryland. "Our men are not moles, and can't dig under the earth," the president told a Maryland delegation on April 22. "They are not birds, and can't fly through the air. There is no way but to march across, and that they must do."[39]

Meanwhile Benjamin Butler, a brigadier general of militia from Massachusetts, had detrained one of his regiments at the head of Chesapeake Bay, commandeered a steamboat, and brought the regiment to Annapolis. From there the Bay Staters, whose ranks included several railroad men, repaired rolling stock, rebuilt the tracks and bridges, and steamed triumphantly into Washington on April 25. By the end of the month some ten thousand loyal militia were in the capital — enough to defend it against anything the Confederates could mobilize at the time.

On May 13 the resourceful Butler occupied Baltimore with two regiments and a battery of artillery. General Scott considered Butler something of a loose cannon and was incensed at him for acting without orders.

But Lincoln regarded Butler (at this stage of the war) as a can-do officer and two days later appointed him as a major general of U.S. volunteers.[40]

These events in Maryland led to a constitutional showdown between the commander in chief and the chief justice of the United States. On April 27 Lincoln authorized General Scott to suspend the writ of habeas corpus on any "military line" between Philadelphia and Washington. Subsequent presidential orders expanded the area where the writ could be suspended, until a proclamation of September 24, 1862, suspended it throughout the whole country.[41] The writ was an ancient Anglo-American protection against arbitrary arrest and detention that required an arrested person to be brought before a court to decide the legality of his detention or imprisonment. The Constitution mandates that the writ "shall not be suspended, unless when in cases of Rebellion or Invasion the public Safety may require it" (Article I, Section 9). The Civil War was a clear case of rebellion, said Lincoln, and the public safety required the detention of those who were aiding and abetting that rebellion.

John Merryman was a wealthy Maryland landowner and lieutenant in a secessionist cavalry company that had torn down telegraph lines near Baltimore. Arrested and confined at Fort McHenry in the city, he petitioned the federal circuit court for a writ of habeas corpus. The senior judge in that circuit was none other than Chief Justice Roger B. Taney, who issued a writ ordering the commanding officer at the fort to bring Merryman before the court to show cause for his arrest. The officer refused, citing the president's suspension of the writ. Taney immediately delivered a ruling denying the president's authority to do so. At issue was not whether the writ could be suspended, but who could suspend it. The suspension clause is in Article I of the Constitution, which deals with the powers of Congress — not of the president. So Taney insisted that only Congress could suspend the writ.[42]

Taney cited several precedents to support his position. In Anglo-American legal history, legislative powers were a check on the arbitrary authority of the executive. On the other hand, at the Constitutional Convention in 1787 the suspension clause was initially placed in the article dealing with the judiciary, and it was eventually moved to Article I by the committee on style. In 1861 several constitutional lawyers (including Attorney General Edward Bates) upheld Lincoln's right to suspend the writ as falling under his responsibilities as commander in chief.[43]

In any event Taney had no power to enforce his ruling, and Lincoln refused to obey it. The president, however, exercised his assumed right to suspend the writ with restraint at this early stage of the war. When some associates suggested that he order General Scott to arrest several Maryland legislators, and to prevent the meeting of the legislature to forestall the state's possible secession, Lincoln refused to do so. "They have a clearly legal right to assemble," he wrote, and "we can not know, in advance, that their actions will not be lawful, and peaceful." There would be time enough to take action if they tried "to arm their people against the United States." Then Scott could "adopt the most prompt, and efficient means to counteract, even to the bombardment of their cities." The legislature reassured the government of its loyalty to the United States.[44] Even in the District of Columbia, where Confederate sympathizers were numerous, Lincoln opposed their arrest unless it was "*manifest, and urgent.*"[45]

The issue of "arbitrary arrests" remained highly controversial, however, especially when their number grew as the war went on. The opposition fastened on Taney's opinion to denounce Lincoln as a tyrant. The president responded in his message to the special session of Congress on July 4, 1861. He noted (without mentioning Taney's name or position) that as president he had been admonished "that one who is sworn to 'take care that the laws be faithfully executed,' should not himself violate them." But he had not violated the law, Lincoln insisted. Confederates in Virginia and secessionists in Maryland had surrounded the capital, whose capture would have brought down the government. Surely this met the constitutional criterion for suspending the writ. "Now it is insisted that Congress, not the Executive, is vested with this power," Lincoln acknowledged. "But the Constitution itself is silent as to which, or who, is to exercise the power; and as the provision was plainly made for a dangerous emergency, it cannot be believed the framers of the government intended, that in every case, the danger should run its course, until Congress should be called together; the very assembling of which might be prevented, as was intended in this case, by the rebellion."[46]

But even if Taney was right that the

Constitution gave only Congress the power to suspend habeas corpus, Lincoln averred a higher constitutional duty to do whatever was necessary to preserve, protect, and defend the nation — including its capital. "The whole of the laws which were to be faithfully executed, were being resisted, and failing of execution, in nearly one-third of the States," he noted. "Must they be allowed finally to fail of execution [because] some single law . . . should, to a very limited extent, be violated? To state the question more directly, are all the laws, *but one* [the privilege of the writ of habeas corpus], to go unexecuted, and the government itself go to pieces, lest the one be violated?"[47]

A master of metaphors designed to make abstruse concepts clear to laymen, Lincoln used the analogy of a surgeon who amputates a limb to save a life. Looking back in 1864 to the early weeks of the war, he asked: "Was it possible to lose the nation, and yet preserve the constitution? By general law life *and* limb must be protected; yet often a limb must be amputated to save a life; but a life is never wisely given to save a limb. I felt that measures, otherwise unconstitutional, might become lawful, by becoming indispensable to the preservation of the constitution through preservation of the nation."[48] Here was the core of Lincoln's concept of his war powers as commander in chief: His supreme constitutional obligation was to preserve the nation by winning the war. Any measures necessary to achieve that purpose overrode lesser constitutional restrictions (the amputated limb) — or, to quote a modern constitutional scholar, *"A part cannot control the whole, to the destruction of the whole."*[49]

Virginia's secession and the fear that Maryland might follow suit temporarily reoriented Lincoln's strategic priority from recapturing federal property to defense of the capital and of the Unionist border states. Kentucky and Missouri as well as Maryland seemed poised on the knife edge of secession. Some of their leaders warned Lincoln that any "invasion" of Confederate states with the purpose of "coercion" would push border states into the arms of their "Southern brethren." With some asperity the president responded to one of them that "the sole purpose of bringing troops *here* is to defend this capital. . . . I have no purpose to *invade* Virginia, with them or any other troops, as I understand the word *invasion.*" But if Confederate troops from Virginia "assail this capital, am I not to repel them, even to the crossing of the Potomac? . . . I do not mean to let them invade us without striking back."[50]

One of the senators from Kentucky likewise said Lincoln had promised him "that until the meeting of Congress he would make no attempt to retake the forts. . . . He did not intend to invade with an armed force, or make any military or naval movement against any state, unless she or her people should make it necessary by a formidable resistance." Kentucky proclaimed its neutrality between the warring sections. Although he considered "neutrality" to be as bad as secession in principle, Lincoln assured the senator that he would respect it "if Kentucky made no demonstration of force against the United States."[51]

Lincoln kept that promise with respect to Kentucky. But elsewhere the hands-off strategy did not last long. By the middle of May, Union troops occupied Baltimore and additional regiments would soon move into other key points in Maryland. In Virginia secessionist militia seized the U.S. naval base at Norfolk and the federal armory at Harpers Ferry. Fort Monroe, across Hampton Roads from Norfolk, remained in Union hands, however, and Lincoln reinforced it in May. When Virginia voters ratified the state's secession in a referendum on May 23, Union troops crossed the Potomac the next day to occupy Alexandria in order to "protect" those Virginians who had voted against secession and remained loyal to the Union. Most such Virginians lived in the region west of the Shenandoah Valley, bordering Ohio and Pennsylvania. Union regiments from Ohio and Indiana under the command of Maj. Gen. George B. McClellan moved into western Virginia in May and began an offensive that would secure this large Unionist region and pave the way for its eventual entry into the Union as the new state of West Virginia.

The convention elected to consider secession in Missouri defied the pro-Confederate governor and voted to remain in the Union. The governor nevertheless began organizing a secessionist militia, while U.S. Representative Frank Blair, Jr., brother of Lincoln's postmaster general, proceeded to organize a Unionist militia. Blair's ally was Capt. Nathaniel Lyon, a red-bearded, hotheaded abolitionist and commander of the St. Louis arsenal. Caught in the middle of this brewing conflict was Brig. Gen. William Harney, commander of the Department of the West, with his headquarters at St. Louis. Harney was a moderate who wanted to reconcile all factions and preserve the peace. But in the volatile political climate of Missouri, his efforts to prevent the mustering of Unionist militia seemed to tilt toward the secessionists. The Blairs persuaded Lincoln to relieve Harney and recall him to Washington. Frank Blair and Lyon mobilized their militia, surrounded the secessionist camp, and captured them. As they were marched through St. Louis on May 10, a riot broke out that left thirty-three people dead, including two of Lyon's soldiers.

General Harney returned to St. Louis and resumed his command on May 11. He tried to calm the volcanic passions that threatened a Missouri civil war within the larger national Civil War. Harney's efforts seemed ineffective, however, so Lincoln gave Frank Blair discretionary orders to relieve him from command again, though cautioning Blair not to issue the orders unless the situation became "very urgent." Blair was chafing at the bit, and on May 30 he removed Harney on Lincoln's authority and replaced him with Lyon, now a brigadier general.[52] Lyon's vigorous offensive, with troops from Iowa and Kansas as well as Missouri, drove the rebels from most of the state but at the cost of his own life at the Battle of Wilson's Creek (August 10, 1861) and of vicious guerrilla warfare that plagued Missouri for years.

The strong-arm strategy that kept Maryland and Missouri precariously under Union control would have been counterproductive in Kentucky. Lincoln remained acutely sensitive to the critical balance of allegiances in his native state. Seven brothers or brothers-in-law of Mary Todd Lincoln fought for the Confederacy. Although Governor Beriah Magoffin proclaimed the state's neutrality, his sympathies leaned southward. Both Lincoln and Jefferson Davis kept their troops out of Kentucky for fear that whichever side first violated its neutrality would force the state over to the other side. Lincoln rejected a request from the governors of Ohio, Indiana, and Illinois to send troops from their states into Kentucky.[53] The president's restraint paid off. Kentucky held three elections from May to August: for delegates to a border-state convention; for representatives in Congress; and for the state legislature. All resulted in Unionist majorities.

Meanwhile Governor Magoffin organized "State Guard" regiments, composed mostly of pro-Southern volunteers. Kentucky Unionists countered by recruiting "Home Guard" regiments and asking Washington for arms. Lincoln authorized the quiet distribution of five thousand muskets to the Home Guards. He also commissioned Maj. Robert Anderson — defender of Fort Sumter and a Kentuckian — a brigadier general and sent him to Cincinnati to muster Kentucky volunteers into the Union army.[54] Confederate officers were similarly mustering Kentucky volunteers into Tennessee regiments in that state.

Kentucky's neutrality was clearly destined to end. On September 3, Maj. Gen. Leonidas Polk sent Confederate troops into the state. Brig. Gen. Ulysses S. Grant immediately countered by ordering some of his Union regiments across the Ohio River into Kentucky. The Unionist legislature passed a resolution demanding that the Confederates leave and inviting the Union troops to stay. Kentucky remained contested ground until the failure of a large-scale Confederate invasion in the fall of 1862. But Lincoln's skillful handling of matters there in the war's early months helped keep the state largely Unionist.[55]

The effective control of most parts of the border states proved to be of great strategic value for the Union cause. But the eleven states that made up the Confederacy covered more than 750,000 square miles — as large as France, Spain, Germany, Italy, and Great Britain combined. They had a functioning government and an army as large as that of the United States in May 1861. To win the war the Confederate States needed only to defend successfully their existing boundaries. For Lincoln, control of the border states and the defense of Washington were crucial, but they hardly constituted a strategy for winning the war and restoring the Union. Even the reconquest of coastal forts in the South would not accomplish that purpose.

As the Northern states filled and even exceeded their quotas of ninety-day militias and also exceeded the 43,000 three-year volunteers Lincoln had called for, the administration searched for a war-winning strategy. In May 1861 General Scott proposed what he considered the right one. It fitted his desire for a restoration of the Union with the least possible violence. As a Virginian, Scott deplored the cry of many Republican politicians and newspapers for an invasion to "crush the rebels." Even if successful, he wrote, an invasion would produce "fifteen devastated provinces [that is, the slave states] not to be brought into harmony with their conquerors, but to be held for generations, by heavy garrisons." Instead of invading the Confederacy, Scott proposed to "envelop the insurgent States" with a blockade by sea and to move down the Mississippi River, establishing "a cordon of posts at proper points" to seal off the Confederacy from the outside world and thus "bring them to terms with less bloodshed than by any other plan."[56]

Scott's strategy rested on a belief in a strong residual Unionism in the Confederate states. The passions of the moment had swept a temporary majority in eleven states into the secession camp, he acknowledged. But he believed that the silent majority were Unionists at heart and would return to their old allegiance if the government pursued a firm but conciliatory strategy. "Invade the South at any point," Scott reportedly told Lincoln, and "I will guarantee that at the end of the year you will be further from a settlement than you are now." But if the envelopment plan was adopted, the South would be "cut off from the luxuries to which the people are accustomed; and . . . not having been exasperated by attacks made on them . . . the Union spirit will assert itself; those who are on the fence will descend on the Union side, and I will guarantee that in one year from this time all difficulties will be settled."[57]

Scott's faith in Southern Unionism was similar to that of Secretary of State Seward. The general's hope of fostering this Union sentiment was a continuation of the "voluntary reconstruction" policy espoused by Seward before the firing on Fort Sumter. Lincoln partly shared this faith in the early months of the war. That was why, in his April 15 proclamation calling up the militia, he promised that they would "avoid any devastation, any destruction of, or interference with, property, or any disturbance of peaceful citizens."[58]

The principal form of property in the South was, of course, slave property. Southern states had seceded because they feared that the Lincoln administration would interfere with the institution — despite the president's repeated assertions, well into the war, that he had neither the intention nor the power to do so. Once Southern whites understood this noninterference policy, Lincoln hoped their residual Unionism would reassert itself. When Union troops occupied Alexandria on May 24, Lincoln was pleased to hear that "when the Stars and Stripes were raised, many people in the town actually wept for joy. . . . This is another proof that all the South is not secessionist." In his message to Congress on July 4, the president said that "it may well be questioned whether there is, to-day, a majority of the legally qualified voters of any State, except perhaps South Carolina, in favor of disunion."[59]

This belief in a Southern Unionist majority turned out to be a delusion. And even those who shared it were critical of Scott's minimalist strategy. Several Northern newspapers mocked it as the "Anaconda Plan," after the South American snake that squeezes its prey. Montgomery Blair believed in Southern Unionists, but he told Lincoln that Scott's do-little strategy would embolden secessionists and discourage those Unionists. "Genl. Scott's system," he said, "is but a continuation of the compromise policy with which his mind and that of all his political associates is imbued." Blair predicted that an invasion deeper into Virginia would be "hailed with joy by the [true] people of the South everywhere," but if "we fail to go to the relief of the people of the South they will be subjugated and the state of consolidation now falsely assumed will be produced."[60]

Lincoln was leaning in this direction by June 1861, despite his earlier assurances that he did not intend to "invade" the South. Just as he had agreed with Montgomery Blair's advice to provision Fort Sumter and with Frank Blair's counsel to take a hard line in Missouri, the commander in chief now decided to use the army he had raised to attack the Confederate force defending the key railroad junction at Manassas, Virginia, twenty-five miles from Washington.

2
THE BOTTOM
IS OUT OF THE TUB

On May 21, 1861, the provisional Confederate Congress made a political decision that would have profound military consequences. The Southern lawmakers accepted Virginia's invitation to locate their capital in Richmond, a hundred miles from Washington. This decision made northern Virginia the main theater of the war. Although Richmond would have been a focal point of conflict in any case because of its war industries, the city's political importance concentrated Confederate strategic thinking on Virginia at the expense of the lower and western Southern states. It also focused Northern attention primarily on Virginia.

The success of Gen. George B. McClellan's small army in western Virginia generated pressure for an advance against the larger Confederate army at Manassas. Lincoln's mailbox was crammed with letters from persons prominent and obscure demanding an offensive. Several state governors met at Cleveland in early May to press the administration for "immediate action." Acting as spokesman for the group, Wisconsin's governor Alexander Randall wrote Lincoln: "There is no occasion for the Government to delay, because the States themselves are willing to act vigorously. . . . There is a spirit evoked by this rebellion among the liberty-loving people of this country that is driving them to action, and if the government will not permit them to act for it, they will act for themselves. It is better for the Government to direct this current than to let it run wild."[1] When the Confederate Congress announced its intention to meet in Richmond on July 20, the Northern press clamored for a campaign to prevent it. FORWARD TO RICHMOND! demanded Horace Greeley's powerful *New York Tribune* in every issue beginning on June 26. "The Rebel Congress Must Not be Allowed to Meet There on the 20th of July. BY THAT DATE THE PLACE MUST BE HELD BY THE NATIONAL ARMY."

General Scott did not want public opinion to dictate military strategy. But Lincoln could not afford to ignore such pressure in a democratic polity whose zeal was vital for the mass mobilization that had already exceeded the president's calls for troops. Lincoln's concern for a national strategy of maximizing public support for the war trumped the narrower concern for a cautious military strategy. By late June some thirty-five thousand Union soldiers were camped across the Potomac from Washington — most of them ninety-day militia whose terms of service would begin to run out in the second half of July. If he did not do something with them soon, they would disappear and any action would be postponed for months until the three-year men could be equipped and trained.

On June 29 Lincoln called a meeting of what amounted to a high-level war council consisting of his cabinet, General Scott, Brig. Gen. Irvin McDowell (who commanded the field army camped near Alexandria), Quartermaster General Montgomery Meigs, and three other generals. Scott made one more pitch for his Anaconda Plan, but bowed to the inevitable when Lincoln and others insisted on a campaign against the twenty thousand Confederates defending Manassas. One of the ablest officers at the meeting was Meigs, whom Lincoln had appointed quartermaster general over Secretary of War Simon Cameron's opposition. Another officer, said

Cameron, had seniority over the forty-five-year-old Meigs. Lincoln disregarded seniority in favor of talent, which Meigs had in abundance.[2] His administrative skills became a key factor in ultimate Union victory. Asked for his opinion at the June 29 meeting, Meigs responded, "I did not think we would ever win the war without beating the rebels. They have come near us. . . . It was better to whip them here than to go far into an unhealthy country to fight them" — as in Scott's proposed expedition down the Mississippi.[3]

Lincoln agreed. He asked McDowell to present a plan of campaign. The general proposed to feint against the defended bridges and fords along Bull Run west of Manassas, while sending an attack column around the Confederate flank to cross at an undefended ford to make the real attack. It was a good plan — for veteran troops. But McDowell's civilians in uniform were still raw. He pleaded for more time to train them. More time, however, would melt away the army by expiration of enlistments. And the enemy soldiers were equally raw. "You are green, it is true," the president acknowledged, "but they are green, also; you are all green alike."[4]

McDowell's plan depended on a simultaneous advance by a small Union force in the Shenandoah Valley against eleven thousand Confederate troops at Winchester to prevent them from reinforcing the main Confederate army at Manassas. The commander of the fifteen thousand Union militia in the valley was Robert Patterson, a sixty-nine-year-old veteran of the War of 1812 and the Mexican War. He failed in his mission to pin down the enemy regiments in the valley. Confederate general Joseph E. Johnston brought most of them to Manassas, where they evened the numerical odds and played a key part in the battle along the banks of Bull Run on July 21.

Despite Patterson's failure, the Union attack on that exceedingly hot Sunday achieved initial success. Telegrams from the Union operator at Fairfax (ten miles from the battlefield) reported that McDowell was driving the enemy. General Scott assured Lincoln that things were going well, and both men went to church. Messages from Fairfax continued to be optimistic until 3:30 P.M., when Lincoln expressed concern about the operator's report that the sound of the guns seemed to be coming nearer. The president went to Scott's office and woke the general from his afternoon nap with this news. Scott said the sounds resulted from a variation in wind and atmosphere. According to John Nicolay, who accompanied Lincoln, "the General still expressed his confidence in a successful result, and composed himself for another nap."[5]

Reassured, Lincoln went on his usual afternoon carriage ride — his only form of relaxation. Meanwhile the battle turned against the Union, as the last Confederate brigade from the Shenandoah Valley detrained and spearheaded a counterattack that drove McDowell's army back in a defeat that turned into a rout. Lincoln received the bad news when he returned from his drive at about six thirty and read a telegram from a captain of engineers: "General McDowell's army in full retreat through Centreville. The day is lost. . . . The routed troops will not re-form."[6]

This battle had a powerful psychological impact in both South and North. In the South it produced exultation and overconfidence. A Georgian pronounced Manassas *"one of the decisive battles of the world."* It *"has* secured our independence." A Mobile newspaper predicted that the Union army would "never again advance beyond cannon shot of Washington."[7]

In the North the news produced panic

and despair but also renewed determination. "We are utterly and disgracefully routed, beaten, whipped," wrote the prominent New York lawyer George Templeton Strong. In a fit of remorse for his "Forward to Richmond" editorials, Horace Greeley wrote Lincoln: "On every brow sits sullen, scorching, black despair. . . . If it is best for the country and for mankind that we make peace with the rebels, and on their own terms, do not shrink even from that."[8] But at the White House and the neighboring War Department Building, grim determination reigned. Orders went out to strengthen the capital's defenses and to bring additional three-year regiments to Washington. At 2:00 A.M. on July 22 Lincoln had the adjutant general send a telegram to General McClellan in western Virginia summoning him to Washington, where he would be placed in command of a reorganized army of three-year volunteers newly named the Army of the Potomac. Lincoln stayed up all night receiving reports and jotting notes that he turned into a memorandum outlining near-term strategy for a revitalized prosecution of the war: strengthen the blockade; reorganize and increase the size of the armies at Washington, the Shenandoah Valley, western Virginia, and Missouri and place them under new commanders; and then advance these armies to capture Manassas, Strasburg in the Shenandoah Valley, Memphis on the Mississippi, and Knoxville in East Tennessee.[9]

The day after Bull Run, Lincoln signed a bill for the enlistment of five hundred thousand three-year volunteers (nearly half of this number were already mustered in); three days later Congress passed and the president signed a second bill authorizing another five hundred thousand. Lincoln's secretary John Nicolay acknowledged that the defeat at Bull Run was humiliating. "But the fat is all in the fire now and we shall have to crow small until we can retrieve the disgrace somehow," Nicolay wrote to his fiancée on July 23. "The preparations for the war will be continued with increased vigor by the government."[10]

The vast expansion of the volunteer army required the commissioning of new officers from lieutenants up to major generals. In most regiments the men elected their company officers, and state governors selected the field officers (colonel, lieutenant colonel, and major). The president appointed brigadier and major generals, subject to confirmation by the Senate. At every level this process was as much political as it was military. While some field officers and an occasional company officer had previous military training or experience, most were commissioned from civilian life without such training. It could scarcely have been otherwise when the tiny antebellum army of 16,000 men had grown to a volunteer force of 637,000 by April 1862.

Two-thirds of the 583 Union generals commissioned during the war had prewar military training and experience. Some of the remaining one-third were promoted on the basis of merit demonstrated in lower ranks during the war. In the first year of the conflict, however, Lincoln appointed several "political generals" whose chief recommendation was their prominence as politicians or as leaders of the German American and Irish American ethnic communities. The rationale for doing so was the same as for the governors who commissioned politicians or other prominent civilians as field officers: to mobilize maximum support and recruitment for this war that was to be fought primarily by citizen soldiers. Some of these political and ethnic generals proved to be incompetent on the battlefield. Professional army officers like Maj. Gen. Henry W. Halleck deplored the political influences that had placed them in high positions. "It seems but little better than murder to give important commands to such men as [Nathaniel] Banks, [Benjamin] Butler, [John] McClernand, and Lew Wallace," sighed Halleck, "but it seems impossible to prevent it."[11]

In a narrow military sense Halleck may have been right — though the war also revealed a good many examples of incompetent professionals. But this was another area where considerations of national strategy trumped military strategy. The mass mobilization that brought 637,000 men into the Union army in less than a year could not have taken place without an enormous effort by local and state politicians as well as by prominent ethnic leaders. In New York City, for example, the Tammany Democrat Daniel Sickles raised a brigade and earned a commission as brigadier general. The Irish-born Thomas Meagher helped raise the Irish Brigade and became its commander. The famous German American leader Carl Schurz helped raise several German regiments and eventually became a major general. Lincoln needed the allegiance of prominent Democratic congressmen John McClernand and John Logan in southern Illinois, where support for the war was shaky. These two men "have labored night and day to instruct their fellow citizens in the true nature of the contest," acknowledged the Republican *Chicago Tribune,* "and to organize their aroused feelings into effective military strength. They have succeeded nobly."[12] Both eventually achieved the rank of major general of volunteers, and Logan proved to be an outstanding commander.

Lincoln commissioned several other prominent Democrats in what was a successful effort to mobilize their constituencies for what some perceived as a Republican war. But of course he could not ignore important Republicans who wanted commissions. His own party supplied most of the energy and manpower for the war effort. Lincoln appointed John C. Frémont, who had been the first Republican presidential candidate in 1856, and Nathaniel P. Banks, former Speaker of the House and governor of Massachusetts, as major generals early in the war. Frémont became commander of the Department of the West with headquarters in St. Louis, and Banks replaced the hapless Robert Patterson as commander in western Maryland. Northern state governors, nearly all Republicans, played an essential part in raising and organizing volunteer regiments, and claimed the right to recommend candidates for brigadier generalships. So did key senators and congressmen. Sometimes this system of politicomilitary patronage paid off in a big way. Ulysses S. Grant and William Tecumseh Sherman might have languished in obscurity had it not been for the initial sponsorship of Grant by Elihu B. Washburne, chairman of the House Military Affairs Committee, and of Sherman by his brother John, chairman of the Senate Finance Committee.

Some of the political generals caused Lincoln nagging problems — Frémont in Missouri and McClernand in the Tennessee-Mississippi theater, for example. But by far the most problematical was a thoroughgoing professional who graduated second in his West Point class and had been a rising star in the antebellum army: George B. McClellan. When he arrived in Washington on July 26, McClellan received a hero's welcome and excessive praise for his small victories in western Virginia. The press lionized him as "the young Napoleon"; the correspondent of *The Times* of London described him as "the man on horseback" to save the country; the president of the U.S. Sanitary Commission said that "there is an indefinable *air of success* about him and something of 'the man of destiny.' "[13]

This adulation surprised McClellan and then went to his head. The day after reaching Washington he wrote to his wife that "I find myself in a new & strange position here — Presdt, Cabinet, Genl Scott & all deferring to me — by some strange operation of magic I seem to have become *the* power of the land." Three days later he went to Capitol Hill and was "quite overwhelmed by the congratulations I received & the respect with which I was treated." Congress seemed willing to "give me my way in everything." McClellan developed what can only be called a messiah complex during those first weeks in Washington. "God has placed a great work in my hands," he wrote. "I was called to it; my previous life seems to have been unwittingly directed to this great end."[14]

Lincoln was far from considering himself God, but on July 27 he did place an important work in McClellan's hands. The president asked him to present a strategic plan for winning the war. McClellan's quick response was breathtaking in its grandeur. On August 2 he handed Lincoln a paper outlining a strategy for all theaters of the war from the Atlantic coast to Texas. The main effort would be in Virginia, where McClellan would train and lead an army of 273,000 men supported by a large naval fleet to capture Richmond and then move south to occupy other major cities down to New Orleans. Another army-navy task force would thrust down the Mississippi, while a smaller force would drive southward from Kansas to Texas. Yet another army would move out from Kentucky (once it was firmly in the Union camp) or western Virginia to liberate Unionist East Tennessee and push on to Memphis.[15]

Lincoln's response to this wholly unrealistic plan is unknown. McClellan's proposed campaigns would require at least five hundred thousand trained soldiers — twice the number of three-year recruits then in their training camps. The plan implied a delay of six or eight months until these troops could be organized, trained, and equipped, and for the huge logistical apparatus required to support them to be put in place. The most immediate consequence of McClellan's paper, however, was to create a potential conflict with Winfield Scott. McClellan's strategic outline poached on Scott's territory as general-in-chief responsible for all theaters of the war. This was probably not Lincoln's intention — though he had become disillusioned with Scott and had over-ruled him on both the reprovisioning of Fort Sumter and the advance against Manassas.

In any case McClellan soon became convinced that God had not only called him to his great work; He had also placed obstacles in his path. The first of them was Scott, whose age, obesity, and infirmities limited his workday to a few hours, while the energetic and charismatic Young Napoleon put in sixteen-hour days organizing and drilling his new army. McClellan bypassed Scott frequently, communicating directly with the president and members of the cabinet. Serious tensions soon developed between the old and new military titans.

McClellan's action that most angered Scott was a memorandum he sent Lincoln on August 8. It highlighted what turned out to be McClellan's main defect as a military commander — an alarmist tendency to inflate enemy strength and intentions. The Confederate army in his front only twenty miles from Washington, McClellan claimed, had one hundred thousand men (their real numbers were about forty thousand). Reinforcements were passing through Knoxville to join them (not true). Washington was in danger of attack by this huge force.

"Our present army in this vicinity is entirely insufficient for the emergency," McClellan warned, so he advised Scott to order forward all troops scattered in other places within reach of the capital to meet this "imminent danger."[16]

Scott regarded this communication as an insult to his own authority and to his management of the army. He also scoffed at McClellan's estimate of enemy numbers and his fears of an imminent attack. He called McClellan to his headquarters and apparently dressed him down. At the same time Scott asked to be placed on the retired list because of age and poor health — in effect submitting his resignation.[17]

Lincoln was upset by this contretemps between his two top commanders. With skill and sensitivity he intervened to smooth over the quarrel — for the time being, at least. He persuaded Scott to stay on and persuaded McClellan to withdraw the offending memorandum. In what passed for an apology, McClellan promised Lincoln to "abstain from any word or act that could give offense to General Scott or embarrass the president." He also offered his "most profound assurances of respect for General Scott and yourself."[18]

At this very time, however, McClellan was

writing privately that the Confederate army in his front now numbered 150,000 men. "I am here in a terrible place," he fumed. "The enemy have 3 to 4 times my force. . . . Genl Scott is the most dangerous antagonist I have . . . a perfect imbecile. . . . He will not comprehend the danger & is either a traitor or an incompetent. . . . The president is an idiot, the old General is in his dotage — they cannot or will not see the true state of affairs."[19]

McClellan's chronic overestimation of enemy numbers is often attributed to Allen Pinkerton, the Chicago detective whom McClellan summoned to Washington in August 1861 to head his intelligence service. But the general was making these grossly inflated estimates before Pinkerton submitted his first reports at the end of August. Thereafter Pinkerton did deserve part of the blame. His method of counting enemy regiments without recognizing that the effective strength of such units rarely equaled more than half of their paper strength doubled the estimate of the actual numbers of enemy troops ready to fight.

However, Pinkerton, who was well aware of McClellan's own beliefs in this regard, told his chief what he wanted to hear. The real problem lay in McClellan's personality and the position in which he found himself. The son of an eminent Philadelphia physician, McClellan had been educated in private schools and entered West Point by special permission at the age of fifteen. Graduating second in his class of 1846, he earned two brevet promotions in the Mexican War and won plum assignments in the regular army during the 1850s. Promotion was slow, however, and McClellan resigned from the army in 1857 and served with a large salary as superintendent of two Midwestern railroads during the next four years. He returned to the army when the war began in 1861, and at the age of thirty-four became its second-ranking general, behind only the seventy-five-year-old Scott. Having known nothing but success in his meteoric career, McClellan came to Washington as the Young Napoleon destined by God to save the country. These high expectations paralyzed him. Failure was unthinkable. Never having experienced failure, he feared the unknown. To move against the enemy was to risk failure. So McClellan manufactured phantom enemies to justify his demands for more troops, to explain his inaction against the actual enemy, and to blame others for that inaction.

Blaming Lincoln and Scott was not

enough to absolve McClellan of the heavy weight of responsibility. He convinced himself that several cabinet members were also against him. The cabinet, he wrote his wife, contained some of the "greatest geese . . . I have ever seen." Seward was "a meddling, officious, incompetent little puppy," Secretary of the Navy Gideon Welles was "weaker than the most garrulous old woman," while Lincoln was "nothing more than a well meaning baboon."[20]

Given these convictions, it is not surprising that McClellan's relations with Scott — not to mention with the administration — remained strained. As summer turned into autumn, several Republican leaders and broad segments of the Northern press grew restless as McClellan continued to train his expanding army and to hold impressive reviews but did nothing to advance against the main Confederate army. Nor did he prevent the enemy from establishing batteries on the Potomac below Washington to blockade the river. McClellan declined to cooperate with the navy in an expedition to capture these batteries and end what had become a national humiliation. When Assistant Secretary of the Navy Gustavus Fox informed Lincoln of McClellan's failure to provide troops for this purpose the president, according to Fox, "manifested more feeling and disappointment than I have ever seen him exhibit."[21]

McClellan refused to divert any of his troops because he feared an invasion of Maryland by an enemy force he now estimated at 170,000 (more than three times their actual numbers). The general's intelligence sources indicated that the invasion would be timed to coincide with a secessionist riot in Baltimore and the scheduled meeting of the legislature in Frederick on September 17. The legislature would then vote to secede and join the Confederacy. Swayed by this intelligence, Lincoln approved a plan to prevent the legislature from meeting and to arrest suspected pro-Confederate legislators along with other like-minded public officials — including the mayor of Baltimore. These arrests, said McClellan, "will go far toward breaking the backbone of the rebellion."[22]

The operation went like clockwork. At least twenty-seven members of the Maryland legislature plus several other officials were arrested and subsequently detained at Fort McHenry for periods ranging from two to fourteen months. When pressed to explain the grounds for these arrests, Lincoln issued a statement that "at the proper time they will be made public. . . . In no case has an arrest been made on mere suspicion, or through personal or partisan animosities, but in all cases the Government is in possession of tangible and unmistakable evidence . . . [of] complicity with those in armed rebellion against the Government."[23]

But neither Lincoln nor anyone else ever publicly presented evidence of this complicity. There was no riot in Baltimore and no Confederate invasion of Maryland in 1861. Northern Democrats made the administration's "arbitrary arrests" of war opponents a major political issue. When McClellan ran for the Democratic presidential nomination in 1864, he was forced to explain his leading role in this affair. He did not apologize. The intelligence on which the operation was based "seemed at the time to be thoroughly reliable. The danger was great — in a military point of view we were not prepared to resist an invasion of Maryland — the only chance was to nip the whole affair in the bud — which was promptly done."[24]

McClellan did act promptly in this operation against supposed (and unarmed) Rebel sympathizers in Maryland. Leading Republicans wondered why he continued to delay operations against genuine armed Rebels in Virginia. In early October the radical Republican senator Benjamin Wade wrote to his equally radical colleague Zachariah Chandler: "The present state of things must not be suffered to continue. . . . We have vast armies in the field maintained at prodigious and almost ruinous expense. Yet they are suffered to do nothing with the power in our hands to crush the rebellion. . . . We are in danger of having our army set into winter quarters with the capitol in a state of siege for another year." McClellan met with the senators and told them that he wanted to advance, but Scott, still enamored of his Anaconda Plan, held him back. They went to Lincoln and pressed him to force Scott out. The president had Scott's earlier request for retirement on his desk. The general-in-chief renewed the request, citing continuing deterioration of his health.[25]

McClellan was pulling every string he could find to get himself appointed Scott's successor. But the old general wanted that job to go to Henry W. Halleck, author and translator of books on military strategy, who had resigned from the army in the 1850s to pursue a more rewarding civilian career in California as an expert in mining law. Nicknamed "Old Brains" because of his high, domed forehead and his reputedly powerful intellect, Halleck returned to the army in August with a commission as major general in the regular army (ranking just behind McClellan and Frémont). Scott hoped that Halleck could get to Washington from California in time for Lincoln to appoint him rather than McClellan as Scott's successor.

But it was not to be. On October 18 Lincoln and the cabinet decided to accept Scott's request to retire. McClellan learned of this decision from one of his sources in the cabinet — probably Montgomery Blair, but perhaps Treasury Secretary Chase, a McClellan supporter at this time. The general wrote to his wife on October 19: "It seems to be pretty well settled that I will be Comdr in Chf within a week. Genl Scott proposed to retire in favor of Halleck. The Presdt and Cabinet have determined to accept his retirement, but *not* in favor of Halleck," who was at sea and would not arrive for several weeks.[26]

On November 1 McClellan achieved his goal. Scott retired and at the age of thirty-four McClellan became the youngest general-in-chief of United States armies in history — as well as field commander of the Army of the Potomac. Lincoln expressed some concern that "this vast increase in responsibilities . . . will entail a vast labor upon you." "I can do it all," McClellan replied.[27]

Having convinced Republican senators — and perhaps Lincoln — that it was only Scott's inertia that had kept him on a leash, McClellan now faced expectations that he would advance. But in conversations with the president he immediately began backtracking. In his mind the Confederate forces in Virginia outnumbered his by almost two to one (in reality it was the reverse). He reminded Lincoln of what had happened at Bull Run in July, when the Union army fought a battle before it was trained and disciplined. Probably feeling responsible for having pushed the army into that battle, Lincoln was inclined to defer to McClellan's professional opinion.

The disastrous outcome of a reconnaissance in force toward Leesburg on October 21, when several Union regiments were ambushed at Ball's Bluff and Lincoln's friend Col. Edward Baker was killed, lent legitimacy to McClellan's counsel of caution. "Dont let them hurry me," the general urged Lincoln. "You shall have your own way in the matter," the president assured him. But he also warned McClellan that the pressure for the army to do *something* more than dress parades and reviews was "a reality and should be taken into account. At the same time General you must not fight till you are ready."[28]

McClellan proved to have a tin ear about the ever-present "reality," which the president could not ignore. But the general heard loud and clear Lincoln's injunction not to fight until he was ready. The problem was that he was perpetually *almost* but not *quite* ready to move. The enemy always outnumbered him, and his own army always lacked something. In response to Lincoln's request, the new general-in-chief prepared a memorandum explaining his plans. His paper stated that "winter is approaching so rapidly" that unless the Army of the Potomac could be increased from its current effective strength of 134,000 men to 208,000, the only alternative to taking the field "with forces greatly inferior" to the enemy was "to go into winter quarters."[29] Since Lincoln was well aware that the army could not be increased by that much before the end of the year (if ever), his shoulders must have slumped when he read these words. They slumped more as week after week of unusually mild and dry weather slipped by in November and December with no advance in Virginia and no significant military success elsewhere except the capture of Port

Royal Bay in South Carolina and the adjacent sea islands by a navy-army task force.

Lincoln began dropping by McClellan's headquarters near the White House almost daily to consult with him. The general grew to resent these visits as a waste of time or an unwanted form of pressure. More than once he hid himself away "to dodge all enemies in shape of 'browsing' Presdt etc."[30] On the evening of November 13 Lincoln and Seward, along with the president's secretary John Hay, called unannounced on McClellan at home but learned that he was at a wedding. When the general returned an hour later, the porter told him that Lincoln was waiting to see him. McClellan said nothing and went upstairs. The president, secretary of state, and Hay waited another half hour before a servant deigned to tell them that the general had gone to bed.

Hay was furious at "this unparalleled insolence of epaulettes." But as they walked back to the White House, Lincoln told him that it was "better at this time not to be making points of etiquette and personal dignity." Significantly, however, from then on Lincoln almost always summoned McClellan to his office when he wanted to talk with the general. After one such occasion four days later McClellan wrote to his wife that at the White House "I found 'the original gorilla,' about as intelligent as ever. What a specimen to be at the head of our affairs!"[31]

About December 1, despairing of any initiative by McClellan, Lincoln drafted a proposal for half of the Army of the Potomac to make a feint toward Centreville to hold the enemy in place while the other half moved in two columns south along the Potomac — one by road and the other by water — to turn the Confederate flank. The moving columns would push up the Occoquan Valley in the enemy's rear to destroy the railroad supplying the Confederate army at Manassas and trap that army between the converging Union forces. This proposal reflected the crash course of reading on military history and strategy that Lincoln had recently begun. It was a bold and well-conceived strategic plan that threatened Confederate communications while protecting those of Union forces, and avoided a frontal assault on Confederate defenses, which McClellan claimed were impregnable.[32]

Lincoln's proposed move was precisely what Confederate commander Joseph E. Johnston most feared. A week earlier Johnston had informed Jefferson Davis that his forces were "too weak to observe the Occoquan and prevent the landing of a Federal army on the shores of the Potomac." The enemy's "great advantage over us," wrote Johnston, was his ability "to move on the water while we struggle through deep mud. . . . The enemy's new base would be far better than his present one, for from it he could easily cut our communications . . . and seriously threaten our right."[33] But McClellan did not see it that way. The enemy's greatly superior numbers (of which Lincoln had grown skeptical) would enable Johnston to detach his mobile reserves to defeat the flanking force, said McClellan. Besides, he told Lincoln, "I have now my mind actively turned toward another plan of campaign that I do not think at all anticipated by the enemy nor by many of our own people."[34]

Lincoln would have to wait almost two months to learn what "plan of campaign" McClellan had in mind. The weather finally turned bad and the army went into winter quarters. A few days before Christmas, McClellan fell ill with typhoid fever. During this time Lincoln was preoccupied with the diplomatic crisis over the seizure of Confederate envoys James Mason and John Slidell from the British passenger ship *Trent.* Fears of a war with Britain dried up the sale of bonds to finance the war against the Confederacy. To defuse the crisis Lincoln and the cabinet decided on Christmas Day to release Mason and Slidell. This decision proceeded from a vital principle of national strategy: One war at a time. The release of the Confederate envoys improved Anglo-American relations and disappointed Confederate hopes for an Anglo-American war that might assure their independence. But it also left a sour taste in the mouths of many Northerners. And the whole affair deepened Lincoln's despondency at the end of 1861, unrelieved by military success in any theater except the capture of Port Royal.

Next to McClellan, Gen. John C. Frémont caused Lincoln more headaches than anyone else in the second half of 1861. Famed as the "Pathfinder of the West," Frémont had led two major explorations into western territories as a topographical engineer in the army during the 1830s and 1840s. He had taken part in the California Bear Flag revolution against Mexican rule and had served as acting governor and a senator from that state. Frémont had been the Republican Party's first presidential candidate, and he retained widespread support in the party, especially among radicals. Because of his military reputation and political prominence, Lincoln appointed him commander of the Department of the West (mainly Missouri). Frémont's mission was to secure the state for the Union and then to launch a campaign down the Mississippi River. The Blair family had played a major part in persuading Lincoln to give Frémont this important command. Frank Blair, Jr., now a colonel, was Frémont's main ally in Missouri.

But from almost the moment Frémont arrived at St. Louis on July 25, things began to go wrong. Guerrilla warfare plagued all parts of the state. Two Confederate armies were gathering on the southern border for an invasion. A Rebel force of six thousand crossed the Mississippi from Tennessee, occupied New Madrid, and threatened the Union base at Cairo, Illinois. Frémont reinforced Cairo, which left him with no troops to reinforce Nathaniel Lyon's small army in southwest Missouri. The Confederates defeated that army and killed Lyon at Wilson's Creek on August 10, then moved north and laid siege to Independence. The reinforcements Frémont sent to that post were too few and too late. The garrison surrendered on September 20. In two months

Frémont had lost a substantial part of Missouri.

And that was not the worst of his perceived deficiencies. Frémont faced complex administrative problems without much help from Washington, a thousand miles away. War contracts had to be negotiated; supplies, arms, horses, and wagons had to be obtained in a hurry; gunboats for the river navy had to be built; new recruits had to be organized and trained; transport bottlenecks had to be overcome; and quarreling Unionists had to be kept in line. Frémont turned out to be a terrible administrator. Contractors cheated him. Many of his subordinates were corrupt. Reports of graft found their way to Washington. Frémont had a proconsular personality and an outsize ego. He surrounded himself with a large staff of German and Hungarian soldiers of fortune in gaudy uniforms who turned away many people who had legitimate business with the general.

Frank Blair lost faith in Frémont and wrote a critical letter to his brother Montgomery recommending his removal from command.[35] Montgomery showed the letter to Lincoln. When Frémont learned of this letter he had Frank Blair arrested for insubordination. That was his worst mistake.

It was said of the Blairs that when they went in for a fight they went in for a funeral. Lincoln dispatched a succession of high-level delegations to Missouri to sort out the mess: Gen. David Hunter, Secretary of War Cameron, Quartermaster General Meigs, Adjutant General Lorenzo Thomas, and Montgomery Blair. All sent or brought back devastating reports.[36] The House Committee on Contracts also investigated Frémont's department. Elihu Washburne, a member of the committee who was close to Lincoln, wrote the president on October 21 that "the disclosure of corruption extravagance and peculation are utterly astounding. We think the evidence will satisfy the public that a most formidable conspiracy has existed here to plunder the Government and that high officials have been prominently engaged in it."[37]

Three days later Lincoln issued orders replacing Frémont with General Hunter as interim commander of the department.[38] The president instructed Hunter to pull back from a dangerously extended position in southern Missouri, where Frémont had led his troops in a desperate effort to keep his command by provoking a battle. The enemy eventually withdrew into Arkansas. When General Halleck finally reached

Washington, Lincoln appointed him commander of the renamed Department of Missouri, which stretched as far east as the Cumberland River in Kentucky. Halleck proved to be the right man in the right place. An excellent administrator, he soon brought order out of the organizational chaos in Missouri and consolidated his forces for an effective defense of the state.

Frémont had not helped his cause by issuing an order on August 30 that placed Missouri under martial law, proclaimed the death penalty for guerrillas captured behind Union lines, and confiscated the property and freed the slaves of all Confederate sympathizers in the state.[39] Lincoln immediately ordered Frémont to execute no one without the president's consent. But the most controversial part of Frémont's edict was the liberation of Rebel-owned slaves. For the past five months the administration had been walking a tightrope on the sensitive issue of slavery. Lincoln's national strategy of maximizing support for the war would be jeopardized by any sign of an antislavery policy. A war to restore the Union united the North; a war against slavery would divide it. Border-state Unionists and Northern Democrats were suspicious of the Republican Party's designs on slavery. The strategy of conciliation of the presumed silent majority of Unionists in the Confederate states would also be wrecked by the first hint of an emancipation policy. Lincoln had lost some faith in that silent majority. But he very much wanted to keep Democrats and border-state Unionists in his war coalition.

A majority of congressional Republicans also supported this national strategy in the war's early months. All but a handful of them voted in July for a resolution sponsored by U.S. Representative John J. Crittenden of Kentucky and Senator Andrew Johnson of Tennessee (the only senator from a seceded state who remained loyal to the United States). This resolution affirmed that the war was being fought not for the purpose "of overthrowing or interfering with the rights or established institutions of those States," but only "to defend and maintain the supremacy of the Constitution and to preserve the Union."[40]

Some cracks in this policy had appeared by the time of Frémont's edict, however. Abolitionists, black leaders, and many Republicans viewed the war as potentially one against slavery from the beginning. They cheered the action of an unlikely but apparent convert to this position, Gen. Benjamin Butler — a former proslavery Democrat. After securing Baltimore, Butler had been assigned to command the Union toehold in tidewater Virginia at Fort Monroe. There on May 23 three slaves had escaped to Butler's lines. Their owner was a Confederate colonel, who came to Butler under flag of truce and demanded the return of his property under the Fugitive Slave Law! With as deadpan an expression as possible (given his cocked eye), Butler informed him that since Virginia claimed to have left the United States, the Fugitive Slave Law no longer applied.

Butler also learned that these slaves had worked for the Confederate army. An astute lawyer, he declared them contraband of war — enemy property subject to seizure. It was an inspired phrase. Northern newspapers picked it up, and it was used thereafter to describe all slaves who came under Union control. Word quickly spread among slaves on the Virginia Peninsula near Butler's lines, and scores of them began escaping to the Yankees. Butler put many of them to work for his own army, and also received their wives and children — the latter of whom could by no stretch of the imagination be defined as having worked on Confederate fortifications. Butler notified the War Department of his actions and requested approval. The cabinet discussed the matter on May 30. Lincoln joked about "Butler's fugitive slave law," and the cabinet fully sanctioned the contraband policy.[41]

Only two weeks after passing the Crittenden-Johnson resolution, Congress in effect ratified the contraband policy by enacting (over Democratic and border-state opposition) a Confiscation Act that authorized the seizure of all property used in military aid of the rebellion — including slaves. Lincoln signed the bill without comment.[42] The law carefully did not specify the permanent future status of the contrabands, but few expected they would ever be returned to slavery. Lincoln told his diary-keeping confidant, Senator Orville Browning, that "the government neither should nor would send back to bondage such as come to our armies."[43]

Frémont's blanket order declaring *all slaves* owned by Confederate activists in Missouri to be free went considerably beyond this policy. It provoked an instant outcry from border-state Unionists, while many Northern Republicans praised it. Fearing the defection of Kentucky, which still sat on the fence of neutrality, Lincoln sent a letter to Frémont by special messenger asking him to modify his order concerning slavery to conform with the more limited terms of the Confiscation Act. As it stood, the order "will alarm our Southern Union friends," wrote the president, "and turn them against us — perhaps ruin our rather fair prospect for Kentucky."[44]

Any other general would have treated this request as an order. But not Frémont. Instead he sent his wife, Jessie Benton Frémont (daughter of the famed Missouri senator Thomas Hart Benton), to Washington with a letter stating his refusal to modify the emancipation clause without a direct order. Lincoln was understandably angered by this refusal. He could barely hold his temper as the sharp-tongued Jessie gave him the rough side of that tongue. As Lincoln later recalled this confrontation, "She sought an audience with me at midnight and taxed me so violently with many things that I had to exercise all the awkward tact I have to avoid quarreling with her. . . . She more than once intimated that if Gen Fremont should conclude to try conclusions with me he could set up for himself."[45]

Mrs. Frémont obviously did not help her husband's cause. Lincoln publicly ordered the general to modify his edict. Border-state men expressed satisfaction, but the president came in for vigorous criticism from Republicans. This issue produced more letters to Lincoln, pro and con, than any other event of his presidency. One critical letter came from an unexpected source, Lincoln's friend Orville Browning, who was usually found in the conservative camp. Lincoln felt impelled to write a lengthy reply, which outlined his national strategy at this stage of the war. There was a great deal of credible evidence, the president told Browning, that Kentucky would have gone over to the Confederacy if Frémont's proclamation had stood. "I think to lose Kentucky is nearly the same as to lose the whole game. Kentucky gone, we can not hold Missouri, nor, as I think, Maryland. These all against us, and the job on our hands is too large for us. We would as well consent to separation at once, including the surrender of this capitol."

Lincoln also raised a constitutional objection to Frémont's edict. He acknowledged that a general might, on grounds of military necessity, seize enemy property including slaves, "but when the need is past, it is not for him to fix their permanent future condition. . . . You speak of it as being the only means of *saving* the government. On the contrary it is itself the surrender of government. Can it be pretended that it is any longer the government of the U.S. — any government of Constitution and laws, — wherein a General, or a President, may make permanent rules of property by proclamation?"[46]

The date of this letter to Browning is ironic: September 22, 1861, one year to the day before Lincoln did precisely what he said a general or a president could not do — proclaim slaves in rebellious states "forever free" unless those states returned to the Union within one hundred days. But the war intensified and took on a new character between those two Septembers that changed policies — and constitutional interpretations. Meanwhile, during the remainder of 1861 Lincoln confronted frustrating military delays not only with McClellan in Virginia but also with his commanders in the West.

When Tennessee seceded, three of the state's congressmen plus Senator Andrew Johnson remained loyal to the Union and took their seats in the Congress that met at Washington instead of at Richmond. All four were from East Tennessee, a region of mountains and valleys with few slaves. Two-thirds of the voters in East Tennessee had cast their ballots against secession in the referendum held on June 8, 1861. This pattern duplicated events in western Virginia. And perhaps the process of creating a new Union state in western Virginia could be applied in East Tennessee as well. Once Kentucky's neutrality came to an end in September, Lincoln outlined a plan for Union troops to invade East Tennessee through the Cumberland Gap from Kentucky. Federal agents established contacts with Unionists in East Tennessee to coordinate a local uprising with the invasion.[47]

The logistical problems in this region were much greater than those in western Virginia, where two railroads, a navigable river, and a macadamized turnpike could carry soldiers and supplies to the theater of operations. No such routes ran from Union bases in eastern Kentucky 150 miles over the rugged Cumberland Mountains to Knoxville. Nevertheless, in expectation of an invasion the Tennessee Unionists rose in November, attacked Confederate outposts, and burned five bridges on the railroad used by Confederates through the Tennessee Valley. There was no invasion, however, because Gen. William T. Sherman and his successor as commander in the Department of the Ohio, Gen. Don Carlos Buell, had called it off. Confederate troops rounded up scores of Unionists, hanged five of them, and imprisoned the rest.[48]

Lincoln was disconsolate at this turn of events. For reasons of both national and military strategy he placed a high priority on liberating East Tennessee: It would strengthen Unionism there and by encouragement perhaps elsewhere; and it would cut the Confederacy's main east–west railroad from Virginia to Memphis where it ran between Knoxville and Chattanooga. On these matters Lincoln and his new general-in-chief saw eye to eye. McClellan wanted Knoxville occupied to prevent Confederate reinforcements from coming to Virginia on that route and also to threaten the rear of the Confederate army at Manassas.

McClellan telegraphed Buell repeatedly to urge an advance into East Tennessee; just as often Buell replied to him, and to Lincoln, that logistical difficulties, especially with winter coming on, would make it impossible to march an army on terrible roads through the barren mountains or to keep it supplied even if it could get to Knoxville.[49] An advance on Nashville using the Louisville and Nashville Railroad and the Cumberland River, said Buell, was the true line of operations in Tennessee. From his sickbed McClellan dictated a letter to Buell on January 6, 1862: "I was extremely sorry to learn from your telegram to the President that you had *from the beginning attached little or no importance* to a movement in East Tennessee. . . . It develops a radical difference between your views and my own, which I regret."[50]

That same day Lincoln also wrote Buell that his dispatch explaining why he could not invade East Tennessee "disappoints and distresses me." Lincoln said he "would rather have a point on the Railroad south of Cumberland Gap, than Nashville, first, because it cuts a great artery of the enemies' communication, which Nashville does not, and secondly because it is in the midst of a loyal population, who would rally around it, while Nashville is not." Lincoln's great "distress is that our friends in East Tennessee are being hanged and driven to despair, and even now, I fear, are thinking of taking rebel arms for personal protection. In this we lose the most valuable stake we have in the South."[51]

Buell got the message — at least in part. He sent a small army under Gen. George H. Thomas toward East Tennessee. Thomas's force met and defeated a Confederate army of similar size at Logan's Crossroads near Mill Springs in southeastern Kentucky on January 19. Despite this victory Thomas could advance no farther over wretched roads in the harsh mountain winter. Lincoln's cherished dream of liberating East Tennessee would not be fulfilled for another twenty months.

On January 7 Lincoln sent a telegram to Buell pointedly asking him, since he preferred to advance against Nashville, when he planned to get started. The commander in chief sent an identical telegram to General Halleck, whose forces based at Cairo, Illinois, would have to cooperate with Buell. "Delay is ruining us," Lincoln told both generals. "It is indispensable for me to have something definite."[52] From Halleck came word that his troops still lacked sufficient arms and equipment and that he knew nothing of Buell's plans. Lincoln wrote a note on the back of Halleck's communication: "It is exceedingly discouraging. As everywhere else, nothing can be done."[52] That same day, January 10, the president dropped in to Quartermaster General Montgomery Meigs's office. "General, what shall I do?" asked Lincoln. "The people are impatient; Chase has no money . . . the

General of the Army has typhoid fever. The bottom is out of the tub. What shall I do?"[53]

3
You Must Act

Lincoln's plaintive question to Meigs echoes down the years. It was one of his low points as commander in chief. Two other important campaigns in which Lincoln had played a significant planning role were also hanging fire in January 1862: a joint army-navy effort to make a lodgment on North Carolina's mainland coast and to control Albemarle and Pamlico Sounds; and an ambitious campaign to capture the South's largest city and port, New Orleans. The president had ordered Benjamin Butler to raise troops in New England for the New Orleans expedition; he had also authorized Gen. Ambrose Burnside to recruit new regiments for the North Carolina campaign.[1] These efforts would bear fruit in important Union victories, but Lincoln could not know that yet. He manifested the same impatience with Burnside he had shown with McClellan, Buell, and Halleck. "It is of great importance you should move as soon as possible," the president wired Burnside on December 26. "Consumption of time is killing us."[2]

Burnside's expedition finally sailed on January 11. The previous day Lincoln had begun to carry out the advice Montgomery Meigs offered in response to the president's lament that the bottom was out of the tub. Meigs urged him to assert his prerogative as commander in chief and set in motion a campaign in Virginia without regard to McClellan, who might not be able to resume duty for weeks.[3]

This counsel echoed similar advice from Attorney General Edward Bates, who had also become disillusioned with McClellan. As " 'Commander in chief' by law," wrote Bates, the president "*must* command" rather than continue "this injurious deference to subordinates."[4] The Joint Committee on the Conduct of the War, created by Congress in December and dominated by radical Republicans, was also pressing Lincoln to prod the army into more vigorous action. Learning at this time that the campaign against New Orleans had been delayed by the army's failure to get the mortar boats ready, Lincoln told Assistant Navy Secretary Fox that he was convinced "he must take these army matters in his own hands."[5]

So Lincoln walked out of Meigs's office on that fateful January 10 and summoned several cabinet members plus Gens. Irvin McDowell and William B. Franklin to the White House for an emergency strategy session. The Army of the Potomac's senior division commander, McDowell was also the choice of the Committee on the Conduct of the War to replace McClellan — despite McDowell's taint of defeat stemming from Bull Run. Franklin was one of McClellan's personal friends and protégés. These two seemed an unpromising combination to carry out Lincoln's insistence on action. Nevertheless the president figuratively knocked their heads together at that January 10 meeting. According to McDowell's notes, the president said that "if General McClellan did not want to use the army, he would like to *borrow* it." Lincoln ordered the two generals to come up with a plan and to meet the next day with him and Meigs (who would be responsible for logistics) plus several cabinet members.[6]

They came up with two plans. McDowell formulated a short-range flanking movement via the Occoquan Valley similar to Lincoln's earlier proposal. Franklin sketched out a deep flanking movement down the Potomac River and Chesapeake Bay (one hundred miles farther) to operate against Richmond from the east. McClellan had been mulling a similar operation for some time, and Franklin was privy to it — while McDowell and Lincoln obviously were not. Most of those present on January 11 favored McDowell's plan. But McClellan got wind of the meeting and, largely recovered from his illness, met with the same group on the thirteenth. Sullen and silent during most of the session, McClellan refused to reveal his own plan because, he whispered to Meigs, he feared that the president would leak it! When McClellan assured the group that he actually *had* a plan and a timetable to carry it out, however, the president once again deferred to him and adjourned the meeting.[7]

McClellan's whispered statement that he feared a leak was a colossal act of hypocrisy. The very next day he had a long interview with a reporter for the *New York Herald,* the country's largest newspaper, and outlined his plans in detail. The *Herald* had influence in Democratic circles, and McClellan wanted to cultivate that influence to offset growing Republican criticisms of his inaction. Lincoln knew none of this, and during the next few days the launching of the

Burnside expedition and Gen. George Thomas's advance toward East Tennessee put the president in a better mood. On January 18 he told Orville Browning that he had "great confidence" in McClellan.[8]

During these mid-January days Lincoln also took another decisive action: He replaced Simon Cameron with Edwin M. Stanton as secretary of war. This move had been building for a long time. Lincoln had been reluctant to appoint Cameron in the first place. But he felt bound by the pledges of his campaign managers in return for Cameron's release of his Pennsylvania delegates to Lincoln on the second ballot at the Republican convention in 1860. Cameron was known sardonically as the "Winnebago Chief" because of his alleged cheating of the Winnebago tribe in financial dealings in the 1830s. He had a perhaps exaggerated reputation for corruption in his antebellum career as a businessman and for spoilsmanship as a politician. As secretary of war he turned out to be a slipshod administrator who awarded lucrative contracts to favorite cronies without competitive bidding.

Favoritism aside, Cameron was clearly not up to the task of overseeing with efficiency the huge military mobilization of 1861. By

October of that year Lincoln was fed up with him. In a conversation with John Nicolay, who took notes, the president complained that Cameron was "utterly ignorant and regardless of the course of things. . . . Selfish and openly discourteous to the President. Obnoxious to the Country. Incapable either of organizing details or conceiving and advising general plans."[9] Lincoln determined to get rid of Cameron but had to tread carefully to avoid alienating his partisans in Pennsylvania. In January the president seized his opportunity. Cameron had made vague references to a desire to resign if he could be appointed to a less stressful but honorable post. When the minister to Russia resigned, the president offered the job to Cameron, who accepted.[10]

Lincoln's choice as Cameron's successor was somewhat surprising. Edwin M. Stanton was a Democrat, a confidant of McClellan who had made no secret of his disdain for the administration in 1861. It was from Stanton that McClellan had picked up the description of Lincoln as "the original gorilla." One of the country's leading trial lawyers, Stanton had snubbed Lincoln when they were associated on a patent infringement case in 1855. But the president admired Stanton's ability and was willing to overlook personal discourtesy — as he had done with McClellan.

The choice of Stanton proved to be an inspired one. Although many people were offended by his brusque manners and suffer-no-fools rudeness, they were often in need of offending. Ruthlessly honest, he brought efficiency and integrity to the business of war contracts. Lincoln and Stanton developed an unexpectedly warm relationship based on mutual respect. They also practiced a sort of good cop/bad cop administrative style: Lincoln would send politicians and others requesting impossible favors to Stanton, who he knew would say no. The disappointed favor seekers would go away blaming Stanton, saving Lincoln from negative political consequences.

McClellan was initially delighted with Stanton's appointment, which he described to a fellow Democrat as "a most unexpected piece of good fortune." But Stanton soon became disillusioned with the general. A few days after taking over at the War Department, he wrote that "as soon as I can get the machinery of office going, the rats cleared out, and the rat holes stopped, we shall *move. This army has got to fight or run away; . . . the champagne and oysters on the*

Potomac must be stopped."[11]

Lincoln thought so too, and at the end of January he issued two orders designed to force Halleck and Buell as well as McClellan into action. General Order No. 1 specified that the "Land and Naval forces" should move "against the insurgent forces" on or before February 22, Washington's Birthday. Special Order No. 1 stated that the Army of the Potomac should move against the railroad supplying Johnston's army at Manassas (the Occoquan operation favored by Lincoln and McDowell) on or before the same date.[12]

Lincoln did not necessarily intend the February 22 date to be taken literally. Rather, as he explained to Orville Browning, he wanted the principal Union armies to advance more or less simultaneously to "threaten all [enemy] positions at the same time with superior force, and if they weakened one to strengthen another seize and hold the one weakened." Lincoln's strategy of coordinated offensives grew out of his correspondence with Buell and Halleck, in which the commander in chief tried to get them to cooperate in movements against Confederate strongpoints in Kentucky and Tennessee. After Halleck explained that he could not move because he lacked arms and equipment (in the letter that Lincoln found "exceedingly discouraging"), the general proceeded to lecture the president: "To operate on *exterior* lines against an enemy occupying a central position, will fail, as it has always failed, in ninety-nine cases out of a hundred. It is condemned by every military authority I have ever read."[13]

By this time Lincoln had read some of those authorities himself in his cram course on strategy, and was prepared to challenge Halleck's reasoning. The president recognized that by the geography of the case, Union forces had to operate from exterior lines around the perimeter of the Confederacy. Lincoln grasped sooner than many of his generals the strategic concept of "concentration in time." Because the Confederacy's basic military strategy was to defend the territory that lay behind its frontier, Southern armies had the advantage of interior lines. That advantage enabled them to shift reinforcements from inactive to active fronts, as they had done at Manassas in July 1861. This concentration in *space* could be overcome only if the Union employed its greater numbers (a reality despite McClellan's belief to the contrary) to attack on two or more fronts at once — concentration in *time.*

No one explained this strategic concept better than Lincoln himself. Three days after receiving Halleck's letter, Lincoln replied to him and sent an identical letter to Buell. "I state my general idea of this war," wrote the commander in chief, "that we have the *greater* numbers, and the enemy has the *greater* facility of concentrating upon points of collision." Union forces could not succeed "unless we can find some way of making *our* advantage an over-match for his; and that this can only be done by menacing him with superior forces at *different* points, at the *same* time; so that we can safely attack, one, or both, if he makes no change; and that if he *weakens* one to strengthen the other, forbear to attack the strengthened one, but seize and hold the weakened one, gaining so much."[14]

If Buell or Halleck acknowledged this good advice, there is no record of it. In any case events in their theaters during the next month proved the soundness of Lincoln's strategy. At the beginning of February, Halleck ordered Gen. Ulysses S. Grant, with fifteen thousand men, to proceed against Fort Henry on the Tennessee River just south of the Kentucky border. Grant would be accompanied by Flag Officer Andrew H. Foote and his fleet of new ironclad river gunboats. Grant and Foote had been urging such an advance; Halleck responded to that urging as well as to Lincoln's General Order No. 1 by turning them loose. The gunboats subdued and captured Fort Henry on February 6, opening up the Tennessee River to the Union fleet all the way to Muscle Shoals at Florence, Alabama. Grant prepared to march his army across the twelve miles that separated Fort Henry from Fort Donelson on the Cumberland River.

This lightning campaign confronted Confederate commander Albert Sidney Johnston with a serious dilemma. Buell menaced his defenses at Bowling Green, Kentucky, at the same time that Grant approached Fort Donelson. Just as Lincoln had predicted, Johnston was forced to weaken one to defend the other from these Union forces converging on exterior lines. Johnston chose to abandon Bowling Green to reinforce Fort Donelson. Grant captured Donelson anyway, which compelled Johnston to abandon Nashville as Buell approached and also to evacuate the Confederate bastion on the Mississippi River at Columbus, Kentucky, which Southerners had proudly labeled "the Gibraltar of the West."

Grant became one of the first Union heroes of the war with his demand for "unconditional surrender" of Fort Donelson. Foote received almost equal acclaim and was soon promoted to become one of the first three rear admirals in American naval history (along with Samuel F. Du Pont, captor of Port Royal, and David G. Farragut, captor of New Orleans). "We all went wild over your success," a lieutenant in the Washington Navy Yard wrote to Foote. "Uncle Abe was joyful, and said everything of the naval boys and spoke of you — in his plain, sensible appreciation of merit and skill."[15]

Halleck tried to take credit for these achievements because Forts Henry and Donelson were in his department. He asked for supreme command in the West as a reward, and also recommended Buell, Grant, and Charles F. Smith (a division commander under Grant) for promotion to major general. Lincoln had a pretty good idea who deserved the credit. He ignored most of Halleck's requests (for the time being) but immediately promoted Grant to major general of volunteers, making him second in seniority only to Halleck in the Western theater.[16]

A misunderstanding between Grant and Halleck — who was perhaps jealous of his subordinate — temporarily threatened

Grant's command. Halleck complained that he had received no reports from Grant for two weeks after the capture of Fort Donelson and that Grant had made an unauthorized trip to Nashville after it fell. Halleck slyly hinted that Grant may have resumed his "old habits" — a reference to the persistent rumors of drunkenness that had supposedly forced Grant to resign from the army back in 1854. McClellan authorized Halleck to remove Grant from command if satisfactory explanations were not forthcoming. Halleck suspended Grant pending further information.[17]

It turned out that Grant had been sending dispatches to Halleck all along, but the telegraph operator at Cairo — a Confederate sympathizer — had not forwarded them. Grant gave copies of them to his congressional sponsor, Elihu Washburne, who in turn showed them to Lincoln. The president had the adjutant general send a telegram to Halleck demanding an official statement of his charges against Grant. Lincoln's intervention was decisive. Halleck backed down, cited the telegrapher's sabotage as the source of the trouble, and ordered Grant to resume his command and "lead [your army] on to new victories."[18]

■ ■ ■ ■

While this contretemps between Halleck and Grant was going on, Lincoln was losing patience with McClellan — again. In response to the president's Special Order No. 1, the general asked for permission "to submit in writing my objections to his plans and my reasons for preferring my own." Lincoln granted the request, and on February 3 McClellan wrote a long memorandum explaining for the first time his proposal for a deep flanking movement to pry the enemy out of his Manassas/Centreville fortifications. As foreshadowed by General Franklin three weeks earlier, McClellan proposed to take the Army of the Potomac down its namesake river and the Chesapeake Bay and up the Rappahannock River to Urbana, some 120 miles by water from Washington. From there he would have a secure base to launch a 50-mile campaign to Richmond. This move, he said, would force Joseph Johnston to evacuate the Manassas line and retreat south to defend Richmond, which McClellan predicted he might reach before the enemy could get there.

Lincoln was not convinced. He was concerned that the enemy might attack Washington before McClellan got anywhere near Richmond. He posed a series of hard questions to the general. In what ways, Lincoln asked, would a victory be more certain and valuable by McClellan's plan than by the president's preferred operation in the Occoquan Valley? In case of defeat, "would not a safe retreat be more difficult by your plan than mine?" Finally, "does not your plan involve a greatly larger expenditure of *time,* and *money,* than mine?"

McClellan largely ignored this last question, but answered the others by assuring the president that his own plan "if successful gives us the capital, the communications, the supplies of rebels; Norfolk would fall; all the waters of the Chesapeake would be ours; all Virginia would be in our power; & the enemy forced to abandon Tennessee & North Carolina." But if not successful, McClellan said he would have a safe line of retreat down the peninsula between the York and James Rivers to Fort Monroe.[19]

Lincoln remained skeptical. Two sound premises that underlay his questions were left unanswered by McClellan: First, the enemy army, not Richmond, should be the primary objective; and second, Lincoln's plan would enable the Army of the Potomac to operate close to its own base

(Alexandria), while McClellan's plan, even if successful, would draw the enemy back to *his* base (Richmond) and greatly lengthen Union supply lines.

Nevertheless Lincoln once again (perhaps unwisely) deferred to McClellan's supposedly superior professional qualifications and tentatively approved the general's plan. Assembling the shipping and other logistical requirements for the operation would take several weeks — one of the reasons, of course, that Lincoln had questioned it. As these February weeks went by, the Union victories in Kentucky and Tennessee as well as the success of Burnside's expedition that gained control of the North Carolina sounds and much of the coast made the Army of the Potomac's apparent continuing inactivity all the more humiliating by comparison.

A fiasco at Harpers Ferry did further damage to McClellan's credibility. Desiring to protect the Baltimore and Ohio Railroad and keep Confederates off his flank on the Potomac above Washington, McClellan planned to cross General Banks's division at Harpers Ferry and occupy Winchester. Banks's troops would be supplied via a pontoon bridge of canal boats towed up the Chesapeake and Ohio Canal from Washington. McClellan went to Harpers Ferry on

February 26 to oversee the operation. But it turned out that the boats were six inches too wide to pass through the outlet locks from the canal to the river. When the embarrassed McClellan telegraphed this news to Stanton, the secretary of war took the telegram to Lincoln. "What does this mean?" asked the astonished president. "It means it is a d[amne]d fizzle," said Stanton. "It means that he does not intend to do anything."[20]

Lincoln usually managed to keep his temper in check. But not this time. He summoned McClellan's chief of staff (who was also the general's father-in-law), Randolph Marcy, and vented his spleen. "Why in [tar]-nation," snapped the president, "couldn't the Gen. have known whether a boat would go through that lock, before he spent a million of dollars getting them there? I am no engineer; but it seems to me that if I wished to know whether a boat would go through a hole, or a lock, common sense would teach me to go and measure it." Lincoln expressed himself as "almost despairing at these results. Everything seems to fail. The general impression is daily growing that the general does not intend to do anything. By a failure like this we lose all the prestige we gained by the capture of Fort Donelson. I am grievously disappointed."[21]

Ugly rumors began to circulate in Republican circles that McClellan, a Democrat, did not really want to crush the rebellion. Lincoln received scores of letters accusing the general of treasonable motives and endured dozens of visits from Republican leaders, some of whom made similar charges. These rumors were a product of politics as well as of the army's inactivity. McClellan had made little secret of his dislike for abolitionists and radical Republicans. His closest political associates were Democrats who wanted to restore the Union on the basis of something like the Crittenden Compromise that would preserve slavery and the political power of Southern Democrats. Some of the generals serving in the Confederate army confronting him "were once my most intimate friends," McClellan had acknowledged (privately) in November 1861. He did not want to fight the kind of war the radicals were beginning to demand — a war to destroy slavery and the power of the planter class. McClellan wrote in November 1861 to an influential Democratic friend: "Help me dodge the nigger. . . . *I* am fighting to preserve the integrity of the Union. . . . To gain that end we cannot afford to raise up the negro question."[22]

Radical Republican senators Benjamin Wade and Zachariah Chandler had played a significant role in boosting McClellan to the position of general-in-chief in November. Four months had passed, and, in their view, McClellan had betrayed them by doing nothing. They were suspicious of his politics and perhaps half believed rumors of his disloyalty. But the main reason for their conversion from supporters of McClellan to his most vocal critics was the general's inactivity. On March 3 Lincoln met with members of the Committee on the Conduct of the War (chaired by Wade). They gave the president an earful of complaints about McClellan. Wade urged Lincoln to remove him from command. If he did so, Lincoln asked, who should replace him? "Why, anybody!" Wade reportedly responded. "Wade," Lincoln supposedly said, "*anybody* will do for you, but not for me. I must have somebody."[23]

This story may be apocryphal. The committee actually had two possible candidates in mind: McDowell or their new favorite, Frémont, whose antislavery credentials seemed more important than military competency. But Lincoln believed that these generals carried too much negative baggage

140

from defeat at Bull Run and failure in Missouri. The president was more receptive to the committee's advice to organize the Army of the Potomac into four corps of three divisions each instead of the twelve discrete divisions whose commanders each reported directly to McClellan. Most of the generals who would presumably become corps commanders by seniority were Republicans or at least nonpartisan, while most of the younger division commanders whom McClellan had placed in their posts were Democrats. That party had dominated Congress most of the time since the 1830s, so a majority of plebes appointed to West Point by congressmen came from Democratic families. For the same reason officers ambitious to get ahead in the antebellum army often cultivated relationships with Democrats who were in a position to help them. One historian has estimated that in 1860 almost three-quarters of regular army officers whose political affiliation could be determined were Democrats.[24]

Despite Lincoln's deflection of Wade, the president was in fact considering the removal of McClellan. A month had gone by since Lincoln had lukewarmly approved the general's Urbana plan. The army was still in winter quarters. The day after his meeting with the committee, Lincoln told a Pennsylvania congressman that unless McClellan moved soon he would be replaced.[25] Secretary of War Stanton had summoned to Washington the sixty-three-year-old retired colonel Ethan Allen Hitchcock, grandson of Revolutionary War hero Ethan Allen. Hitchcock had served in the army for thirty-eight years before resigning after a dispute with Secretary of War Jefferson Davis in 1855. More interested in philosophy and theology than in war, Hitchcock reluctantly accepted a commission as major general and a staff position in the War Department. One day in March, Stanton surprised him by asking if he would be willing to replace McClellan — which Stanton scarcely would have done without Lincoln's approval. Hitchcock wrote in his diary that Stanton told him "the most astounding facts, all going to show the astonishing incompetency of General McClellan. I can not recite them: but . . . I felt positively *sick*. . . . I do not wonder, now, that the Secretary offered me the command of this Army of the Potomac."[26]

Hitchcock declined the offer on grounds of age and health. For better or worse the president decided to stick with McClellan. But on March 7 Lincoln summoned the general to his office and told him with unprecedented bluntness that his tenure was short unless he got moving. The president also hinted — perhaps stated openly — that some influential men believed the real purpose of his Urbana plan was to leave Washington uncovered so the Rebels could capture it. McClellan was outraged, but Lincoln assured him that he did not believe a word of the rumors.[27]

With his tin ear for the political realities of both his and the president's positions, McClellan said he would resolve any doubts about his Urbana plan by submitting it to a vote of his division commanders and the army's chief engineer officer. They voted eight to four in favor of the plan — not surprising, perhaps, since most of those eight owed their positions to McClellan's sponsorship. Three of the four division commanders with the greatest seniority voted against the plan and expressed a preference for Lincoln's and McDowell's Occoquan strategy. Lincoln nevertheless said he would assent to the majority decision. "We can do nothing else than accept their plan," he told Stanton. "We can't reject it and adopt another without assuming all the responsibility in the case of the one we adopt."[28]

Perhaps he should have rejected it. But that probably would have provoked McClel-

143

lan's resignation, demoralization in the Army of the Potomac, and further delay. Lincoln did not have anyone else in whom he had confidence to substitute for McClellan, who had created the Army of the Potomac and enjoyed the adulatory support of the rank and file as well as of most officers. But the day after the generals' vote, Lincoln issued an order organizing the Army of the Potomac into four corps and appointing the four senior generals — including three who had voted against the Urbana plan — as the corps commanders. McClellan had opposed the corps organization until he could make his own recommendations for corps commanders, but was overruled. Lincoln also issued a second order on March 8 approving the Urbana plan on condition that McClellan leave "in, and about Washington" a force sufficient to make the capital "entirely secure." Three days later came another order that relieved McClellan as general-in-chief because, as commander of an army about to take the field, he could no longer "do it all." The same order protected Lincoln's left political flank (the radical Republicans) by creating a new command in western Virginia for Frémont, designated the Mountain Department. This order also gave Halleck command over the vast area west of Frémont's department all the way to Kansas. For the time being Lincoln and Stanton would do the job of general-in-chief themselves.[29]

The impact of these orders was to put McClellan on notice that he would be held accountable for results in his theater, and that Halleck was being rewarded for success in *his* theater and promoted to virtual equality of responsibility with McClellan. But for McClellan the central fact in this flurry of orders was that Lincoln had approved his plan. The general wrote to his friend Samuel L. M. Barlow, a prominent lawyer and Democratic leader in New York: "The President is all right — he is my strongest friend."[30]

The very day that a majority of generals voted for the Urbana plan, however, Joseph Johnston threw a monkey wrench into the operation. He withdrew his army from the Manassas/Centreville line to Culpeper, south of the Rappahannock River, where he was in a position to block McClellan's intention to move toward Richmond from Urbana. Johnston was thus also no longer vulnerable to a turning movement via the Occoquan Valley — which was one of his reasons for the withdrawal.[31]

McClellan immediately led the Army of

the Potomac on what he called a "practice march" to the abandoned Confederate works. Northern journalists who accompanied the army discovered that the Confederate defenses were by no means as formidable as McClellan had claimed, and the camps had room for only about half as many men as McClellan had estimated. Several of the heavy-artillery redoubts mounted logs painted black rather than large-caliber cannons. These "Quaker guns" caused McClellan much embarrassment. Already skeptical of his estimates of enemy numbers and strength, Lincoln and Stanton never again gave credence to the general's perpetual complaints of inferior numbers.

Johnston's retreat compelled McClellan to shift his proposed flanking movement another thirty miles south to Fort Monroe, at the tip of the Virginia Peninsula. This time all four corps commanders voted for the plan, and Lincoln once again reluctantly approved — provided enough troops were left behind to protect Washington.[32] McClellan promised to do so, but failed to consult with Lincoln about what constituted a sufficient force. In fact the general did not even send a list of the units designated for this purpose until he had boarded ship for the Peninsula on April 1. A courier carried back to the War Department a misleading tabulation that counted some nonexistent troops, counting others twice, and included thirty thousand soldiers under General Banks around Harpers Ferry who were as far from Washington as was Johnston's army around Culpeper. Stanton submitted to Hitchcock and Adjutant General Lorenzo Thomas the question of whether these units constituted the sufficient force the president had specified for Washington's defense. They replied on April 2 that "the President's order has not been fully complied with."[33] Described by Senator Charles Sumner as "justly indignant" about this information, Lincoln ordered McDowell's large corps of thirty thousand men temporarily withheld from McClellan and deployed in the vicinity of Manassas.[34]

McClellan was incensed when he received this news. He described it to his wife as "the most infamous thing that history has recorded." He blamed Stanton more than Lincoln. Indeed, the general's bitterness toward Stanton was all the more intense because he had once considered the secretary of war an ally in the struggle against his radical enemies. Stanton was now hand in glove with the "wretches" and "hell hounds" in Washington who wanted him to fail because they disliked his politics. "History will present a sad record of these traitors who are willing to sacrifice the country & its army for personal spite," wrote McClellan. "Stanton is without exception the vilest man I ever knew."[35]

McClellan appealed to Lincoln for a reversal of the order withholding McDowell's corps. "I beg that you will reconsider," he telegraphed the president on April 5. "The enemy are in large force along our front. . . . The success of our cause will be imperiled by so greatly reducing my force. . . . I am now of the opinion that I shall have to fight all the available force of the Rebels not far from here." In an effort to explain why he had held back McDowell's corps, Lincoln summarized the false arithmetic in McClellan's listing of the units left to defend Washington and asked: "Do you really think I should permit the line from Richmond, *via* Manassas Junction, to this city to be entirely open, except what resistance could be presented by less than twenty thousand unorganized troops?" This was, said the commander in chief, "a question which the country will not allow me to evade."[36] McClellan may have been correct in asserting that his offensive on the Peninsula would force Johnston to hasten south to defend his own capital instead of attacking Washington. But Lincoln was right in saying that he could not afford the risk.

When McClellan wrote on April 5 that the enemy was in "large force" on his front, most of Johnston's army was eighty miles away. McClellan had 60,000 men with another 25,000 only a day or two distant, facing about 13,000 Confederates stretched thinly along a dozen miles of defenses behind the Warwick River near Yorktown. Lincoln telegraphed McClellan that with this advantage, "I think you better break the enemies' line . . . at once. They will probably use *time,* as advantageously as you can." McClellan's only reaction to this admonition was a comment to his wife: "I was much tempted to reply that he had better come and do it himself."[37]

The commander of the Confederate force at Yorktown was Gen. John. B. Magruder, who had been known in the old army as "Prince John" because of his taste for the high life, including amateur theatricals. Prince John put on a show for McClellan. He marched some of his troops back and forth behind his lines and shifted his artillery around to give the impression that he had more men than he really did. Whether for that reason or because of his habitual exaggeration of enemy numbers, McClellan believed that "the enemy are in large force along our front," as he told Lincoln.

In a conversation with Orville Browning, the president said that McClellan "had the capacity to make arrangements properly for a great conflict, but as the hour for action approached he became nervous and oppressed with the responsibility and hesitated to meet the crisis." It was an incisive observation, and entirely accurate. In an attempt to help McClellan overcome his nervous hesitation, Lincoln wrote him a fatherly letter on April 9. Now was "the precise time to strike a blow," he said. "By delay the enemy will gain faster, by *fortifications* and *re-inforcements,* than you can by re-inforcements alone." This was exactly right. "And, once more let me tell you," Lincoln continued, "it is indispensable to you that you strike a blow. . . . You will do me the justice to remember I always insisted, that going down the Bay in search of a field, instead of fighting at or near Manassas, was only shifting, and not surmounting, a difficulty — that we would find the same enemy, and the same, or equal, intrenchments, at either place. The country will not fail to note — is now noting — that the present hesitation to move upon an intrenched enemy, is but the story of Manassas repeated." Lincoln assured McClellan that "I have never written you, or spoken to you, in greater kindness of feeling than now, nor with a fuller purpose to sustain you. . . . *But you must act.*"[38]

It was a superb letter, one of Lincoln's best. But McClellan ignored it. And even though one of McDowell's divisions had joined him, he decided to bring up his siege guns to pulverize the Confederate lines — a process that would take weeks just to get the guns and mortars into position. On April 16 a reconnaissance in force by several companies of the Third Vermont discovered a weak point in the Confederate line at Dam No. 1 on the Warwick River. Instead of reinforcing this potential breakthrough, McClellan rode away and subsequently reported that "the object I proposed had been fully accomplished." The only result was to persuade the enemy to reinforce that part of the line.[39] But when General Johnston arrived on April 22 and inspected the Confederate defenses, he reported that "labor enough has been expended here to make a very strong position, but it has been wretchedly misapplied by younger engineer officers. No one but McClellan could have hesitated to attack."[40]

151

■ ■ ■ ■

Lincoln remained preoccupied with Mc-Clellan and the Virginia theater during this period because the war in other theaters was going so well. As usual it was the squeaky wheel that got the grease — and McClellan's wheel was by far the squeakiest. After the capture of Fort Donelson and the occupation of Nashville, General Halleck ordered Grant and Buell to unite their armies at Pittsburg Landing on the Tennessee River for a campaign against the key Confederate railroad junction at Corinth, Mississippi. In northwest Arkansas a small Union army routed the enemy in the Battle of Pea Ridge on March 7–8 and gained control of the northern part of the state. A naval flotilla supported by Gen. John Pope's Army of the Mississippi moved down that river picking off Confederate fortifications on its way to naval capture of Memphis on June 6. Operations along the South Atlantic coast captured islands from South Carolina to Florida and the harbors of New Bern and Beaufort, North Carolina, and closed Savannah and Fernandina, Florida, to blockade-runners by capturing the forts at the entrance to their harbors.

The greatest coup of all was the capture of New Orleans by a fleet under the command of David Glasgow Farragut at the end of April. Benjamin Butler's army occupied the city while Farragut's ships proceeded up the Mississippi, compelling the surrender of Baton Rouge and Natchez on their way to meet the Union river fleet coming down to Vicksburg. That bastion on the bluff held out, but its capture seemed only a matter of time.

The well-oiled Union machinery in these theaters emitted some troubling noises only at Pittsburg Landing, where a Confederate attack almost pushed Grant's army into the Tennessee River on April 6. The next day, however, a counterattack by Grant and part of Buell's Army of the Ohio drove the enemy back to Corinth. This two-day Battle of Shiloh was the largest of the war so far, with almost twenty-four thousand casualties on both sides, of which thirteen thousand were Union. Newspaper correspondents who descended on the field after the battle reported that Grant had been surprised on the first day because he was drunk or incompetent. Neither was true, but the stories gained such wide circulation that several politicians went to Lincoln and demanded Grant's dismissal.

Having personally promoted Grant after Fort Donelson, Lincoln parried the demands. After all, Shiloh *was* a Union victory. And despite the stories, Lincoln learned from official reports and other information that Grant's tactical handling of his army during the battle deserved much of the credit for that victory. On April 23 the president sent an official inquiry to Halleck asking "whether any neglect or misconduct of General Grant or any other officer contributed to the sad casualties that befell our forces on Sunday" (April 6). Halleck replied that several subordinate officers had behaved badly, but the rumors about Grant were false.[41]

Lincoln defended Grant against the shower of criticism. The president probably did not utter the famous words quoted by the Pennsylvania politico Alexander McClure: "I can't spare this man; he fights."[42] But he certainly spoke other words as strong or stronger in Grant's defense. As Elihu Washburne later told Grant, "When the torrent of obloquy and detraction was rolling over you, and your friends, after the battle of Shiloh, Mr. Lincoln stood like a wall of fire between you and it, uninfluenced by the threats of Congressmen and the demands of insolent cowardice."[43] Had it not been for Lincoln's support at this time, the Grant of history would not have existed — and perhaps neither would the Lincoln of history.

During these months of military frustration in Virginia and success elsewhere, Lincoln also had to deal with the escalating issue of slavery. His modification of Frémont's emancipation edict continued to rankle many Republicans. When Congress met in December 1861, a solid Republican vote in the House defeated a motion to reaffirm the Crittenden resolution that had disavowed any antislavery purpose in the war.[44] More and more slaves came into Union lines as Northern armies penetrated into the South, especially in Tennessee and the lower Mississippi Valley. Some generals tried to bar them from entering Union lines, but these efforts seemed little more effective than King Canute's attempt to hold back the waves. On March 13 Congress enacted a new article of war prohibiting army officers, under pain of court-martial, from returning escaped slaves to their masters — even loyal masters. On April 16 Lincoln signed into law a bill abolishing slavery in the District of Columbia.[45] During this session of Congress, bills to expand the Confiscation Act by freeing the slaves of *all* Rebel owners were making their way through congressional committees.

Lincoln recognized that he needed to seize control of the slavery issue before it ran away from him. There was no question about his personal inclinations. He had frequently branded slavery "an unqualified evil to the negro, the white man, and the State. . . . The monstrous injustice of slavery . . . deprives our republican example of its just influence in the world — enables the enemies of free institutions, with plausibility, to taunt us as hypocrites."[46] But Lincoln did not believe that "the Presidency conferred upon me an unrestricted right to act officially upon this judgment and feeling."[47] And he told Congress in December 1861 that "in considering the policy to be adopted for suppressing the insurrection, I have been anxious that the inevitable conflict for this purpose shall not degenerate into a violent and remorseless revolutionary conflict." What he meant by that was not entirely clear. But he seemed to mean that he wanted the purpose of the war to remain restoration of the Union with a minimum of radical transformation in the Southern social order. However, another passage in the same message — little noticed at the time — pushed that minimum beyond what it had been when he signed the Confiscation Act the previous August. He referred to the contrabands affected by that law as "thus liberated" — that is, free people who could not be returned to slavery. Lincoln also hinted in this message at a new border-state strategy that would keep these states in the Union while making progress toward emancipation.[48]

Lincoln believed that the existence of slavery in the border states kept alive Confederate hopes that they would eventually join their slave nation. If the border states could be persuaded to abolish slavery gradually, they would be more firmly welded to the Union, and the Confederacy would be correspondingly weakened. In the fall of 1861 Lincoln tried to test this proposition in the state where slavery had almost disappeared already — Delaware. Only 8 percent of Delaware's black population were enslaved. In November 1861 Lincoln drafted a bill for gradual abolition of slavery in the state, with owners to be compensated by the federal government. Delaware's congressman presented the bill to the legislature, which buried it after Democrats denounced this effort "to place the negro on a footing of equality with the white man."[49]

Lincoln did not give up, however. On March 6, 1862, he sent Congress a special message recommending passage of a joint resolution offering financial aid to any state "which may adopt gradual abolishment of slavery." If all four border states should accept the offer, the cost would be no more than the cost of three months of war. Lincoln predicted (overoptimistically) that if adopted, the measure would "substantially end the rebellion" by depriving the Confederacy of any hope that these states would join them. Lincoln also uttered a thinly veiled warning to the border states. If they refused this offer, he said, "it is impossible to foresee all the incidents which may attend and all the ruin which may follow" if the war continued much longer — in other words, they might lose slavery anyway and have nothing to show for it.[50]

Congress passed Lincoln's resolution, with Republicans unanimously in favor and Democrats 85 percent opposed. But the president's meeting with border-state congressmen on March 10 was discouraging. They complained of federal coercion, bickered about the amount of compensation, questioned the measure's constitutionality, and predicted racial strife and economic ruin.[51] Two months later an action by Gen. David Hunter, commander of Union forces occupying the South Atlantic coast, should have reminded them of Lincoln's warning. On May 9 Hunter issued an edict declaring free all slaves in South Carolina, Georgia, and Florida. Lincoln knew nothing of this order until he read it in the newspapers. He promptly rescinded it, telling Secretary of the Treasury Chase (who urged him to let it stand) that "no commanding general shall do such a thing, upon my responsibility, without consulting me."[52]

In his rescindment order, however, the president again signaled the border states — and everyone else — with a carrot and a stick. "You can not," he told border-state representatives, "be blind to the signs of the times." The changes brought about by compensated, gradual emancipation "would come gently as the dews of heaven, not rending or wrecking anything," while "the strong tendency to a total disruption of society in the South" would get even stronger if the war continued. Lincoln also hinted ominously, in his comment on the substance of Hunter's order, that "whether at any time, in any case, it shall have become a necessity indispensable to the maintenance of the government, to exercise such supposed power, are questions which, under my responsibility, I reserve to myself" and not to commanders in the field.[53]

In May 1862, however, the chances that a prolonged war would erode slavery appeared remote. The remarkable string of Union victories everywhere but in Virginia encouraged many in the North and discouraged others in the South with the prospect that the war was almost over. After the capture of New Orleans the *New York Herald* exulted that "we are within a month, or perhaps two weeks, of the end of the war." Other Northern newspapers echoed this optimism. The capture of Island No. 10 on the Mississippi, declared the *New York Times,* "must utterly discourage the rebels and show the futility of further resistance to the Government."[54]

Many Rebels were indeed disheartened. A Georgia officer acknowledged that "our recent disasters are appalling. . . . The valley of the Mississippi is virtually lost, and our entire seacoast and Gulf coast with but few exceptions are completely in the power of the enemy." The fall of New Orleans profoundly depressed even the firebrand Edmund Ruffin, who had proudly claimed to have fired the first shot at Fort Sumter. "I

160

cannot help admitting," Ruffin wrote in his diary, "the *possibility* of the subjugation of the southern states."[55]

Even in Virginia matters were looking up for the Union cause. As McClellan prepared to open his siege guns on Confederate lines at Yorktown, Johnston pulled out on the night of May 3–4 and retreated toward Richmond. McClellan considered his monthlong siege to be a triumph at minimal cost in casualties. Lincoln was not convinced, for the enemy lived to fight another day. By coincidence Lincoln plus Stanton and Chase arrived at Fort Monroe two days after the Confederate evacuation of Yorktown. They had come, in part, to prod McClellan into action. But they did not see the general because he had gone forward to supervise the pursuit after the Confederates had fought a rearguard action at Williamsburg on May 5.

Norfolk was still in enemy hands, however, and the feared CSS *Virginia* (formerly the USS *Merrimack*) was still docked there. On May 7 the commander in chief took direct operational control of a drive to capture Norfolk and to push a gunboat fleet up the James River. Lincoln ordered Gen. John Wool, commander at Fort Monroe, to land troops on the south bank of Hampton

Roads. The president even personally carried out a reconnaissance to select the best landing spot. On May 9 the Confederates evacuated Norfolk before Northern soldiers could get there. Two days later the *Virginia*'s crew blew it up to prevent its capture. An officer on the USS *Monitor* wrote that "it is extremely fortunate that the President came down as he did — he seems to have infused new life into everything." Nothing was happening, he said, until Lincoln began "stirring up dry bones."[56] Chase was usually sparing of praise for Lincoln (to put it mildly), but on May 11 he wrote to his daughter: "So has ended a brilliant week's campaign of the President; for I think it quite certain that if he had not come down, Norfolk would still have been in possession of the enemy, and the 'Merrimac' as grim and defiant and as much a terror as ever."[57]

Lincoln was willing to take some of the credit for these events.[58] But the Confederates would have abandoned Norfolk anyway to avoid being cut off when Johnston's army retreated up the Peninsula. As it did so, morale in the South plunged further, and hopes in the North for an imminent victory rose correspondingly. An officer in the Seventy-first Pennsylvania boasted that when the Army of the Potomac attacked

Richmond, "we will just go right over the works, for I do not think it possible to stay this enthusiastic army." A Wisconsin soldier wrote home on May 25 that "the next letter I send you will be mailed from Richmond." General McClellan's wife was confident that "the war would be over by the Fourth of July."[59]

Dispirited Confederates were afraid she was right. Jefferson Davis was "greatly depressed in spirits," according to one observer. The Confederate president's niece was visiting his household during these tense days. She wrote to her mother in Mississippi: "Oh, mother, Uncle Jeff. is miserable. . . . Our reverses distressed him so much. . . . The cause of the Confederacy looks drooping and sinking. . . . I am ready to sink with despair."[60] A Virginia cavalry captain wrote to his wife that "our cause is hopeless," but added: "unless some great change takes place."[61]

Great changes *were* about to take place, most of them in Virginia. They would turn the war around in the short run but ensure the death of both slavery and the Confederacy in the end.

4
A QUESTION OF LEGS

By the third week of May 1862 the Army of the Potomac with 105,000 men was closing in on Richmond defended by 60,000 soldiers. Claiming that he faced "perhaps double my numbers," McClellan continued to clamor for reinforcements. Lincoln responded by ordering McDowell's corps from Fredericksburg to link up with McClellan's right flank a few miles northeast of Richmond.[1] One division of McDowell's corps had been drawn from Nathaniel Banks's small army in the Shenandoah Valley, leaving Banks with only 8,000 men to face Gen. Thomas J. "Stonewall" Jackson's 17,000 Confederate troops in the valley.

Gen. Robert E. Lee, Jefferson Davis's military adviser, had instructed Jackson to create a diversion in the valley to prevent the very reinforcements that Lincoln ordered. Jackson was just the man for this task. Secretive, crafty, a master of strategic deception and misdirection, an austere Presbyterian in his personal life, a hard fighter and harder disciplinarian as a commander, he pushed his troops into such long and fast marches that they became known as "Jackson's foot cavalry." On May 8 Jackson defeated two brigades of Frémont's army in the western Virginia mountains. The foot cavalry then marched quickly down the valley (northward) toward Banks's force at Strasburg, swerved suddenly to cross Massanutten Mountain into the Luray Valley, struck Banks's outpost at Front Royal on May 23, and then routed the retreating Northerners at Winchester on May 25. They fled north across the Potomac River into Maryland, leaving the valley and the south bank of the Potomac wide open to the enemy.

Alarm bells about the safety of Washington went off in the War Department. Stanton sent out a call for the mobilization of emergency militia.[2] And on May 24 Lincoln suspended McDowell's movement toward McClellan and ordered him instead to send two divisions to the valley. McClellan was outraged. He insisted (correctly) that the purpose of Jackson's movements "is probably to prevent reinforcements being sent to me." He vented his spleen in letters to his wife. Lincoln "is terribly scared about Washington," he wrote. "Heaven help a country governed by such counsels! . . . It is perfectly sickening to deal with such people. . . . I get more sick of them every day — for every day brings with it only additional proof of their hypocrisy, knavery, and folly."[3]

Lincoln was of course concerned about a potential threat to the capital. But that was not his main reason for suspending McDowell's movement. Rather, he intended to trap Jackson in the valley by having Frémont take up a blocking position to the south and having McDowell hit Jackson in the flank before he could retreat to the safety of the upper valley. Recognizing that Jackson was one of the Confederacy's most dangerous commanders, Lincoln hoped to snare him and cripple his army. He believed this to be a better strategic use of McDowell's troops than reinforcing McClellan, who would still maintain that "their numbers [are] greatly exceeding our own."[4] Lincoln no longer took such claims seriously. He was convinced that no matter how many troops McClellan had, he would not attack Richmond but would bring up his heavy artillery and lay siege to it, as he had done at Yorktown.

So the commander in chief acted as his own general-in-chief. For the next several days — and nights — Lincoln spent most of his time in the War Department telegraph office firing off dispatches to Frémont, McDowell, and other generals. He ordered Frémont to cross the Bull Pasture Mountains with his fifteen thousand men "to move against Jackson at Harrisonburg and operate against the enemy in such a way as to relieve Banks. This movement must be made immediately." Frémont replied that he would "move as ordered." Lincoln thanked him and urged that "much — perhaps all — depends upon the celerity with which you can execute it. Put the utmost speed into it. Do not lose a minute."[5]

To McDowell went orders to march two of his divisions to Strasburg in the valley "to capture the forces of Jackson & Ewell, either in cooperation with Gen Fremont" or, if Frémont was delayed (Lincoln's confidence in him was minimal), "it is believed that the force with which you move will be sufficient to accomplish the object alone." McDowell obeyed the order, but added a protest that the suspension of his move toward Richmond "is a crushing blow to us." McDowell told Lincoln that "I am entirely beyond helping distance of General Banks. . . . I shall gain nothing for you there, and shall lose much for you here." Lincoln responded that "the change was as painful to me as it can possibly be to you." But he wanted no excuses for failure; he had had enough of those from McClellan. He did not want to hear any such word as "can't." If McDowell marched his men half as fast as Jackson, he could catch that wily general. "Everything now depends on the celerity and vigor of your movement," Lincoln told McDowell. "It is, for you a question of legs. Put in all the speed you can."[6] McDowell adopted Lincoln's terminology in telegrams to the commander of his lead division, James Shields (who had almost fought a duel with Lincoln twenty years earlier). "The question now seems to be one of legs — whether we can get to Jackson and Ewell before they can get away," said McDowell. "We must not disappoint the expectations of the President."[7]

Frémont and Shields failed Lincoln. Instead of marching to Harrisonburg south of Strasburg, Frémont moved to Moore-field, thirty-five miles to its northwest. In reply to a dispatch received from Frémont at Moorefield on May 27, Lincoln de-manded: "What does this mean? . . . You were expressly ordered to march to Harrisonburg." Frémont offered what to Lincoln surely seemed a lame explanation that the route through Moorefield Valley was easier for his tired, hungry troops than the shorter but rough going over the Bull Pasture Mountains to Harrisonburg. Nothing could be done about it now, so Lincoln ordered Frémont to close on Strasburg immediately to catch Jackson in a vise between Frémont's fifteen thousand and Shields's division of ten thousand coming from the east.[8] With considerably farther to go, Jackson's foot cavalry again outmarched the ponderous Yankees and slipped through the trap on May 31.

Lincoln was disgusted, but he did not give up the effort to get his generals to chase down and attack Jackson, whom they now outnumbered by almost two to one. Stanton wired Frémont and McDowell on June 2: "The President tells me to say to you do not let the enemy escape from you."[9] But the slippery Stonewall outdistanced his pursuers to Port Republic, 135 miles from where he had begun his epic retreat. There he gained control of the bridge over the south fork of the Shenandoah River, which separated the two Union forces. The Confederates repulsed a feeble attack by Frémont on June 8 and then crossed the river to defeat Shields on June 9. Jackson's storied Shenandoah Valley campaign was over, and he prepared to join the Confederate army facing McClellan at Richmond.

Perhaps Lincoln had expected too much of his generals. And perhaps he failed to appreciate that logistical problems and frequent rains slowed their movements. But the same rain fell on Confederate troops, whose logistical problems were even more difficult. Then and later Lincoln could not understand why Northern armies could not march as fast as the enemy. General Shields seemed to share Lincoln's sentiments. In his official report on the campaign, Shields wrote that Lincoln's "plan for Jackson's destruction was perfect. The execution of it, from inexplicable causes, was not what was to be expected."[10]

Shields by implication blamed Frémont for the failure. So did Lincoln. Without directly rebuking the general — who still had powerful Republican supporters — the president made clear his disapproval in a series of dispatches to Frémont, which also instructed him to keep a close watch on Jackson to prevent him from doing more mischief.[11] On June 26 Lincoln created the Army of Virginia, to be composed of the commands of Frémont, Banks, and the portion of McDowell's corps that had not already reinforced McClellan. Lincoln called Gen. John Pope from the West, where he had done well, to command this army. Refusing to serve under Pope, who was his junior in rank, Frémont submitted his resignation, which Lincoln promptly accepted.[12]

Several historians have echoed McClellan's criticism of Lincoln's diversion of McDowell on what they considered a wild-goose chase at the expense of what should have been the primary strategic objective of Richmond. But General Shields was right; there was a real chance to hurt and perhaps even capture Jackson, with incalculable benefits to the Union cause. The conclusion offered by the most recent historian of McClellan's Peninsula campaign seems sound: "The notion that McDowell's corps was essential to victory on the peninsula is nonsense. McClellan always greatly overestimated his opponents, and McDowell would not have made a difference. . . . There is absolutely no reason to think that if [McClellan] had been . . . given everything he wanted in the Peninsula Campaign it would have made any difference."[13]

While Jackson was making his escape from Lincoln's trap, important events were taking place in two other theaters. After the Battle of Shiloh, General Halleck had come from his St. Louis headquarters to take command of the combined armies of Grant and Buell as well as that of John Pope after he captured Island No. 10. This force of 110,000 men advanced at a glacial pace to invest the rail junction at Corinth defended by 70,000 Confederates under the command of Gen. Pierre G. T. Beauregard. Although Halleck had defended Grant from criticism after Shiloh, he still had reservations about Grant and relegated him to the largely meaningless position of second in command. Grant almost resigned, but was talked out of it by his friend Sherman, with whom he had forged a close bond at Shiloh. On the night of May 29–30 the Confederates evacuated Corinth before Halleck could strike. Lincoln was pleased with this almost bloodless victory, even though the enemy lived to fight another day, just as Joseph Johnston's army did after it had similarly evacuated Yorktown four weeks earlier. Secretary of War Stanton reported the president to be especially "delighted" with Halleck's plan to send Buell with 30,000 men to capture Chattanooga and "liberate" East Tennessee.[14]

As before, however, the commander in chief remained preoccupied with events on McClellan's front. On May 31 Johnston attacked part of the Army of the Potomac south of the Chickahominy River six miles east of Richmond. In the two-day Battle of Seven Pines and Fair Oaks, the Federals repulsed and punished the attackers. The battle had a profound impact on the opposing commanders. It confirmed McClellan's belief that the enemy was concentrating all its forces against him; but perhaps more important, he was unnerved by the sight of "mangled corpses" and wounded men on the battlefield. "Victory has no charms for me when purchased at such a cost. . . . Every poor fellow that is killed or wounded almost haunts me."[15] McClellan's sentiments did credit to him as a human being and help explain why his soldiers idolized him. But they also reinforced his intention to capture Richmond by maneuver and siege rather than by hard fighting. On the Confederate side, Joseph Johnston was wounded in the Battle of Seven Pines, and Jefferson Davis replaced him with Robert

E. Lee. No one knew it yet, but this move ensured that hard fighting would become the norm for the rest of the war.

Most of a wet June passed as Lee prepared a counteroffensive. Lincoln ordered one of McDowell's divisions plus some additional regiments to join McClellan, bringing his effective strength to at least 106,000 men. The president also authorized McClellan to call on Gen. Ambrose Burnside for reinforcements from his army in North Carolina. McClellan failed to appreciate these additions. Much of his energy went into a series of telegrams to Washington complaining that he lacked this and that, the roads were too wet to move up his heavy artillery, and he faced 200,000 enemy troops (the maximum number that Lee would be able to bring against him was 92,000). If these "vastly superior" forces overwhelmed him, McClellan told Lincoln and Stanton, "I will in no way be responsible for it, as I have not failed to represent repeatedly the need of reinforcements. . . . The responsibility cannot be thrown on my shoulders; it must rest where it belongs." To this astonishing accusation, Lincoln responded only that it "pains me very much. I give you all I can . . . while you continue, ungenerously I think, to assume that I could give you more if I would. I have omitted and shall omit no opportunity to send you reinforcements whenever I possibly can." McClellan told his wife that "Honest A[be] has again fallen into the hands of my enemies."[16]

On June 23 Lincoln made an unannounced trip by special train to West Point to consult Gen. Winfield Scott, who was summering there. What Scott advised is not clear, but it may have included a recommendation to create the Army of Virginia under Pope, which the president did the day after he returned to Washington. Scott also probably renewed his old suggestion to appoint Henry W. Halleck as general-in-chief. Two weeks later the president did just that. A great deal happened during those two weeks that changed the course of the war.[17]

While McClellan bickered with Washington, Lee acted. On June 26 he launched his counteroffensive against McClellan's right flank north of the Chickahominy. The previous day McClellan had probed Confederate lines south of that river in an operation that in retrospect became known as the first of the Seven Days' battles (June 25–July 1). From June 26 on it was the Army of Northern Virginia that did the attacking — repeatedly, relentlessly, with a courage bordering on recklessness, without regard for heavy casualties that would total about twenty thousand Confederates (and sixteen thousand Federals, of whom six thousand were captured) for the whole Seven Days'.

Even though only one of the four sizable battles during these days was a Confederate tactical victory (Gaines' Mill on June 27), McClellan lost his nerve. He was defeated, even if his army was not. He abandoned all thought of making a stand or ordering a counterattack. While the Confederates assaulted the thirty thousand Federals north of the Chickahominy at Gaines' Mill, McClellan had seventy thousand facing only twenty-five thousand Confederates south of the river. But he wired the War Department that he was "attacked by greatly superior numbers in all directions."[18] He decided to destroy his supply base and retreat south to the James River. "I have lost this battle because my force was too small," he told Stanton. "The Government must not & cannot hold me responsible for the result. . . . I have seen too many dead & wounded comrades to feel otherwise than that the Government has not sustained this army. . . . If I save this army now, I tell you plainly that I owe no thanks to you or any other persons in Washington. You have done your best to sacrifice this army." The colonel in charge of the War Department telegraph office was so shocked by McClellan's final two sentences that he deleted them from the copy he sent on to Stanton, so he and Lincoln did not see them.[19]

Although Lincoln did not read these sentences, he saw plenty of other evidence that McClellan had gone to pieces. And when news of the Seven Days' reached the North in a form that magnified the Union defeat, home front morale plunged. A panic on Wall Street sent stocks as well as the value of the new greenback dollar (introduced in February 1862) into a temporary free fall. Newspapers described the public mood as "mortified" by this "stunning disaster" which had caused "misery" and "revulsion" throughout the North.[20] A State Department translator wrote in his diary that this Fourth of July was "the gloomiest since the birth of this republic. Never was the country so low, and after such sacrifices of blood." Lincoln told a Connecticut congressman that when he learned of McClellan's retreat to Harrison's Landing on the James River, "I was as nearly inconsolable as I could be and live."[21]

But the president refused to panic. He did what he could to calm McClellan. He telegraphed the general to "maintain your ground if you can. . . . Save the Army, material and personal; and I will strengthen it for the offensive again, as fast as I can. . . . We still have strength enough in the country, and will bring it out."[22] Lincoln ordered several thousand troops from the coast of the Carolinas to reinforce the Army of the Potomac.[23] The president also asked General Halleck if he could spare some troops from his western armies to reinforce McClellan — but only if it would not jeopardize the campaign to liberate East Tennessee. Halleck replied that such a detachment would indeed jeopardize that campaign, so Lincoln dropped the matter.[24]

McClellan was not the only one whom Lincoln had to calm and reassure. On the night of July 4–5 the normally unflappable Montgomery Meigs awakened the president at the Soldiers' Home cottage that the Lincolns used as a summer White House. Meigs said excitedly that the Army of the Potomac must be evacuated from the Peninsula at once before the enemy captured it, all supplies must be destroyed, and all the horses killed because they could not be gotten away. Lincoln sent Meigs home and went back to sleep. The president later told John Hay of the incident, and added: "Thus often I who am not a specially brave man have had to sustain the sinking courage of these professional fighters in critical times."[25]

Lincoln also tried to reassure the public. He announced that "I expect to maintain this contest until successful, or till I die, or am conquered, or my term expires, or Congress or the country forsakes me." He had Seward instruct Northern governors to ask the president to call for three hundred thousand new three-year volunteers so "the recent successes of the Federal arms may be followed up . . . to bring this unnecessary and injurious civil war to a speedy and satisfactory conclusion." Lincoln issued the call on July 1, 1862.[26]

Lincoln decided to visit the Army of the Potomac to see its condition for himself. Arriving on July 8, he reviewed the troops and found their morale to be better than he expected. The next day he met with McClellan and five corps commanders. The president asked their opinion about removing the army from the Peninsula. Most said it could be done, but McClellan plus three corps commanders said that to do so would be ruinous to the cause. Only one (Gen. William B. Franklin) wanted to withdraw and start a new overland campaign from the region between Washington and the Rappahannock River. Lincoln was noncommittal about his intentions but returned to Washington "in better spirits" than before he went, according to John Nicolay.[27]

The same could not be said of McClellan. "I do not know what paltry trick the administration will play next," he wrote his wife. "I did not like the Presd't's manner — it seemed that of a man about to do something of which he was much ashamed. . . . [He] *is* 'an old stick' — & of pretty poor timber at that."[28] The first thing Lincoln did after getting back to Washington was to appoint Halleck as general-in-chief. McClellan considered this appointment "a slap in the face. . . . It *is* grating to have to serve under the orders of a man whom I know by experience to be my inferior."[29]

McClellan reserved his bitterest rhetoric for Stanton, whom he professed to blame even more than Lincoln for undercutting his Peninsula campaign by withholding reinforcements. One of Stanton's greatest sins, according to McClellan, was to have challenged the general's claim that the Confederates had outnumbered him. Stanton's (quite accurate) statement that Union forces were larger than the enemy's "is simply false," fumed McClellan. "They had more than two to one against me."[30] When one of Burnside's divisions from North Carolina went to Pope instead of to McClellan, the latter as usual blamed Stanton. The secretary of war was "the most depraved hypocrite & villain" he had ever known, McClellan wrote. If he "had lived in the time of the Saviour, Judas Iscariot would have remained a respected member of the fraternity of Apostles."[31]

The outcome of the Seven Days' battles produced a flurry of scapegoating in the press as well as within the Army of the Potomac. Republican newspapers blamed McClellan, but their criticism was muted compared with the opposition's tirades against Stanton. Democratic newspapers — especially the powerful *New York Herald* — took their cue from McClellan. The secretary of war, announced the *Herald,* was "the tool of abolitionists, the organizer of disasters, the author of defeats." His "reckless mismanagement and criminal intrigues" caused "thousands of lives" to be "thrown away, unnecessarily sacrificed, wantonly squandered, heedlessly murdered."[32]

Many officers and men in the Army of the Potomac echoed the *Herald.* McClellan remained their hero. For them as for him, it was an article of faith that they had not been outfought or outgeneraled but beaten by superior numbers because traitors in Washington withheld reinforcements. A soldier in the crack Eighty-third Pennsylvania, which had suffered 65 percent casualties in the Seven Days' (including 111 killed), wrote that "no one thinks of blaming McClellan. His men have the fullest confidence in his ability. . . . Anyone who saw how the rebels . . . pour five different lines of fresh troops against our one, can tell why he does not take Richmond." A Massachusetts officer considered Stanton "the great murderer of the age, for to him are fairly imparted the deaths of all the men who have fallen since the siege of Yorktown."[33]

To prevent the vendetta against Stanton from getting further out of hand, Lincoln used the occasion of a Union rally in Washington on August 6 to defend the secretary as *a brave and able man* who did all he could to support McClellan. If anyone was responsible for withholding troops, said Lincoln, it was himself — because those soldiers were needed elsewhere. It was time to stop blaming Stanton *for what I did myself.* And it was also time to stop this internecine fault-finding and move forward together against the real enemy. "I know Gen. McClellan wishes to be successful, and I know he does not wish it any more than the Secretary of War for him, and both of them together no more than I wish it."[34]

Political polarization with respect to the Army of the Potomac was closely related to the increasing intensity of the slavery issue. As the war entered its second year Lincoln pretty much gave up his earlier hope that a conciliatory policy might coax supposed Unionists in the Confederacy out of the closet. Guerrilla attacks behind Union lines in the West and cavalry raids in Tennessee and Kentucky by Confederate troopers under Gens. Nathan Bedford Forrest and John Hunt Morgan took place just after the Seven Days'. The success of these Confederate counteroffensives helped to harden the attitudes of Republicans including Lincoln toward "rebels." Senator John Sherman wrote to his brother William of a growing sentiment "that we must treat these Rebels as bitter enemies to be subdued — conquered — by confiscation — by the employment of their slaves — by terror — energy — audacity — rather than by conciliation."[35]

Many soldiers on the front lines espoused this notion of "hard war," even in the Army of the Potomac, where their beloved Mc-

Clellan deplored such attitudes. It was time, they thought, to stop coddling Southern civilians, many of whom Union soldiers considered "bushwhackers" who raided behind Union lines, fired at Northern soldiers from their houses, and harassed Union operations in any way they could. "The star of the Confederacy appears to be rising," wrote an Ohio colonel about these Southern counteroffensives, "and I doubt not it will continue to ascend until the rose-water policy now pursued by the Northern army is superseded by one more determined and vigorous." An Illinois officer believed that "the iron gauntlet must be used more than the silken glove to crush this serpent."[36] A lieutenant in the Tenth Massachusetts complained of McClellan's conciliatory policy toward civilians on the Peninsula. "The whole aim [of] this kid glove war," he wrote, "seems to be to hurt as few of our enemies and as little as possible." Even General Halleck, previously a sharp critic of such hard-war ideas, became a convert. After he moved to Washington as general-in-chief, one of his first orders to Grant, now commander of occupation forces in western Tennessee and northern Mississippi, was to "take up all active [Rebel] sympathizers, and either hold them as prisoners or put them beyond our lines. Handle that class without gloves, and take their property for public use. . . . It is time that they should begin to feel the presence of the war."[37]

"Take their property." The principal form of property in the South was slaves. They were also an essential part of the Confederacy's labor force and of the logistical operations of Confederate armies. A Wisconsin major insisted that "the only way to put down this rebellion is to hurt the instigators and abettors of it. Slavery must be cleaned out." The colonel of the Fifth Minnesota, stationed in northern Alabama, wrote that "I am doing quite a business in the confiscation of slave property. . . . Crippling the institution of slavery is . . . striking a blow at the heart of the rebellion."[38]

One prominent advocate of hard war was Gen. John Pope. Soon after becoming commander of the newly formed Army of Virginia in June 1862, Pope issued a series of orders authorizing his officers to seize enemy property without compensation, to hold civilians responsible for guerrilla attacks on Union communications or personnel, to shoot civilians caught firing on Union soldiers, to expel from occupied territory any civilians who refused to take an oath of allegiance, and to treat them as spies if they returned.[39]

Lincoln approved of these orders, which were based in part on the Second Confiscation Act passed by Congress and signed by the president on July 17. Lincoln issued separate orders, milder than Pope's and also based on the Confiscation Act, that among other provisions authorized the employment of confiscated slaves "for Military and Naval purposes, giving them reasonable wages for their labor."[40]

The *New York Times,* which represented the views of moderate Republicans (including Lincoln), considered Pope's orders just the ticket. "The country is weary of trifling," declared the *Times.* "We have been afraid of wounding rebel feelings, afraid of injuring rebel property, afraid of using, or under any circumstances, of freeing rebel slaves. Some of our Generals have fought the rebels — if fighting it be called — with their kid gloves on" — a thinly veiled allusion to McClellan. But now, said the *Times,* "there is a sign of hope and cheer in the more warlike policy which has been inaugurated."[41]

McClellan bitterly opposed these steps toward hard war. If the government "adopts these radical and inhuman views to which it seems inclined, & which will prolong the struggle," he wrote, "I cannot in good conscience serve the Govt any longer." He did not resign, however, but sought to push his own views of how the war should be fought. "The people of the South should understand that we are not making war upon the institution of slavery," he instructed the new general-in-chief, Halleck. "Private persons and property should enjoy all the protection we can afford them" in order to prove to Southern civilians that the government "is, as we profess it to be, benign and beneficent."[42] McClellan issued his own set of orders to the Army of the Potomac intended to have the opposite effect from that of Pope's "infamous orders" to *his* army. "I will not have this army degenerate into a mob of thieves," McClellan declared. "We are not engaged in a war of rapine, revenge, or subjugation," he informed his soldiers. "This is not a war against populations, but against armed forces."[43]

Before the Seven Days' battles McClellan had asked Lincoln for permission to lay before the president some suggestions about how the war should be fought. Lincoln acquiesced, and when he came to visit the army at Harrison's Landing, McClellan handed him a letter dated July 7. "The time has come when the Government must determine upon a civil and military policy," the general told his commander in chief. "It should not be a war looking to the subjugation of the Southern people . . . and it should be conducted upon the highest principles known to Christian civilization. . . . Neither confiscation of property . . . nor forcible abolition of slavery should be contemplated for a moment. Military power should not be allowed to interfere with the relations of servitude. . . . A declaration of radical views, especially upon slavery, will rapidly disintegrate our present armies."[44]

Lincoln read this extraordinary document in McClellan's presence and pocketed it without comment — then or later. But his thoughts can be guessed. Several months earlier he might have agreed with much of what McClellan wrote. In his message to Congress back in December he too had expressed a hope that the war would not "degenerate into a remorseless and revolutionary struggle." But since then the conflict *had* become remorseless, and Lincoln was about to embrace the revolution. Democrats and border-state Unionists who expressed alarm about what the *New York Times* was calling "an active and vigorous war policy" now elicited an exasperated response from the president. The demand of professed Southern Unionists "that the government shall not strike its open enemies, lest they be struck by accident," wrote Lincoln in July 1862, had become "the paralysis — the dead palsy — of the government in this whole struggle." The war could no longer be fought "with elder-stalk squirts [that is, squirt guns], charged with rose water," Lincoln said sarcastically. "This government cannot much longer play a game in which it stakes all, and its enemies stake nothing. Those enemies must understand that they cannot experiment for ten years trying to destroy the government, and if they fail still come back into the Union unhurt."[45]

Lincoln was about to commit himself to a historic shift in national strategy toward slavery. But first he decided to give the border states one last chance to accept his offer of compensated emancipation, which had lain dormant since March. The "signs of the times" he had warned them about in May were even more obvious now. "You can form no conception of the change of opinion here as to the Negro question," Senator Sherman wrote to his brother. "I am prepared for one to meet the broad issue of universal emancipation." A conservative

Boston newspaper conceded that "the great phenomenon of the year is the terrible intensity that this [emancipation] resolution has acquired. A year ago men might have faltered at the thought of proceeding to this extremity, [but now] they are in great measure prepared for it."[46] Lincoln summoned border-state representatives to the White House on July 12 and laid out the "unprecedentedly stern facts of the case." The pressure for emancipation was increasing, he pointed out. If they did not make "a decision at once to emancipate *gradually* . . . the institution in your states will be extinguished by mere friction and abrasion." But once again the border-state men turned him down, by a margin of two to one.[47]

Disappointed and frustrated, Lincoln made up his mind that very evening to go ahead with a proclamation of emancipation. His thinking on this question had come a long way since his denial the previous September (to Orville Browning) that he had any constitutional power to do so. Lincoln may have been influenced by a pamphlet titled *The War Powers of the President, and the Legislative Powers of Congress in Relation to Rebellion, Treason, and Slavery,* first published in the spring of 1862. Its author was William Whiting, a Boston abolitionist and one of the leading lawyers in New England. Whiting's pamphlet went through seven editions in little more than a year. On the strength of it he was appointed solicitor of the War Department. Lincoln's own legal mind grasped Whiting's argument that the laws of war "give the President full belligerent rights" as commander in chief to seize enemy property (in this case slaves) being used to wage war against the United States. "This right of seizure and condemnation is harsh," wrote Whiting, "as all the proceedings of war are harsh, in the extreme, but is nevertheless lawful." And once the slaves were "seized," the government surely would never allow them to be re-enslaved.[48]

The day after his frustrating session with border-state representatives, Lincoln shared a carriage with Secretaries Seward and Welles on their way to a funeral for Secretary Stanton's infant son. The president startled his seatmates with an announcement of his intention to issue an emancipation edict. As Welles later recounted the conversation, Lincoln said that this matter had "occupied his mind and thoughts by day and night" for several weeks even as he spent many hours in the War Department telegraph office trying to manage his generals in Virginia. According to Welles, Lincoln said that an emancipation policy had been "forced on him by the rebels." They "had made war upon the government . . . and it was our duty to avail ourselves of every necessary measure to maintain the Union." The border states "would do nothing" on their own; perhaps it was unrealistic to have expected them to give up slavery while the Rebels retained it. Therefore "the blow must fall first and foremost" on the enemy. Emancipation was "a military necessity, absolutely necessary to the preservation of the Union. The slaves were undeniably an element of strength to those who had their service, and we must decide whether that element should be for us or against us. . . . We wanted the army to strike more vigorous blows. The administration must set the army an example and strike at the heart of the rebellion."[49]

Nine days later Lincoln called the full cabinet together to announce his decision. Congress had just passed the Second Confiscation Act, which included a provision to free the slaves of owners who had engaged in rebellion. Lincoln considered this measure unworkable, however, and also believed that his more sweeping proclamation freeing all slaves in areas at war with the United

States rested on the surer foundation of his war powers as commander in chief.

Most cabinet members expressed varying degrees of qualified support for a proclamation. Montgomery Blair, however, opposed it. He said the Democrats would capitalize on the unpopularity of such a measure in the border states and parts of the North to gain control of the House in the fall elections. Seward said that he approved of the proclamation but opposed its issuance during this time of public discouragement after the Seven Days'. He advised Lincoln to postpone it "until you can give it to the country supported by military success." Otherwise the world might view it as an incitement for slave insurrections, "as the last measure of an exhausted government, a cry for help . . . our last *shriek,* on the retreat."[50]

The wisdom of this advice "struck me with very great force," Lincoln said later.[51] So he put the proclamation away to wait for a military victory. It would prove to be a long, dismal wait.

5
DESTROY THE REBEL ARMY, IF POSSIBLE

Commander in Chief Lincoln had high hopes for Henry W. Halleck as general-in-chief. Halleck was the apparent organizer of major Union victories in the West. As the president pondered what to do with McClellan and the Army of the Potomac after the Seven Days', he pressed Halleck to put Buell and Grant in charge in the West and to get to Washington as soon as possible. "I am very anxious — almost impatient — to have you here," Lincoln telegraphed Halleck on July 14. Orville Browning, who saw the president often during these dispiriting July days, wrote in his diary that he "looked weary, care-worn and troubled." Browning tried to cheer him up. Lincoln "held me by the hand, pressed it, and said in a very tender and touching tone — 'Browning I must die some time.' . . . There was a cadence of deep sadness in his voice. We parted both of us I believe with tears in our eyes."[1]

Halleck finally arrived on July 23 and met with Lincoln, Stanton, and Generals Pope and Burnside. "Old Brains" looked less like a fighting general than any of them. Lincoln, however, discounted the paunchy figure, fishlike eyes, irritable personality, and off-putting mannerism of constantly scratching his elbows that caused others to dislike Halleck. The president wanted his new general-in-chief to make decisions, give orders, take actions to relieve Lincoln of the everyday supervision of military events. The day after Halleck arrived, Lincoln sent him to visit McClellan and to decide (a) whether to keep him in command; and (b) whether to withdraw the Army of the Potomac from the Peninsula or to reinforce it to renew the campaign from there.

Accompanied by Burnside and Meigs, Halleck held intensive discussions with McClellan. Give me 30,000 more men, said McClellan, and I will resume the offensive even though Lee has 200,000. Halleck said that he could scrape together no more than 20,000. If that was not enough the Army of the Potomac would have to be withdrawn to combine with Pope's army along the Rappahannock. McClellan agreed to 20,000. As soon as Halleck got back to

Washington, however, he received a telegram from McClellan asking in effect for 50,000. That was the final straw. Both Lincoln and Halleck were already inclined toward withdrawal. Now McClellan had been hoist with his own petard. If Lee really did have 200,000 men holding a position between McClellan's 90,000 and Pope's 40,000, Halleck pointed out, the Confederates could use their interior lines to strike McClellan and Pope in turn with superior numbers. Thus it was imperative to combine the two Union armies to shield Washington.[2]

After returning to the capital Montgomery Meigs made his own calculations of probable Confederate numbers in the Army of Northern Virginia. He came up with an estimate of 105,000 men (which was in fact about 30,000 too high).[3] Meigs had great credibility with Lincoln. His estimate further undermined McClellan's credibility. After a conversation with Lincoln on July 25, Orville Browning wrote in his diary that the president "was satisfied McClellan would not fight and that he had told Halleck so. . . . If by magic he could reinforce McClellan with 100,000 men today he would be in ecstacy over it . . . and tell him that he would go to Richmond tomorrow, but that when tomorrow came he would telegraph that he had certain information that the enemy had 400,000 men, and that he could not advance without reinforcements."[4]

Sometime between July 23 and 27 Lincoln offered command of the Army of the Potomac to Burnside, whose success in North Carolina had impressed the president. Lincoln took a risk with this offer. McClellan had a powerful constituency in the army and the polity that would resent — perhaps even resist — his removal from command. Most of the corps and division commanders were McClellan men. Northern Democrats embraced McClellan, and even many non-Democratic readers of newspapers like the *New York Herald* believed that the general was more sinned against than sinning. In any case Burnside declined the offer and urged the president to give McClellan another chance. The two generals were close friends at this time. They addressed each other as "Dear Burn" and "Dear Mac." Burnside genuinely believed that he was unqualified to command so large a force as the Army of the Potomac, which was McClellan's creation and was still fiercely loyal to him.[5]

McClellan bitterly protested the order to withdraw from the Peninsula. To give up his own campaign in order to reinforce Pope added insult to injury in McClellan's eyes. When Pope had taken command of the Army of Virginia, he had issued a bombastic address to his troops. "I have come to you from the West, where we have always seen the backs of our enemies." Here in the East, Pope continued, he had heard too much about holding strong positions and securing lines of retreat. "Let us discard such ideas" and instead "study the probable lines of retreat of our opponents, and leave our own to take care of themselves."[6]

McClellan rightly read these words as an indictment of himself and of his army. Whether consciously or subconsciously, he was not likely to exert himself to reinforce Pope. That attitude soon bore bitter fruit. In early August, General Lee concluded that McClellan's inactive army posed little danger, so he shifted twenty-four thousand troops under Jackson to confront Pope along the Rappahannock. Rumor magnified this force — Jackson's reputation was worth several divisions. On August 9 near Culpeper, the Confederates clashed with part of Pope's army commanded by Jackson's old victim in the Shenandoah Valley, Nathaniel Banks. The Rebels again defeated Banks in the Battle of Cedar Mountain.

McClellan learned of this outcome with satisfaction. He predicted that Pope "will be badly thrashed within two days . . . very badly whipped he will be & ought to be — such a villain as he is ought to bring defeat upon any cause that employs him." Then "they will be very glad to turn over the redemption of their affairs to me. I won't undertake it unless I have full and entire control."[7]

These words help explain why McClellan seemed to be in no hurry to obey orders to reinforce his despised rival. He received these orders from Halleck on August 3. The first units did not leave until August 14. The last troops finally embarked at Fort Monroe for Washington on September 3. "I cannot get General McClellan to do what I wish," complained Halleck.[8] Lincoln was not surprised; he had been having the same problem for the past year. McClellan himself left the Peninsula on August 23, uncertain whether he or Pope would command the united armies. "I don't see how I can remain in the service if placed under Pope — it would be too great a disgrace," he wrote to his wife. But if "Pope is beaten," which McClellan expected, "they may want me to save Washn. again." Once they "suffer a terrible defeat" and Pope is "disposed of . . . I *know* that with God's help I can save them."[9]

As general-in-chief, Halleck was also having trouble getting Gen. Don Carlos Buell to do what he — and Lincoln — wished. Buell had several things in common with McClellan. He was a Democrat who did not believe in a hard war against Southern civilians or against slavery. He was an efficient organizer and disciplinarian whose Army of the Ohio was a fine body of troops. Like McClellan, Buell preferred a strategy of maneuver and siege to one of all-out battle. "The object is," he had written in December 1861, "not to fight great battles, and storm impregnable fortifications, but by demonstrations and maneuvering to prevent the enemy from concentrating his scattered forces."[10] But Buell lacked McClellan's charisma. While he commanded the loyalty of his men, he did not command their affection.

Before going to Washington, Halleck had ordered Buell to move east along the Memphis and Charleston Railroad to capture Chattanooga and drive the enemy out of East Tennessee. Buell's snail's-pace advance illustrated the problems of railroad logistics in enemy territory swarming with guerrillas and vulnerable to cavalry raids. The general's belief in a "soft" war prevented him from dealing harshly with the civilian population that sheltered guerrillas who destroyed bridges and tore up rails in his rear. Buell refused to subsist his army on the country it marched through. In three weeks he had advanced only ninety miles from Corinth and was still less than halfway to Chattanooga. On July 8 Lincoln warned Buell (through Halleck) that "your progress is not satisfactory and that you should move more rapidly. The long time taken by you to reach Chattanooga will enable the enemy to anticipate you by concentrating a large force to meet you."[11]

Buell responded that "the dissatisfaction of the President pains me exceedingly." He tried to explain his logistical problems, but having had a bellyful of excuses from McClellan, Lincoln was in no mood to hear them from Buell. The president had approved Pope's hard-war orders in Virginia; he suggested that Buell try the same approach in Tennessee and northern Alabama. But Buell continued to dawdle along at four or five miles a day until enemy cavalry raids on his communications almost stopped him altogether. As Lincoln had predicted, the Confederate Army of Tennessee, now commanded by Gen. Braxton Bragg, reached

Chattanooga and fortified its defenses before Buell got close.

Through Halleck, who was now in Washington, Lincoln in mid-August again expressed himself "greatly dissatisfied" with the "want of energy and activity" in Buell's operations. The president wanted to replace Buell, but Halleck persuaded him to give the general one more chance. Nevertheless Halleck reflected the mood in the White House when he informed an officer in Buell's department that unless that general "does something very soon" he would be removed. "The Government seems determined to apply the guillotine to all unsuccessful generals" (figuratively, one hopes). "Perhaps with us now, as in the French Revolution, some harsh measures are required."[12]

Buell found himself forced to "do something very soon," but not what Lincoln had hoped. In late August the Confederates launched a two-pronged invasion from Chattanooga through East Tennessee into Kentucky. Instead of liberating East Tennessee, Buell was compelled to backtrack northward in a race to defend Nashville and then to prevent the enemy from "liberating" Kentucky. Two garrisons of newly recruited Union troops defending Munfordville, Tennessee, and Richmond, Kentucky, were gobbled up by the invading Confederate armies — a total of almost eight thousand Northern captives.

Once again Lincoln haunted the telegraph office sending and reading dispatches to and from Buell's army and other Union officers in Kentucky.[13] The president's hope that he could let Halleck run the war while he attended to other duties had not lasted long. It was Halleck, however, who reported Lincoln's sentiments in a telegram to Buell on September 20: "The immobility of your army is most surprising. Bragg in the last two months has marched four times the distance you have."[14] Four days later Lincoln gave up on Buell and ordered him to turn over his command to George Thomas. When the courier carrying this order gave it to Buell in Louisville, the general promptly obeyed it. But Thomas protested that Buell was about to attack Bragg, and asked that the order be suspended. Lincoln complied. With this new lease on his command, Buell moved out and stopped the Confederate invasion at the Battle of Perryville on October 8.[15]

Buell's problems were far from over, however. From Washington came a continuing shower of telegrams ordering him not to let the retreating enemy get away without further damage. Buell's command still hung by a thread.

So did McClellan's during those tense months from August to October 1862. Having detected the start of the Army of the Potomac's departure from his front in mid-August, Robert E. Lee also moved north with most of his army to attack Pope before McClellan's troops could reinforce him. Demoralization in the North encouraged Southern hopes. From Washington on August 27 Lt. Charles Francis Adams, Jr., of the First Massachusetts Cavalry wrote to his father, the U.S. minister to Britain: "The air of this city seems thick with treachery; our army seems in danger of utter demoralization and I have not since the war began felt such a tug on my nerves. . . . Everything is ripe for a terrible panic."[16]

Stonewall Jackson's foot cavalry logged fifty miles in a two-day march around Pope's right flank to destroy his supply base at Manassas on August 27. Part of the Army of the Potomac had joined Pope by then, and McClellan was at Alexandria, charged with the task of forwarding additional reinforcements to Pope as they arrived. From Pope's headquarters on August 28 poured a series of confusing orders to his own Army of Virginia and to four divisions of the Army of the Potomac (plus two from Burnside's army that had been transferred from North Carolina). If and when united, these reinforcements would give Pope some seventy-five thousand men (to Lee's fifty thousand). But these Union troops from three different armies had never fought together before, and the jealousies among some of their generals did not augur well. McClellan's opinion of Pope was scarcely a secret, nor was that of Gen. Fitz-John Porter, McClellan's protégé and commander of two Army of the Potomac divisions that had joined the Army of Virginia. "Pope is a fool," wrote Porter, and the administration that had appointed him was no better. In a sentence that could be construed as treasonable, he added: "Would that this army was in Washington to rid us of incumbents ruining our country."[17]

On August 29 Pope launched piecemeal attacks on Jackson's corps holding a position next to the Bull Run battlefield of the previous year. For two days Halleck had been sending repeated telegrams to McClellan ordering him to push forward William B. Franklin's and Edwin V. Sumner's corps to help Pope. Back from McClellan came as many telegrams explaining why "neither Franklin's nor Sumner's corps is now in condition to move and fight a battle" — because their artillery and cavalry had not arrived. Pope did not need cavalry and had enough artillery, said Halleck; what he needed was the infantry of these two veteran corps. "There must be no further delay in moving Franklin's corps toward Manassas," Halleck wired McClellan on the evening of August 28. McClellan replied that Franklin would march in the morning. But the next day he halted Franklin six miles out, in direct disobedience of Halleck's orders and within hearing of Pope's battle.[18]

The general-in-chief, exhausted from sleepless nights dealing not only with this crisis but also with the simultaneous Confederate invasion of Kentucky, could not budge McClellan. Lincoln was present with Halleck in the telegraph office much of the time. He witnessed what amounted almost to a nervous breakdown by Halleck under the stress. The president later told John Hay that Halleck "broke down — nerve and pluck all gone — and has ever since evaded all possible responsibility — little more than a first-rate clerk."[19] What Lincoln probably did not know was that Halleck suffered severely from hemorrhoids, which grew even more painful under stress, and that he was taking opium to ease the pain.[20] The general-in-chief's incapacity forced Lincoln once again to take on the responsibilities of that position.

In the midst of this crisis McClellan sent a telegram to Lincoln that seemed to reveal his real reason for halting Franklin's corps and failing to hurry up Sumner's. Although McClellan acknowledged that he was under orders "to open communication with Pope," he implied that a better alternative might be "to leave Pope to get out of his scrape & at once use all our means to make the capital perfectly safe." Lincoln was shocked by these words. McClellan "wanted Pope defeated," he told John Hay.[21] Circumstantial evidence seems to support Lincoln's accusation. General Sumner expressed anger when he learned that McClellan had held him back because his corps was not in shape to go forward. "If I had been ordered to advance right on," Sumner told the Committee on the Conduct of the War, "I should have been in that second Bull Run battle with my whole force." As Pope's army retreated toward Washington after its defeat on August 30, it encountered Franklin's corps coming up — two days too late. One of Pope's division commanders overheard some of Franklin's subordinates voice "their pleasure at Pope's discomfiture without the slightest concealment, and [they] spoke of our government in Washington with an affectation of supercilious contempt."[22]

These were dark, dismal days in the North. "For the first time," wrote the Washington bureau chief of the *New York Tribune* on September 1, "I believe it possible that Washington may be taken."[23] Newspapers of various political stripes agreed that "the Country is in extreme peril. The Rebels seem to be pushing forward their forces all along the border line from the Atlantic to the Missouri." "Disguise it as we may, the Union arms have been repeatedly, disgracefully, and decisively beaten." Unless there was some change, "the Union cause is doomed to a speedy and disastrous overthrow."[24] The *New York Times* reported that many people were asking: "Of what use are all these terrible sacrifices? Shall we have nothing but defeat to show for all our valor?"[25]

Demoralization on the home front was bad enough. Demoralization in both the Army of Virginia and the Army of the Potomac was worse. A New Hampshire captain whose regiment had lost heavily at Bull Run declared that "the whole army is disgusted. . . .You need not be surprised if success falls to the rebels with astonishing rapidity." "Our men are sick of the war," wrote Washington Roebling, a New Jersey officer and future builder of the Brooklyn Bridge. "They fight without an aim and without enthusiasm; they have no confidence in their leaders." A brigade commander shared "a general feeling that the Southern Confederacy will be recognized and that they deserve to be recognized."[26]

No one was more aware of the army's demoralization than Lincoln. And as commander in chief, his was the responsibility for doing something about it. A newspaper reporter who spoke with Lincoln on August 30 had never seen the president so "wrathful" toward anyone as he was toward McClellan. Lincoln seemed to think that the general was "a little crazy," according to John Hay, but he agreed with Hay that "envy jealousy and spite are probably a better explanation."[27] The president received plenty of advice on what to do about the matter. Stanton wanted McClellan court-martialed; Chase said he should be shot. Four members of the cabinet signed a memorandum urging the president to dismiss McClellan. Secretary of the Navy Welles did not sign but agreed with the sentiments in the memorandum.[28]

So did Lincoln, but he knew that he would have an army mutiny on his hands if he retained Pope in command. At 7:30 A.M. on September 2 Lincoln and Halleck called on McClellan at his house during breakfast and asked him to take command of all the troops as they retreated into the Washington defenses — Pope's army as well as his own. Three days later, after Burnside had again declined command of a field army to be formed from the troops now in those defenses, Lincoln saw no alternative to McClellan as commander of the merged armies. "Again I have been called upon to save the country," McClellan wrote his wife. "My enemies are crushed, silent & disarmed" (he meant Stanton, Chase, and radical Republicans). He accepted because "under the circumstances no one else *could* save the country."[29]

At a cabinet meeting on September 2, Stanton and Chase protested Lincoln's action; Chase said "it would prove a national calamity." Lincoln's decision caused an estrangement with Stanton that lasted for several weeks. Two cabinet members who kept diaries described the president as "extremely distressed" during the meeting. "He seemed wrung by the bitterest anguish

— said he felt ready to hang himself." That mood was general. "There was a more disturbed and desponding feeling than I have ever witnessed in council," wrote Welles. Lincoln agreed that McClellan "had acted badly in this matter." There was "a design, a purpose, in breaking down Pope, without regard to the consequences to the country," admitted the president. "It is shocking to see and know this." But the army was "utterly demoralized," and Mc-Clellan was the only one who could "reorganize the army and bring it out of chaos," said Lincoln. "McClellan has the army with him . . . [and] we must use the tools we have. There is no man . . . who can . . . lick these troops into shape half as well as he. . . . If he can't fight himself, he excels in making others ready to fight."[30]

The extraordinary response of soldiers to McClellan's resumption of command confirmed Lincoln's judgment. As the dispirited troops trudged back toward Washington on the "cold and rainy" afternoon of September 2, a veteran recalled years later, "everything had a look of sadness in union with our feelings." Everyone "looked as if he would like to hide his head somewhere from all the world." Many soldiers then and later described what happened next. An officer mounted on a dark bay horse with a single escort met the first of the retreating soldiers. A startled captain took one look and ran back to his colonel shouting, "General McClellan is here. 'Little Mac' is on the road." Other soldiers heard the cry. "From extreme sadness we passed in a twinkling to a delirium of delight. A Deliverer had come. . . . Men threw their caps high in the air, and danced and frolicked like schoolboys." Word quickly spread. "Way off in the distance as he passed the different corps we could hear them cheer him. . . . The effect of this man's presence . . . was electrical, and too wonderful to make it worth while attempting to give a reason for it."[31] The Washington correspondent for the *Chicago Tribune,* no partisan of McClellan, witnessed this event. "I have disbelieved the reports of the army's affection for McClellan," he wrote, "being entirely unable to account for the phenomenon. I cannot account for it to my satisfaction now, but I accept it as a fact."[32]

Like the *Tribune* reporter, historians have found it difficult to explain McClellan's popularity with his soldiers. Part of it stemmed from his undeniable charisma, which is not captured by the paper trail on which historians rely but clearly existed in the flesh-and-blood reality of 1862. McClellan possessed an indefinable charm and magnetism that caused Lincoln (and many others) to like him personally even as the president expressed frustration with his behavior. Then, too, McClellan had *created* the Army of the Potomac. They had gone through thick and thin together. He had instilled in them a sense of identity and pride; they reciprocated by identifying with him and his claim that their defeats were caused by lack of support from Congress and the War Department. McClellan was their man, and they were his boys.

In any event McClellan did bring order out of chaos and lick the troops into shape, as Lincoln hoped. Within a few days he reorganized and amalgamated the disparate armies and corps. He got them ready to fight. Whether he would actually lead them into battle would soon be determined, for on September 4 the Army of Northern Virginia began crossing the Potomac into Maryland looking for a fight.

Lincoln once again saw this Confederate offensive as an opportunity more than as a threat — an opportunity to cut off the invading enemy far from his base and if possible prevent him from getting back. Lincoln urged McClellan to go after Lee in strong force. The general started well. But as he probed northward in the second week of September looking for the enemy, McClellan once more began to inflate their numbers by a factor of two or three. Lee's exhausted army was leaking stragglers on every mile of road. Starting with 55,000 men, the Army of Northern Virginia was down to fewer than 45,000 before its first contact with the Union army. McClellan estimated their numbers at 110,000.

On September 13, however, McClellan had a stroke of luck such as few generals have ever had. In a field near Frederick, where the Army of Northern Virginia had camped a few days earlier, a Union corporal found a copy of Lee's Special Orders No. 191 wrapped around three cigars, evidently lost by a careless Confederate courier. These orders detailed a plan for almost two-thirds of Lee's army under Stonewall Jackson to converge from three directions and capture the Union garrison at Harpers Ferry, which stood athwart Lee's supply line from the Shenandoah Valley. This lucky find quickly made its way up the chain of command to McClellan. It gave him a picture of the Army of Northern Virginia divided into four or five parts, each several miles from any other, and the most widely separated units thirty miles apart with the Potomac River between them. No Civil War general had a better chance to destroy an enemy army in detail before it could reunite. McClellan was jubilant. At noon on September 13 he wired Lincoln: "I think Lee has made a gross mistake and that he will be severely punished for it. . . . I have the plans of the Rebels and will catch them in their own trap if my men are equal to the emergency."[33]

Yet, typically, McClellan himself did not seem to feel any sense of urgency. Six more hours went by before he issued orders to his corps commanders to break through the gaps in the South Mountain range. And these orders did not specify an assault at first light the next day, but only that Union troops begin their march *toward* the attack points at first light. This eighteen-hour delay was just enough for Lee to avoid disaster. On September 14 Confederate defenders at Fox's, Turner's, and Crampton's Gaps held off the attacking Federals, while Jackson completed his encirclement of Harpers Ferry and captured it the following morning. Confederate troops evacuated the gaps overnight on September 14–15. The next morning McClellan telegraphed to Washington greatly exaggerated reports of a "rout &

demoralization of the rebel army" that was retreating "in a perfect panic. . . . It is stated that Lee gives his loss as fifteen thousand."[34] (Confederate casualties were actually about 2,700, which were more than counterbalanced by Jackson's capture of 12,500 Federals at Harpers Ferry, which McClellan neglected to mention.)

Lincoln wired congratulations to McClellan: "God bless you, and all with you." Then the president added: "Destroy the rebel army, if possible." Unwisely casting aside his skepticism about anything he heard from McClellan, Lincoln sent a jubilant telegram to the state auditor of Illinois, which quickly found its way into the newspapers: "Gen. McClellan has gained a great victory over the rebel army in Maryland. . . . He is now pursuing the flying foe."[35]

But the foe was not flying nor was McClellan pursuing him. Instead, Lee concentrated his army on the high ground east of the village of Sharpsburg to accept battle if McClellan offered it. The Union general approached cautiously on September 15, studied the situation on the sixteenth, and attacked on the seventeenth. For twelve hours on that bloodiest single day of the Civil War (indeed, in all of American history), repeated assaults by 60,000 of

McClellan's 80,000 men forced back but did not break through the 37,000 Confederates (whom McClellan estimated to be 110,000). The Union attacks came one corps at a time, enabling Lee to shift his troops from one flank to the other to shore up threatened positions.

On two occasions in the early and late afternoon, Union assaults on the enemy center and right achieved potential breakthroughs that might have cut Lee off from his retreat route over a single ford on the Potomac. But McClellan, certain that the Confederates outnumbered him and that Lee was holding back large reserves, refused to commit his own reserves. Never during this long day did more than 15,000 Union infantry go into action simultaneously, and almost 20,000 of McClellan's infantry and cavalry never fired a shot at all. After a night of horror in which 4,000 Rebels and Yankees lay dead on the field and 2,000 of the 17,000 wounded would soon die, the morning of September 18 dawned with the Confederates still standing defiantly in place. Although McClellan wired Halleck at 8:00 A.M. that "the battle will probably be renewed today," it was not.[36] That night the Army of Northern Virginia crossed the Potomac to its namesake state. Except for a

feeble pursuit on the nineteenth and twentieth that was easily repulsed, the Battle of
Antietam was over.

McClellan telegraphed news of "a complete victory" to Washington. "The enemy is
driven back into Virginia." Forgotten was
Lincoln's injunction to "destroy the rebel
army." Gideon Welles probably echoed the
president's sentiments when he wrote in his
diary on September 19: "Nothing from the
army, except that instead of following up
the victory, attacking and capturing the
Rebels, they . . . are rapidly escaping across
the river. . . . Oh dear."[37] But McClellan
believed that "I fought the battle splendidly
& that it was a masterpiece of art." He also
thought that he now had the upper hand
over his "enemies" in Washington. "Thro'
certain friends of mine . . . I have insisted
that Stanton shall be removed & that Halleck shall give way to me as Comdr. in
Chief. . . . Unless these conditions are
fulfilled I will leave the service."[38]

Seldom had even McClellan been so blind
to reality. His fantasy was fed by a letter
from Allan Pinkerton, his chief of intelligence, who reported a conversation with
Lincoln on September 22. The lawyer-
president asked Pinkerton a series of probing questions in such a mild manner that

the detective did not realize he was being cross-examined. Had everything possible been done to prevent the capture of Harpers Ferry? asked Lincoln. Yes, of course, answered Pinkerton. How had McClellan handled himself during the battle? With great skill and courage. Why didn't the army renew the attack on September 18? The odds were too great, Pinkerton replied. "He next enquired regarding the Rebels escaping across the Potomac," the detective reported, and the president was satisfied with the explanation that the Union forces faced "many very great obstacles" to preventing it. "I must say General," concluded Pinkerton, "that I never saw a man feel better than he did with these explanations. He expressed himself as highly pleased and gratified with all you had done . . . to push the Rebels back to Maryland . . . and free the Capitol from danger."[39]

Pinkerton's report that Lincoln was "highly pleased" with all McClellan had done was about as accurate as his intelligence estimates of the numbers of Confederate troops. But much of the Northern public seemed highly pleased. The press magnified Antietam into a great victory, all the more heartening because of the pessimism that had preceded it. "At no time since the war commenced did the cause of Union look more dark and despairing than one week ago," declared the *New York Sunday Mercury* on September 21, but now "at no time since the first gun was fired have the hopes of the nation seemed in such a fair way of realization as they do today." The *New York Times* proclaimed that this great victory would be "felt in the destinies of the Nation for centuries to come."[40]

The *Times* was right about the long-term consequences of Antietam. Among other results it caused the British government to back away from a joint French-British project to recognize the Confederacy as an independent nation and to offer to mediate an end to the war. But perhaps the most momentous consequence was the opening it provided for Lincoln to issue a preliminary Emancipation Proclamation.

That document had remained in his desk since the cabinet meeting of July 22, when Seward persuaded him to wait for a Union victory. During those two months the pressure for emancipation had continued to build. But so had opposition, as the issue threatened to polarize the North — and its armies, in which many soldiers agreed with a private from Indiana who declared that "if emancipation is to be the policy of this war . . . I do not care how quick the country goes to pot."[41] Democrats made political headway in 1862 with the demagogic argument that if slaves were freed they would come North and take the jobs of white men — perhaps even marry their daughters. "Shall the Working Classes Be Equalized with Negroes?" blared the headline of one Northern newspaper. "Workingmen! Be Careful! Organize yourselves against this element which threatens your impoverishment and annihilation." Lyman Trumbull of Illinois, chairman of the Senate Judiciary Committee, confessed with mortification in July 1862 that "there is a very great aversion in the West — I know it to be so in my State — against having free negroes come among us. Our people want nothing to do with the negro."[42]

As commander in chief, Lincoln could not ignore such sentiments lest a Northern backlash undermine the positive benefits he hoped to achieve with a national strategy of emancipation. Like Trumbull, the president recognized with regret that white racism was a stumbling block to emancipation. Thus he endorsed the colonization of freed slaves abroad as a way of defusing white fears of an influx into the North of freedpeople. An

Illinois soldier who approved of emancipation nevertheless declared in October 1862 that "I am not in favor of freeing the negroes and leaving them to run free and mingle among us nether is Sutch the intention of Old Abe but we will Send them off and colonize them."[43]

Such indeed was Lincoln's expressed intention during the weeks he waited for an opportunity to proclaim emancipation. He invited five black men from Washington to the White House on August 14 and urged them to consider the idea of emigration. The "substance" of Lincoln's remarks was written down by a reporter for the *New York Tribune* whom the president had invited to be present. Slavery was "the greatest wrong inflicted on any people," Lincoln told the delegation. But even if slavery were gone, white prejudice and discrimination would remain. "Your race suffer very greatly, many of them, by living among us, while ours suffer by your presence." Black people had little chance for equality in the United States. More than that, "There is an unwillingness on the part of our people, harsh as it may be, for you free colored people to remain with us. . . . I do not mean to discuss this, but to propose it as a fact with which we have to deal. I cannot alter it if I would. . . . It is better for us both, therefore, to be separated."[44]

This meeting bore little fruit either in assuaging white anxieties about emancipation or in recruiting blacks for emigration. It also earned Lincoln public denunciations by several black and abolitionist leaders and a private complaint by Salmon P. Chase in a diary entry: "How much better would be a manly protest against prejudice against color! — and a wise effort to give freemen homes in America!"[45] The president's next venture in preparing public opinion for the proclamation resting in his desk was more successful. On August 19 the *New York Tribune* published an open letter to Lincoln by editor Horace Greeley titled "The Prayer of Twenty Millions." Greeley chastised the president for "a mistaken deference to Rebel Slavery" and urged him to heed the prayers of twenty million loyal Northerners for the abolition of slavery. In an unusual public response, the commander in chief carefully explained: "My paramount object in this struggle *is* to save the Union, and is *not* either to save or destroy slavery. If I could save the Union by not freeing *any* slave I would do it, and if I could save it by freeing *all* the slaves I would do it; and if I could save it by freeing some and leaving others alone I would also do that. What I do about slavery and the colored race, I do because it helps save the Union." In closing Lincoln said that these statements represented "my view of *official* duty; and I intend no modification of my oft-expressed *personal* wish that all men every where could be free."[46]

This presidential letter was a stroke of genius. To conservatives who insisted that preservation of the Union must be the sole purpose of the war, Lincoln said that such *was* his purpose. To radicals who wanted him to proclaim emancipation in order to save the Union, he hinted that he might do so. To everyone he made it clear that partial or even total emancipation might become necessary (as of course he thought it had) to accomplish the purpose on which they all agreed.

The same intentional ambiguity characterized Lincoln's interview on September 13 with a group of clergymen who presented him with a petition for emancipation. This event took place at a time of what John Hay described as "fearful anxiety" and "almost unbearable tension" for the commander in chief, who was preoccupied with military crises in Maryland and Kentucky. Lincoln agreed with the delegation that "slavery is the root of the rebellion" and that "emancipation would help us in Europe, and convince them that we are incited by something more than ambition. . . . And then unquestionably it would weaken the rebels by drawing off their laborers, which is of great importance." On the other hand, with Confederate armies on the offensive, "what *good* would a proclamation of emancipation from me do? . . . I do not want to issue a document that the whole world will necessarily see must be inoperative. . . . Would *my* word free the slaves, when I cannot even enforce the Constitution in the rebel states?"[47]

Here too was something for everybody: an assertion that emancipation would benefit the Union cause but also an acknowledgment that in the present military circumstances a proclamation would be worse than useless. Four days later at Antietam those circumstances changed. So on September 22 Lincoln called a special meeting of the cabinet. He reminded them of the decision exactly two months earlier to postpone issuance of an Emancipation Proclamation. "I think the time has come now," he said. "I wish it were a better time. I wish we were in better condition. The action of the army against the rebels has not been quite what I should have best liked. But they have been driven out of Maryland, and Pennsylvania is no longer in danger of invasion." When the enemy was at Frederick, said the president, he had made a "promise to myself and (hesitating a little) — to my Maker" that "if God gave us the victory in the approaching battle, [I] would consider it an indication of Divine will" in favor of emancipation. The Battle of Antietam was God's sign that "he had decided this question in favor of the slaves." Therefore he intended to issue a proclamation warning Confederate states that unless they returned to the Union by January 1, 1863 (which scarcely anyone expected), their slaves "shall be then, thenceforward, and forever free."[48]

Montgomery Blair was the only cabinet member who objected. He had changed during the past year from one of the cabinet's most radical members to its most conservative. Blair repeated his warning that the proclamation would drive border-state elements into the Confederacy and give Northern Democrats "a club . . . to beat the Administration" in the forthcoming congressional and state elections. Lincoln replied that he had done everything he could to bring the border states along. "They [will] acquiesce, if not immediately, soon; for they must be satisfied that slavery

[has] received its death-blow from slave-owners — it could not survive the rebellion." As for Northern Democrats, Lincoln no longer intended to indulge them, for "their clubs would be used against us take what course we might."[49]

GOD BLESS ABRAHAM LINCOLN! proclaimed Horace Greeley's *New York Tribune,* which a month earlier had damned the president for his "mistaken deference" to slavery. The proclamation "is the signal gun of a new era of energy, resolution, and triumph," declared the *Tribune.* It "is one of those stupendous facts in human history which marks not only an era in the progress of the nation, but an epoch in the history of the world."[50]

The *Tribune* was right. The proclamation completed the transformation of Lincoln's policy and national strategy from a war for restoration of the old Union into a war to give the nation a new birth of freedom. Three days after signing the preliminary proclamation, Lincoln told an unsympathetic official of the Interior Department, as the latter paraphrased the president's words, that "the character of the war will be changed. It will be one of subjugation. . . . The [Old] South is to be destroyed and replaced by new propositions and ideas."

General-in-Chief Halleck got the message. "The character of the war has very much changed in the last year," he told General Grant in March 1863. "There is now no possible hope of reconciliation with the rebels. . . . We must conquer the rebels or be conquered by them. . . . Every slave withdrawn from the enemy is the equivalent of a white man put hors de combat."[51]

As if to reinforce the New York Tribune's prediction about the administration's new energy and resolution, Lincoln issued a second proclamation two days after the preliminary emancipation edict. On September 24 he suspended the writ of habeas corpus throughout the country and authorized trials by military commissions of "all Rebels and Insurgents, their aiders and abettors within the United States, and all persons discouraging volunteer enlistments, resisting militia drafts, or guilty of any disloyal practice."[52]

This draconian decree was a response to attacks and riots against military recruiters and against efforts to enforce militia drafts in several Northern states. Congress had passed a new militia law in July making the states liable to calls for militia to serve for nine months (instead of the ninety days under the previous law). In August the War

Department had issued such a call and mandated a federally enforced draft in states that did not meet their quotas. Resistance to this quasi draft occasioned Lincoln's order, which gave Democrats another civil liberties "club" with which to beat the administration in the fall elections.

High-ranking Democrats in the Army of the Potomac reacted with anger to these twin presidential proclamations — especially the first one. Gen. Fitz-John Porter, McClellan's favorite subordinate, denounced the Emancipation Proclamation as the act "of a political coward" that was "ridiculed in the army — causing disgust, discontent, and expressions of disloyalty to the views of the administration." McClellan told his wife that he was thinking of resigning because the Emancipation Proclamation and "the continuation of Stanton & Halleck in office render it almost impossible for me to retain my commission & self-respect at the same time."[53]

McClellan wrote to his friend William Aspinwall, a wealthy New York businessman, for advice on what he should do in response to Lincoln's proclamations "inaugurating servile war" (emancipation) and "changing our free institutions into a despotism" (suspending habeas corpus). Rather than responding in writing, Aspinwall traveled down to see McClellan personally. He was "decidedly of the opinion," McClellan reported, "that it is my duty to submit to the Presdt's proclamation & quietly continue doing my duty as a soldier." The general told Aspinwall that he would think it over.[54]

McClellan received similar advice from other quarters, and decided to heed it — especially when he learned what happened to Maj. John Key, a staff member in the War Department and brother of Col. Thomas Key of McClellan's own staff. Word reached Lincoln several days after the Battle of Antietam that in a private conversation Major Key had said that the reason the Rebel army was not "bagged" before recrossing the Potomac was "that is not the game. The object is that neither army shall get much advantage of the other; that both shall be kept in the field till they are exhausted, when we will make a compromise and save slavery." Lincoln called Key on the carpet and cross-examined him. When the major admitted making this remark, Lincoln cashiered him on the spot. If this was the "game" of some army officers, Lincoln wrote, it was his intention "to break up the game." The president told John Hay that he had heard similar rumors about "staff talk" in the Army of the Potomac, so he cashiered Key to send a message.[55]

McClellan got the message. On October 7 he issued a general order (a copy of which he sent to Lincoln) pointing out that the army was the servant of government. Civil authorities made policy; the army executed it. "Armed forces are raised and supported simply to sustain the Civil Authorities and are to be held in strict subordination thereto in all respects. . . . The Chief Executive, who is charged with the administration of the National affairs, is the proper and only source through which the views and orders of the Government can be known to the Armies of the Nation." This was excellent, but McClellan could not resist adding a none-too-subtle reference to the forthcoming elections: "The remedy for political errors, if any are committed, is to be found only in the action of the people at the polls."[56]

McClellan talked no more of resigning. But the president in effect put him on notice that unless he showed more initiative as a commander, his tenure was limited. The previous July, Lincoln had said, with respect to his intention to issue an emancipation edict, that "we wanted the Army to strike more vigorous blows. The Administration must set an example, and strike at the heart of the rebellion." The Emancipation Proclamation struck such a blow. Now it was McClellan's turn. For him the heart of the rebellion in October 1862 was the Army of Northern Virginia a few miles across the Potomac River. On October 6 he received an order from the president, through Halleck, that McClellan should have considered peremptory: "Cross the Potomac and give battle to the enemy. . . . Your army must move now."[57]

6
THE PROMISE MUST NOW BE KEPT

For Lincoln the dispatches between Washington and the armies commanded by McClellan and Buell in October 1862 must have left a strong feeling of déjà vu. From the White House and the War Department went repeated messages urging action to follow up the limited victories of Antietam and Perryville and do more damage to the enemy. Back to Washington came as many telegrams filled with explanations and excuses for why the armies could not do what Lincoln and Halleck wanted: The roads were bad, supplies were short, the men were tired, horses and mules were worn out, the men needed new uniforms and shoes — on and on. The only general in charge of one of the principal Union armies who did not bombard Washington with excuses and complaints was Ulysses S. Grant, commander of the Army of the Tennessee, which had stopped a Confederate counteroffensive at the Battles of Iuka and Corinth. Lincoln would remember this fact.

As the exhausted and outnumbered Confederate Army of Tennessee retreated to its namesake state after the Battle of Perryville, Lincoln urged Buell to pursue and attack again and to secure East Tennessee. But even though more than half of Buell's Army of the Ohio had not fought at Perryville, the general considered it necessary to reorganize and refit before he could renew the offensive. Lincoln did a slow burn. "I am directed by the President to say that your army must enter East Tennessee this fall," Halleck wired Buell. "Neither the Government nor the country can endure these repeated delays." The president "does not understand why we cannot march as the enemy marches, live as he lives, and fight as he fights, unless we admit the inferiority of our troops and generals."[1]

Lincoln made the same point to McClellan. He visited the Army of the Potomac near the Antietam battlefield during the first four days of October. In conversations with McClellan he tried to prod the general into action. A week later, after reading McClellan's excuses for inaction, Lincoln wrote him a gentle admonition. "You remember me speaking to you of what I called your over-cautiousness," said the president. "Are you not over-cautious when you assume that you can not do what the enemy is constantly doing? Should you not claim to be at least his equal in prowess, and act upon the claim?" A campaign to cripple Lee's damaged army was possible "if our troops march as well as the enemy; and it is unmanly to say they can not do it."[2]

McClellan and Buell believed that the armchair commander in chief just did not understand the logistical requirements of moving and supplying a large army. But Lincoln *did* know that Confederate armies moved faster and lighter than Union armies — faster *because* lighter. The president understood all too well that Union armies were bogged down by the very abundance of their supplies. He probably never heard of Confederate general Richard Ewell's dictum that "the road to glory cannot be followed with much baggage."[3] But he certainly was familiar with the observation by the Army of the Potomac's quartermaster about McClellan's endless requests for more of everything before he could advance: "An army will never move if it waits until all the different commanders report that they are ready and want no more supplies."[4]

Lincoln may also have read the testimony

of Gen. Irvin McDowell before the Committee on the Conduct of the War back in December 1861. "There never was an army in the world that began to be supplied as well as ours is," said McDowell. Thus Union soldiers "have got into the way that they require and insist upon having an immense deal provided for them. They must have from thirty wagons to a regiment before they will start," while the enemy moved twice as fast because they got along with half as much. In his crash course of reading military history, Lincoln may have learned that the standard ration of a soldier in Napoleon's armies was half that of the Union ration and that Napoleonic regiments had only one-third the number of wagons per thousand soldiers as the Union standard.[5] In any event the president told one of his generals in November 1862 that "this expanding, and piling up of *impedimenta,* has been, so far, almost our ruin, and will be our final ruin if it is not abandoned. . . . You would be better off . . . for not having a thousand wagons, doing nothing but hauling forage to feed the animals that draw them, and taking at least two thousand men to care for the wagons and animals, who otherwise might be two thousand good soldiers."[6]

Grant and Sherman eventually learned this lesson. Buell and McClellan never did. And by the time Lincoln wrote this letter, both were gone. Buell's decision to bring his army back to its base in Nashville for rest and refitting instead of pushing on to East Tennessee was the last straw. Midwestern governors demanded Buell's removal. Two governors were about to start for Washington to press Lincoln on this matter when news arrived that the president on October 23 had replaced Buell with Gen. William S. Rosecrans, who had won the Battle of Corinth three weeks earlier. At Lincoln's direction, Halleck ordered Rosecrans to go after Braxton Bragg's Army of Tennessee at Murfreesboro and secure control of East Tennessee. "I need not urge upon you the necessity of giving active employment of your forces," Halleck told Rosecrans. "Neither the country nor the Government will much longer put up with the inactivity of some of our armies and generals."[7]

Buell was not particularly popular with his soldiers or in the Midwestern states from which most of them came. McClellan was another matter. Although some soldiers and junior officers in the Army of the Potomac expressed frustration with their commander's sluggishness after Antietam, most retained their loyalty to him. Lincoln noticed, however, that when he visited the army in early October the men cheered him as loudly as they cheered McClellan. A bond was forming between common soldiers and "Old Abe," whose plebeian background was similar to theirs and whose kindly chats with wounded as well as healthy soldiers inspired affection.[8] Nevertheless McClellan possessed a powerful constituency among conservatives in the officer corps and on the home front. Early one morning during his visit to the army, Lincoln asked a friend as they strolled through the camps: "Hatch, what do you suppose all these people are?" Why, the Army of the Potomac, a surprised Ozias Hatch replied. "No, you are mistaken," said the president. "That is General McClellan's body guard."[9]

Lincoln's disappointment with McClellan was echoed by a growing clamor of Northern opinion. WILL THE ARMY OF THE POTOMAC ADVANCE? asked a *New York Times* headline. "Why Should There Be Delay?" "What devil is it that prevents the Potomac army from advancing?" asked the editor of the *Chicago Tribune.* "What malign influence palsies our army and wastes these glorious days for fighting? If it is McClellan, does not the President see that he is a traitor?"[10] General Halleck figuratively threw up his hands in exasperation. "I am sick, tired, and disgusted" with McClellan's delays, Halleck wrote privately. "It requires the lever of Archimedes to move this inert mass."[11]

John Hay wrote an unsigned newspaper article that anonymously but intentionally expressed Lincoln's sentiments on this subject. If McClellan had a million men, said Hay, "he would find a place where just another regiment was absolutely essential, and say he could not fight until he got it." The general had "an inherent vice of mind . . . which makes him never ready to act. . . . He works and toils unceasingly to bring an army to a pitch of perfection, which can never be reached." Hay/Lincoln hit the nail on the head. After returning from his visit to McClellan and the army, the president told a colleague that the general was "a ruined man if he did not move forward, move rapidly and effectually."[12]

The president made one more effort with McClellan. The general's demand for a full logistical pipeline before he could advance, said Lincoln, "ignores the question of *time*," which benefited the enemy more than the Army of the Potomac. If McClellan crossed the river quickly and got between the enemy and Richmond, said Lincoln, he could force Lee into the open for a decisive battle. "We should not so operate as to merely drive him away. . . . If we can not beat the enemy where he now is [near Martinsburg, west of Harpers Ferry], we never can, he again being within the entrenchments of Richmond." McClellan should "at least, try to beat him to Richmond on the inside track. I say 'try': if we never try, we shall never succeed."[13]

As Lincoln was writing this letter, news came of a Confederate cavalry raid into Pennsylvania. Jeb Stuart's horsemen rode entirely around the immobile Union army, evaded the Northern cavalry that chased them, and brought away twelve hundred horses and dozens of prisoners. McClellan blamed this embarrassing incident on his own lack of cavalry and good horses. An irritated Lincoln had Halleck telegraph to McClellan that the president "directs me to suggest that, if the enemy had more occupation south of the river, his cavalry would not be so likely to make raids north of it." Quartermaster General Meigs was angered by McClellan's complaint about a lack of horses and pointed out that he had shipped thirteen thousand of them to the Army of the Potomac in the past seven weeks.[14]

When McClellan transmitted to the War Department a report about lame and sore-tongued horses "absolutely broken down from fatigue and want of flesh," Lincoln lost his temper. He fired back a telegram to McClellan: "Will you pardon me for asking what the horses of your army have done since the battle of Antietam that fatigue[s] anything." McClellan vented his anger about this dispatch in a letter to his wife: "The good of the country requires me to submit to all of this from men whom I know to be greatly my inferior socially, intellectually & morally! There never was a truer epithet applied to a certain individual than that of the 'Gorilla.' "[15]

In a direct reply to Lincoln, however, McClellan restrained his temper and detailed the endless picketing and scouting duties carried out by his cavalry. He concluded: "If any instance can be found where overworked Cavalry has performed more labor than mine since the battle of Antietam I am not conscious of it." In truth, however, McClellan did not make good use of his cavalry, and Lincoln knew it. The president telegraphed McClellan a quasi apology for

241

his sarcastic question, but added that "Stuart's cavalry outmarched ours, having certainly done more marked service on the Peninsula, and everywhere since."[16]

During this exchange of telegrams the Army of the Potomac finally began crossing the river into Virginia. Lincoln said he was "rejoiced to learn" of this movement.[17] The rejoicing did not last long, however, as it took the army six days to get across a river that Lee's forces had crossed in one night after Antietam. And the lumbering Army of the Potomac required another six days to move south forty miles to the vicinity of Warrenton. During those twelve days Lieut. Gen. James Longstreet's corps marched almost twice as far to take up a blocking position to the south, while Jackson's corps remained in place to threaten the Union flank. Lincoln's patience finally snapped. He prepared an order replacing McClellan with Burnside. Francis Preston Blair tried to persuade Lincoln not to issue the order. But the president had made up his mind. He had "tried long enough to bore with an auger too dull to take hold," the commander in chief told Blair. "I said I would remove him if he let Lee's army get away from him, and I must do so. He has got the 'slows,' Mr. Blair."[18]

A War Department courier with the rank of brigadier general carried this order by special train in a snowstorm to Warrenton, where he went first to Burnside's headquarters. For the third time that general tried to refuse, but the courier told him that if he did so the command would go to Joseph Hooker (whom Burnside disliked and distrusted). So "Burn" reluctantly accepted and at midnight went with the courier to McClellan's tent to give him the order.[19]

Nothing in McClellan's tenure of command became him like the leaving of it. Despite emotional pleas from some officers to defy Lincoln's order and "change front on Washington," McClellan discountenanced such talk and turned the army over to his successor. "Stand by General Burnside as you have stood by me, and all will be well," he told his soldiers as thousands yelled their continuing affection for him and others wept unashamedly. McClellan boarded a train for New Jersey, where he would sit out the rest of the war except for a run against Lincoln in the election of 1864. In that effort, as a Union naval officer wryly put it, he met "with no better success as a politician than as a general."[20]

Lincoln had waited until after the fall elections to remove McClellan. The president knew that a backlash against the Emancipation Proclamation and his order authorizing military commissions to try civilians would hurt the Republicans. So would failure to make more headway in the war. He did not want to give the Democrats an opportunity to make a martyr of McClellan. As it was, the Republicans lost the governorships of New York and New Jersey, the legislatures of Illinois, Indiana, and New Jersey, and thirty-four seats in the House of Representatives. But it could have been worse. Lincoln's party retained all the other Northern state governments, a comfortable majority in the House, and an increased majority in the Senate.

This continuing political support would sustain the commander in chief in his strategy of "hard desperate fighting."[21] After the elections, Lincoln told a delegation from the Western Sanitary Commission (a soldiers' aid society) that "the people . . . haven't buckled down to the determination to fight this war through; for they have got the idea into their heads that we are going to get out of this fix by . . . *strategy!*" What the president meant by "strategy" in this context was maneuver and siege — the Buell and McClellan strategy. "The army has got the same notion. They have no idea that the war is to be carried on and put through by hard, tough fighting that will hurt somebody."[22] In his conception of military strategy Lincoln was Clausewitzian. The Prussian theorist of war had written that "the destruction of the enemy's military force is the leading principle of war," and it "is principally effected only by means of the engagement" — that is, by "hard, tough fighting."[23] With McClellan and Buell gone, that is what Lincoln now expected from his new commanders.

Burnside did his best to give the president what he wanted but seemed to get off on the wrong foot. He proposed to change the line of operations from a southward move against Longstreet's corps using the rickety single-track Orange and Alexandria Railroad as his supply line. Instead, Burnside wanted to move east to Fredericksburg, where he could open a more secure supply line via the lower Potomac River and then the railroad through Fredericksburg toward Richmond.[24] Halleck did not like this plan. On November 12 he traveled to Warrenton for consultations with Burnside. Halleck took with him Montgomery Meigs and Gen. Herman Haupt, who was in charge of railroad logistics. Haupt agreed with Burnside about the inadequacy and vulnerability of the Orange and Alexandria. Halleck finally agreed to take a modified version of Burnside's plan to Lincoln, who had already expressed skepticism because it seemed to make Richmond rather than the enemy army the main strategic objective.

Halleck and Burnside somehow misunderstood each other on the precise nature of the modified plan. Halleck assumed that most of the Army of the Potomac would cross the Rappahannock River at fords above Fredericksburg and seize the heights there from the rear. This was the operational plan that Halleck presented to Lincoln. On November 14 he telegraphed Burnside: "The President has just assented to your plan. He thinks it will succeed if you move very rapidly; otherwise not."[25]

Burnside did move rapidly. His lead units marched forty miles in two days. But they marched to Falmouth on the north bank of the Rappahannock, across from Fredericksburg, where the river was too deep to ford. Burnside expected pontoons for bridging the river to meet him there; Halleck had understood that Burnside would already be across the river and that the pontoons would be needed only later to open the new supply line. By the time the pontoons finally arrived on the north bank, Longstreet's corps had occupied the heights on the south bank.[26]

There was plenty of blame to go around for this fiasco. But Lincoln was more interested in salvaging the operation than in assigning blame. So he boarded a boat for the trip down the Potomac to consult with Burnside. In Lincoln's summary of this discussion, he said that Burnside thought he could cross the river and drive the enemy south. Lincoln told him, however, that "I wish the enemy to be prevented from falling back, accumulating strength as he goes, into his intrenchments at Richmond." Instead, the president outlined a complicated operational plan whereby two auxiliary forces (part of them to be drawn from Burnside's main army) would move with gunboat support to the head of navigation on the Rappahannock and Pamunkey rivers south of Fredericksburg to catch Lee in a pincers as he retreated from Burnside's attack at Fredericksburg. Halleck and Burnside convinced Lincoln that it would take too long to organize the auxiliary forces and get them in place, and that in any event something was bound to go wrong with such an intricate plan.[27] For better or for worse Burnside was left to carry out whatever plan he could devise.

It turned out to be for the worse. Believing that Lincoln wanted him to cross the river and attack, Burnside reconnoitered possible crossing points both downriver and upriver from Fredericksburg, but decided to cross at the town itself. Except for the harassing fire of one brigade, the Confederates did not contest the crossing but awaited Burnside's December 13 assault on the line of hills behind Fredericksburg. Gen. George G. Meade's Union division achieved a temporary breakthrough against Jackson's corps on the Confederate right. But Gen. William B. Franklin, commanding the Union left, failed to reinforce this potential success and also refused to renew the attack despite Burnside's repeated orders to do so. Assaults by the Union right on Marye's Heights directly behind the town were repulsed with heavy Union casualties. When darkness descended on this short December day, the Army of the Potomac had suffered a disastrous and demoralizing defeat.

Burnside manfully accepted responsibility, unlike McClellan, who had always found someone else to blame. In this case, however, many blamed Lincoln for having forced Burnside to fight a battle he could not win. When the president learned of the outcome, he said: "If there is a worse place than hell, I am in it." Nevertheless, as a gesture to buck up morale and show his support for both Burnside and his soldiers, Lincoln issued a congratulatory proclamation to the army (which he had not done after Antietam): "Although you were not successful, the attempt was not an error." The "courage with which you, in an open field, maintained the contest against an entrenched foe . . . show[s] that you possess all the qualities of a great army, which will yet give victory to the cause of the country."[28]

The Battle of Fredericksburg brought to a head a political crisis in the Republican Party that had been brewing for some time. The military defeat was a catalyst for all the rumors and discontent among Republicans, especially in the Senate. William H. Seward was the principal target of this discontent. Many Republicans, particularly radicals, considered him the "evil genius" of the cabinet — the "unseen hand" whose conservative sway over Lincoln had delayed emancipation, kept McClellan in command too long, and prevented vigorous prosecution of the war. In two long caucus meetings on December 16 and 17, an overwhelming majority of Republican senators voted to press for a reorganization of the cabinet to secure "unity of purpose and action" — mainly by getting rid of Seward. Much of the impetus for this effort had come from Chase, Seward's cabinet rival, who resented the secretary of state's supposed influence with Lincoln.

This affair was the greatest challenge thus far to Lincoln's leadership. If the president "caved in" (his words) to the senators' demand, he would lose control of his administration. His power as leader of his party, head of government, and commander in chief would be gravely weakened. When word of the senatorial caucus leaked out, rumors swept Washington that the whole cabinet — perhaps even Lincoln himself — would resign. The president was "awfully shaken" by the crisis. Branding the charge of Seward's "malign influence" an "absurd lie," Lincoln unburdened himself to Senator Orville Browning (who had voted against the caucus resolution). "What do these men want?" Lincoln asked Browning, and answered his own question. "They wish to get rid of me, and I am sometimes half disposed to gratify them. . . . Since I heard last night of the proceedings of the caucus I have been more distressed than by any event of my life. . . . We are now on the brink of destruction. It appears to me that the Almighty is against us, and I can hardly see a ray of hope."[29]

Lincoln pulled himself together and met with a delegation of nine senators on the evening of December 18. He did not tell them that Seward had submitted his resignation in order to take the pressure off the president (who had not accepted it). Lincoln listened quietly to the senators' speeches "attributing to Mr. Seward a lukewarmness in the conduct of the war, and seeming to consider him the real cause of our failures." Without committing himself the president invited them back for further discussion the next day. When they arrived, the senators were surprised to find the entire cabinet present except Seward. In a brief speech Lincoln said that whenever possible he consulted the cabinet about important decisions but that he alone made the decisions, especially on matters concerning slavery and on questions of military strategy and command; that members of the cabinet sometimes disagreed but they all supported a policy when it was decided upon; and that Seward was a valuable member of the administration. Then Lincoln turned to the cabinet for confirmation. All eyes looked to Chase, who was neatly put on the spot. He had told the senators that Seward was a marplot; if he now agreed with Lincoln he would lose face with them; if he did not he would lose the confidence of the president. Chase mumbled a brief endorsement of Lincoln's statement but tried to save face by expressing regret that major decisions were not more fully discussed by the cabinet. Deflated by the whole experience and no doubt impressed by Lincoln's political skills, the senators quietly left.

Much embarrassed, Chase came to the White House the next morning to offer his resignation. "Let me have it," said Lincoln as he extended his long arm to receive the letter of resignation from the reluctant treasury secretary. "This cuts the Gordian knot." Mixing his metaphors, Lincoln added: "Now I can ride; I have a pumpkin in each end of my bag." The senators could not have Seward's head without losing Chase as well. The president refused both resignations; the cabinet remained unchanged; the political fallout from the Battle of Fredericksburg was contained.[30]

But not the military fallout. On the same day that Lincoln solved his cabinet crisis by declining both resignations, two generals in the Army of the Potomac wrote him a long letter criticizing Burnside and urging a change of strategy to take the army again to the Peninsula. They were Maj. Gens. William B. Franklin and William F. Smith, commanders of the army's left wing and Sixth Corps. Both were McClellan protégés who had never really accepted his removal. Lincoln saw their recommendation as a thinly veiled move to get McClellan restored to command. He rejected the suggestion of a return to the Peninsula.[31]

This exchange did not end the matter. On December 30 Brig. Gens. John Newton and John Cochrane, commanders of a division and a brigade in Smith's corps, appeared at the White House and told Lincoln that the army was demoralized, that Burnside was preparing to cross the Rappahannock again, and that disaster would result if he did so. Lincoln saw through this affair as another ploy by the pro-McClellan cabal. But he wired Burnside: "I have good reason for saying you must not make a general movement of the army without letting me know." Burnside obligingly canceled his orders for a movement and telegraphed that he would come to Washington to see the president.[32]

Burnside arrived at the White House early on the morning of January 1. It would be an eventful day for the commander in chief.

He put the finishing touches on the Emancipation Proclamation. At eleven he would take his stand to shake hands for three hours in the traditional New Year's Day reception, after which he gathered with a small group to sign the proclamation. Bad news was coming from Union armies in Mississippi and Tennessee. But the meeting with Burnside, who was soon joined by Stanton and Halleck, was undoubtedly the worst part of Lincoln's day. The general acknowledged that his senior commanders lacked confidence in him and offered to resign. Before Stanton and Halleck arrived, Burnside had also suggested that they ought to resign as well because they lacked the confidence of the army and the country. When those two men arrived, all four discussed Burnside's proposed move across the Rappahannock but came to no conclusion.[33]

After they left, Lincoln sat down and wrote a letter to Halleck instructing him to go to the army with Burnside, examine the ground, consult with the generals, and make a decision whether or not to authorize the movement. "If in such a difficulty you do not help," the president told his general-in-chief, "you fail me precisely in the point for which I sought your assistance. . . . Your military skill is useless to me, if you will not do this."[34]

When he read these words, Halleck immediately submitted his resignation. Lincoln had not meant to provoke such a response, however; he agreed to withdraw the letter "because considered harsh by Gen. Halleck."[35] It was harsh, and deservedly so. Halleck claimed that the commanding general of a field army should be given the authority and responsibility to determine operations and tactics because he was the man on the ground, while the general-in-chief was miles away — sometimes hundreds of miles. "I have always . . . avoided giving positive instructions to generals commanding departments," Halleck had written to one of them in November, "leaving them the exercise of their own judgment, while giving them my opinion and advice."[36] Lincoln recognized that Halleck's statement of this philosophy was a rationalization to escape the responsibility of making decisions. As the president later told John Hay, Halleck had turned out to be nothing but a first-rate clerk. But Lincoln needed a military clerk, so he kept him on. The problem of what to do about Burnside had to be postponed, however, because of ominous military developments in the West.

■ ■ ■ ■

The most successful theater of Union military and naval operations in 1862 had been the Mississippi River valley and the adjacent regions drained by the great river's tributaries. Yet these conquests attracted less attention at home and abroad than frustration and failure in the East. Lincoln noted this contrast in a letter of August 4 to Count Agénor-Etienne de Gasparin, a Union supporter in France. Gasparin had warned the president that Northern military victories were necessary to forestall European recognition of the Confederacy. Lincoln agreed, but added: "It seems unreasonable that a series of successes, extending through half-a-year and clearing more than a hundred thousand square miles of country, should help us so little, while a single half-defeat [the Seven Days'] should hurt us so much."[37]

Yet Lincoln himself found it necessary to devote most of his attention to the Eastern theater and to events in Middle and East Tennessee. When a prominent judge in St. Louis accused the president of neglecting the Mississippi Valley, he responded that he was strongly committed to opening the river, but he had to focus on the threats to Kentucky as well as to Maryland and Pennsylvania. "The country will not allow us to send our whole Western force down the Mississippi," wrote the commander in chief, "while the enemy sacks Louisville and Cincinnati."[38]

Lincoln was well aware of the strategic importance of the great river he had twice descended on a flatboat in his youth. The success of the Union river navy that fought its way down to Vicksburg, and of David G. Farragut's blue-water navy that fought its way up to the same Confederate bastion in the spring of 1862, had given early promise of opening the whole river from Minnesota to the Gulf. But the reinforced strength of this new "Gibraltar of the West" at Vicksburg and the summer drop in the river level, which threatened to ground Farragut's deep-draft vessels, ended that effort in August 1862. The military crises in Kentucky and Maryland, as well as a combined attempt by two smaller Confederate armies under Gens. Earl Van Dorn and Sterling Price to drive Grant out of northern Mississippi, prevented any renewed Union effort against Vicksburg until November. And when that effort finally began, it was initially plagued by a divided Union command for which Lincoln was partly responsible.

In November 1862 Lincoln decided to replace the controversial Benjamin Butler with Nathaniel P. Banks as commander of Union army forces in southern Louisiana. Banks's record in Virginia, where he had been roughly handled by Stonewall Jackson, offered dubious promise of success as a combat commander in Louisiana. Nevertheless Lincoln and Halleck gave Banks the mission of opening the Mississippi River — which would require the capture of Vicksburg and of Port Hudson, a second fortified bastion two hundred miles south of Vicksburg. On November 9 Halleck instructed Banks that "the President regards the opening of the Mississippi River as the first and most important of all our military and naval operations, and it is hoped that you will not lose a moment in accomplishing it."[39]

Many of the regiments from New England recruited in response to Lincoln's July 1 call for new three-year volunteers, plus several nine-month militia regiments organized in the fall of 1862, were assigned to Banks. His Army of the Gulf grew into a sizable force. Banks outranked Grant at the time, so Halleck told him that "as the ranking general in the Southwest, you are authorized to assume control of any military forces from the Upper Mississippi which may come within your command. The line of division between your department and that of Major-General Grant is therefore left undecided for the present, and you will exercise superior authority as far as you may ascend the river."[40]

Lincoln overrated Banks's abilities, as future events would show.[41] At this time he also overrated the capacity of another general who would complicate the command situation in the Vicksburg campaign: Maj. Gen. John A. McClernand, who did not outrank Grant but thought he should.

Lincoln had known McClernand since they served together in the Illinois legislature in the 1830s. Although Lincoln was a Whig and then a Republican while McClernand was a Democrat, they remained friends across the political divide. The president commissioned McClernand as a brigadier general in 1861 and was gratified by his success in mobilizing Democrats in Illinois for the war. McClernand commanded a brigade under Grant at the Battle of Belmont (November 7, 1861) and a division at Fort Donelson and Shiloh. His performance in these battles was mixed, but he showed an aggressive spirit that Lincoln initially admired.[42] As a subordinate, however, McClernand was a loose cannon and tended to act without orders or contrary to orders. He was also something of a glory hunter and had a habit of issuing congratulatory orders to his own commands and taking credit for the success that Grant's armies achieved. Not surprisingly Grant disliked him — and the feeling was mutual.

McClernand presumed on his friendship with Lincoln to go outside channels and write directly to the president asking for an independent command. He also got eight governors to petition Lincoln to give him command "either of a Department or army, in some active field of operations, particularly in the Mississippi Valley."[43] McClernand came to Washington in September 1862 and personally lobbied the president to put him in charge of new three-year regiments being raised in the Midwest for a campaign down the Mississippi to capture Vicksburg.

McClernand's request was grounded in political as well as military arguments. Some "Copperhead" Democrats — the antiwar wing of the party — were talking of forming an independent "Northwest Confederacy" of Midwestern states to make a separate peace with the Confederacy in order to open the Mississippi River to shipment of

Midwestern farm products. This conspiracy might gain powerful support, McClernand warned Lincoln, unless Union military forces opened the river. How seriously Lincoln took this supposed plot for a Northwest Confederacy is unclear. But significant Democratic electoral gains in the Midwest in 1862 were a danger signal. In any event, at a cabinet meeting on October 7 Lincoln announced the plan to give McClernand his independent command.[44]

Lincoln and Stanton apparently kept Halleck out of the loop on this matter. They were well aware of Halleck's negative opinion of political generals. For their part the president and secretary of war had become skeptical of the professionals, particularly Buell and McClellan, whom Lincoln was soon to sack. The nonprofessional McClernand won their support because he promised an aggressive campaign. On October 20 Lincoln endorsed an order by Stanton for McClernand to organize the troops from several Midwestern states for a campaign "to clear the Mississippi River and open navigation to New Orleans." Lincoln's endorsement stated that "I feel deep interest in the success of the expedition, and desire it to be pushed forward with all possible despatch." But by this time Halleck may have learned of the proposed expedition. Two significant qualifying clauses in Stanton's order bear the earmarks of Halleck's phrasing: "The forces so organized will remain subject to the designation of the General-in-Chief," and McClernand should begin his campaign "when a sufficient force, not required by the operations of General Grant's command, shall be raised."[45]

If Halleck was the author of these loopholes, he proved to be a stronger supporter of Grant than he had previously been. Within a week of Stanton's order Grant heard rumors of the McClernand expedition. On November 10 Grant sought clarification from Halleck of his authority in this theater, especially as he was planning his own campaign against Vicksburg. Halleck wired back: "You have command of all the troops sent to your Department, and have permission to fight the enemy when you please." Grant immediately telegraphed General Sherman to "move on the enemy so soon as you can leave Memphis with two full Divisions" — including the regiments that McClernand had organized and sent to Memphis with the expectation that he would soon follow and take command. On December 9 Grant informed Halleck that "a letter from General McClernand, just received states that he expects to go forward in two days. Sherman has already gone."[46] The West Pointers Grant and Halleck had outwitted the politician McClernand and hijacked the army he expected to command.

Lincoln's role in this hijacking is unclear. He was aware of the telegraphic exchanges between Halleck and Grant. Halleck rarely issued important orders without the president's knowledge and approval. So it seems likely that Lincoln endorsed a command situation in the Department of the Tennessee that was contrary to McClernand's belief that he had been given an independent command. That general fired off a series of bitter protests to the president.

In the midst of this controversy Grant's campaign came crashing down because of the same kind of Confederate cavalry raids against his communications that had doomed Buell's advance on Chattanooga the previous summer. Nathan Bedford Forrest cut the railroads and telegraph in West Tennessee, while Earl Van Dorn led a raid that captured Grant's supply depot at Holly Springs, Mississippi. Unaware that Grant's overland advance on Vicksburg had been forced to turn back, Sherman went ahead with his part of the campaign plan with an attack on the Chickasaw Bluffs just north of Vicksburg on December 29. Confederate defenders punished the attackers with a bloody repulse.

The news of these reverses arrived in Washington at the same time as McClernand's denunciations of Halleck for taking away his army. During those dark December days Lincoln was also fending off senators trying to purge his cabinet and dissident generals in the Army of the Potomac trying to purge Burnside. The president was in no mood to indulge McClernand's complaints. He wrote the general a stern letter advising him for his own good to bow to the inevitable and become a loyal corps commander under Grant. "I have too many *family* controversies (so to speak) already on my hands," Lincoln wrote, "to voluntarily take up another. You are now doing well — well for the country, well for yourself — much better than you could possibly be, if engaged in open war with Gen. Halleck. Allow me to beg, that for your sake, for my sake, & for the country's sake, you give your whole attention to the better work."[47] McClernand submitted with ill grace for the time being, but he would be heard from again.

Along with his appointment as the new commander of the renamed Army of the

Cumberland on October 23, General Rosecrans had received a warning from Halleck that neither the country nor the government could tolerate inactivity by that army. Five weeks went by, and the Army of the Cumberland was still in camp at Nashville. Impatient messages from Washington evoked from Rosecrans the same sort of explanations that Lincoln had heard too often from McClellan and Buell: He could not move against the Confederate army at Murfreesboro thirty miles away until he was fully supplied with every necessity. Conveying Lincoln's displeasure, Halleck told Rosecrans that "I must warn you against this piling up of impedimenta. Take a lesson from the enemy. Move light, and supply yourself . . . in the country you move through." Another week went by with no movement. "The President is very impatient with your long stay in Nashville," Halleck wired Rosecrans on December 4. "You give Bragg time to supply himself by plundering the very country your army should have occupied. . . . Twice have I been asked to designate someone else to command your army. If you remain one more week at Nashville, I cannot prevent your removal."[48]

Even though Rosecrans did not begin his advance until the day after Christmas, Lincoln's distractions closer to home forestalled any action for his removal in the interim. On December 31 Bragg anticipated Rosecrans's planned attack at Murfreesboro by striking first. In some of the war's most savage fighting, the Confederate assault drove back the Union right three miles. But the Federals managed to hang on to the railroad and road back to Nashville that was their supply lifeline. Nevertheless Bragg wired Richmond that he had won a victory and implied that the enemy was retreating.[49]

That was not true, however. On New Year's Day both armies held their positions, and on January 2 the Federals knocked back Bragg's final effort to salvage an actual victory. The following night it was Bragg who retreated. In this Battle of Stones River (or Murfreesboro, as the Confederates called it) the two armies suffered combined casualties amounting to 32 percent of their strength — the highest percentage for any battle in the war. This bloodbath left both of them in no shape to renew fighting for a long time. Despite the cost it was a Union victory that cut the gloom that had settled over the North during this dark holiday season. Lincoln telegraphed to Rosecrans "the Nation's gratitude" for his army's "skill, endurance, and da[u]ntless courage." The president later wrote to Rosecrans that "I can never forget, whilst I remember anything . . . you gave us a hard earned victory which, had there been a defeat instead, the nation could scarcely have lived over."[50]

Democrats boasted that their gains in the 1862 elections constituted a negative referendum on the Emancipation Proclamation. Since the Republicans retained control of the House and actually gained five seats in the Senate, that claim seems exaggerated. In any case the Democratic press predicted that Lincoln would not issue the final proclamation on January 1. Even some Republicans expressed doubts. The president's annual message to Congress on December 1 seemed to reinforce these doubts. Lincoln devoted much of the message to a recommendation of a constitutional amendment to offer federal compensation to states that abolished slavery before 1900. Some Republicans wondered: "If the President means to carry out his edict of freedom in the New Year, what is all this stuff about gradual emancipation?"[51]

The doubters missed the point. They may have failed to notice Lincoln's statement that all slaves freed by "the chances of war"

— which would include his Emancipation Proclamation — would remain "forever free." The proclamation was a war measure that applied only to states in rebellion; the proposed constitutional amendment was a measure to encourage the step-by-step abolition of the *institution* of slavery within a finite period of time. The eloquent peroration of Lincoln's message clothed this gradualist proposal with a radical vision: "Fellow-citizens, *we* cannot escape history. . . . The fiery trial through which we pass, will light us down, in honor or dishonor, to the latest generation. . . . The dogmas of the quiet past, are inadequate to the stormy present. . . . In *giving* freedom to the *slave,* we *assure* freedom to the *free. . . .* We must disenthrall ourselves, and then we shall save the country."[52]

Despite the rumors Lincoln never wavered in his determination to issue the proclamation. After talking with the president in late December, Senator Charles Sumner assured abolitionist friends: "The Presdt. is firm. He says he would not stop the Procltn. if he could, & he could not if he would."[53] After shaking hands at the White House reception, Lincoln retired to his office with a few colleagues to sign the final copy of the proclamation. His hand was so sore from its three hours of social duty that he could scarcely hold the pen. Lincoln did not want to sign while his hand was still trembling, because "all who examine the document hereafter will say 'He hesitated.'" That would not do, for "I never in my life felt more certain that I was doing right than I do in signing this paper. . . . If my name ever goes into history it will be for this act, and my whole soul is in it." The president picked up the pen again, but his hand was still unsteady and he put it down. "The South had fair warning," he reflected, "that if they did not return to their duty, I should strike at this pillar of their strength. The promise must now be kept, and I shall never recall one word." Lincoln then picked up the pen once more and signed his name without a tremor. "That will do," he said.[54]

Lincoln warranted his proclamation as both "an act of justice" and a "fit and necessary war measure for suppressing said rebellion" based on his war powers as commander in chief.[55] The proclamation exempted the Union border states and Tennessee plus the portions of Virginia and Louisiana controlled by Federal troops because these areas were not in rebellion against the United States. The cliché that the proclamation "emancipated" only those slaves beyond Northern control and left the others in bondage is misleading. The president's war powers to seize enemy property applied only to the enemy. The proclamation was a promise of freedom to slaves where it applied if and when the United States won the war. And slavery could scarcely survive in the exempted areas if the North did win the war. Thus the proclamation turned the Union army into a potential army of liberation.

The document also contained a provision that augmented that potential. It publicly announced a policy of recruiting freed slaves into the Union army and navy. This policy was not absolutely new. Free blacks and some contrabands had served in the navy from almost the beginning of the war. Union army officers had unofficially recruited black soldiers in Kansas and in occupied portions of South Carolina and Louisiana in 1862. But the administration had not sanctioned these activities. And even after Lincoln had decided to embrace emancipation, he hesitated about recruiting black soldiers — even free blacks from the North. The idea of putting arms in the hands of black men provoked greater hostility from Democrats and border-state Unionists than did emancipation itself. In July

1862 the president told Orville Browning that arming blacks "would produce dangerous & fatal dissatisfaction in our army, and do more injury than good." A month later Lincoln informed a delegation from Indiana that had offered to raise two black regiments that "the nation could not afford to lose Kentucky at this crisis" and that "to arm the negroes would turn 50,000 bayonets against us that were for us."[56]

Later in August, however, the president quietly allowed the War Department to begin organizing black regiments on the South Carolina sea islands. The preliminary and final Emancipation Proclamations publicly changed the commander in chief's national strategy on slavery from conciliating the border states to depriving the Confederacy of slave labor. Mobilizing that manpower for the Union — as soldiers as well as laborers — was a natural corollary. The final proclamation announced that corollary. It also omitted any mention of colonizing freed slaves abroad, which Lincoln never again mentioned publicly. Instead of being induced to leave, freedpeople would be encouraged to work and fight for the Union.

In January 1863 Lincoln authorized the recruitment of a "Corps d'Afrique" in

Louisiana. By March the president had advanced from a position of approval to one of enthusiasm for enlistment of black soldiers. "The colored population is the great *available* and yet *unavailed* of, force for restoration of the Union," he told Andrew Johnson, military governor of occupied Tennessee. "The bare sight of fifty thousand armed, and drilled black soldiers on the banks of the Mississippi, would end the rebellion at once. And who doubts that we can present that sight, if we but take hold in earnest."[57] The government did exactly that. In the next two years the Union mobilized two hundred thousand black soldiers and sailors. They did not end the rebellion at once, but they surely played a major part in ending it eventually.

The international consequences of the Emancipation Proclamation were of equal importance with its domestic impact. Some European cynics had scoffed at the preliminary proclamation as a Yankee trick. They predicted that Lincoln would never follow through with a final edict. When he did so a massive pro-Union reaction occurred in Europe — especially in Britain. Huge pro-Northern meetings passed resolutions supporting the Union and freedom. The largest such rally, at Exeter Hall in London, "has had a powerful effect on our newspapers and politicians," wrote Richard Cobden, a prominent pro-Union British MP. "It has closed the mouths of those who have been advocating the side of the South. Recognition of the South, by England, whilst it bases itself on Negro slavery, is an impossibility." From the American legation in London, Henry Adams, private secretary to his father, agreed with this assessment. "The Emancipation Proclamation," he wrote, "has done more for us here than all our former victories and all our diplomacy. It is creating an almost convulsive reaction in our favor."[58] Similar reports came from elsewhere in Europe. "The anti-slavery position of the government is at length giving us a substantial foothold in European circles," wrote the American minister to the Netherlands. "Everyone can understand the significance of a war where emancipation is written on one banner and slavery on the other."[59]

But none of this would mean much unless the North won the war. And in January 1863 that prospect seemed more remote than ever.

7
LEE'S ARMY, AND NOT RICHMOND, IS YOUR TRUE OBJECTIVE POINT

For President Lincoln and Quartermaster General Meigs, the new year of 1863 started on the same depressing note as the old year twelve months earlier. Then it had been Lincoln who said disconsolately to Meigs that "the bottom is out of the tub." This time it was Meigs who lamented that "exhaustion steals over the country. Confidence and hope are dying. . . . I see greater peril to our nationality in the present condition of affairs than I have seen at any time during the struggle."[1]

Matters would get worse before they got better. As usual for Lincoln, the Army of the Potomac presented his biggest problem. He was well aware that Burnside had lost the confidence of his principal subordinates. Gen. William B. Franklin headed a cabal of generals scheming to have McClellan restored to command. Joe Hooker made little secret of his contempt for Burnside and was intriguing to obtain the command for himself.[2]

Morale in the ranks sank to a new low. A soldier from Maine wrote to his sister that "the great cause of liberty has been managed by Knaves and fools. The whole show has been corruption, the result disaster, shame and disgrace."[3] To make matters worse Burnside was a slack administrator. With the resources of a rich country at his back and army warehouses bulging with supplies, troops in winter quarters at Falmouth suffered from poor food, poor medical care, weak discipline, and sickness. Many soldiers had not been paid for months. In January desertions increased to epidemic proportions.

Dissension climaxed with an aborted movement that became notorious as the Mud March. In an effort to recoup his fortunes by a successful campaign, Burnside ordered the army to move up the Rappahannock, cross at the fords, and strike the Confederate flank above Fredericksburg. The Franklin clique opposed this plan. An artillery colonel who was no partisan of Burnside nevertheless wrote that "Franklin has talked so much and so loudly to this effect that he has completely demoralized his whole command [two corps] and so rendered failure doubly sure. His conduct has been such that he surely deserves to be broken." Hooker also criticized "the absurdity of the movement" and for good measure included the Lincoln administration in his indictment, saying that what the country needed was a dictator.[4]

Despite this poisonous atmosphere, Burnside's movement got off to a good start January 20 on dry roads and in unusually benign weather. But that evening the heavens opened; heavy rain turned the roads into a bottomless ooze and bogged down the whole army in mud. Triple teams of horses could not budge the artillery and the wagons. After two days Burnside gave up and ordered the army back to camp. He then went to Washington bearing an order he wrote on January 23 cashiering Hooker and two other generals and transferring Franklin plus his chief coconspirator, William F. Smith, out of the Army of the Potomac. Burnside of course had no authority to make these dismissals, so he confronted Lincoln with this order and with his own resignation. Either the dissident generals had to go, he said, or he would. Lincoln agreed — and accepted Burnside's resignation. The president also transferred Franklin and his fellow pro-McClellan schemers to other assignments.

The president's choice of Hooker to replace Burnside came as a surprise. Stanton and Halleck favored General Meade for the command. Halleck had disliked Hooker since they had known each other in California before the war. But Lincoln consulted neither Halleck nor Stanton about the appointment.[5] Meade was only a division commander, while Hooker was one of the army's senior corps commanders. The president admitted to editor Henry Raymond of the *New York Times,* who had told Lincoln of Hooker's loose talk about the need for a dictator, that "Hooker does talk badly, but the trouble is, he is stronger in the country than any other man."[6] Hooker was also popular with many soldiers, if not with his fellow generals. He had a good record as a brigade, division, and corps commander. Lincoln considered him an aggressive, hard-driving general (the press had dubbed him "Fighting Joe") and hoped that Hooker could infuse that spirit into the army.

The president summoned Hooker to Washington for a frank discussion. The exact nature of this interview is unknown. Hooker may have sought and obtained from Lincoln a commitment to protect him from

Halleck's disfavor. Hooker did get the president's permission to communicate directly with him instead of going through Halleck. Lincoln had lost confidence in Halleck and may have preferred this arrangement himself.

In their conversation Lincoln probably told Hooker the substance of what the president wrote that day in an extraordinary letter — a letter that Hooker later said was just what a wise father might write to his son. "There are some things in regard to which, I am not quite satisfied with you," the president said. "I think that during Gen. Burnside's command of the Army, you have taken counsel of your ambition, and thwarted him, as much as you could, in which you did great wrong to the country, and to a most meritorious and honorable brother officer." As for the report of Hooker's words about the country needing a dictator, "of course it was not *for* this, but in spite of it, that I have given you the command. Only those generals who gain successes, can set up dictators. What I ask of you is military success, and I will risk the dictatorship." Lincoln warned Hooker of the possibility that "the spirit which you have aided to infuse in the Army, of criticizing their Commander, and withholding confidence from him, will now turn upon you. I shall assist you, as far as I can, to put it down. Neither you, nor Napoleon, if he were alive again, could get any good out of an army, while such a spirit prevails in it." Lincoln concluded on a positive note: "Beware of rashness, but with energy, and sleepless vigilance, go forward, and give us victories."[7]

Hooker started off with a great deal of energy and vigilance. He shook up the commissary and quartermaster services, got rid of corrupt supply officers, upgraded the food, cleaned the unhealthy camps, improved field hospitals, and cut the sick rate in half. He tightened discipline but also granted furloughs liberally. He increased unit pride by devising insignia badges for each corps. Paymasters finally appeared and brought the men's pay up to date. Morale rose, desertions declined, and thousands of absentees rejoined their regiments after Lincoln on March 10 promised amnesty to deserters who returned by April 1.[8] In his first two months Hooker produced a remarkable transformation in the army's spirit. Even one of the generals who disliked Hooker admitted that "I have never known men to change from a condition of lowest depression to that of a healthy fighting state in so short a time."[9]

Lincoln did not recover his spirits as readily as the army did during this winter of discontent. The president was impressed by Hooker's achievements but disturbed by his gasconade. He had created "the finest army on the planet," Hooker boasted. The question was not whether he would take Richmond, but when. He hoped that God Almighty would have mercy on the Rebels, because Joe Hooker would have none. After visiting the army for several days in early April, Lincoln confided in a friend: "That is the most depressing thing about Hooker. It seems to me that he is overconfident."[10]

Lincoln's depression was compounded by lack of success in other theaters. Adm. John Dahlgren, head of the Washington Navy Yard, who had become a close friend of Lincoln, reported in February that "the President never tells a joke now." The commissioner of public buildings met with Lincoln on February 18. "He looked worn & haggard," wrote the commissioner in his diary. "His hand trembled as I never saw it before."[11]

The president was upset by repeated delays in the projected attack on Fort Sumter and Charleston by a fleet of eight ironclads. He was also concerned about Admiral Du Pont's pessimistic predictions that Confederate defenses were too strong for the attack to succeed. Secretary of the Navy Welles discussed this matter with Lincoln several times in March. "The President, who has a sort of intuitive sagacity, has spoken discouragingly of operations at Charleston," wrote Welles in his diary. "Du Pont's dispatches and movements . . . remind him of McClellan." In mid-March, Lincoln sent word to Du Pont that "I fear neither you nor your officers appreciate the supreme importance of *time.* The more you prepare, the more the enemy will be prepared."[12] Two more weeks went by, and Lincoln again told Welles that "the long delay of Du Pont, his constant call for more ships, more ironclads, was like McClellan calling for more regiments." The president "thought the two men were alike and was prepared for a repulse at Charleston."[13] It came on April 7 when Confederate guns drove back the Union ironclad fleet in a one-sided battle that seemed to confirm Du Pont's pessimism. Lincoln, Welles, and Assistant Secretary of the Navy Fox believed that Du Pont had not pushed the attack with sufficient determination. Whether their assessment was unfair or not, within three months Du Pont, like McClellan, was removed from command.[14]

Another high-ranking officer whose apparent failures in the winter and spring of 1863 threatened his tenure was, surprisingly, Ulysses S. Grant. That general was well aware of Lincoln's desire for the capture of Vicksburg. Although John McClernand had been made subordinate to Grant, the Illinois political general kept open his direct pipeline to the president and played on Lincoln's anxiety about this theater. In a conversation with another general Lincoln had said that "if Vicksburg can be taken and the Mississippi successfully kept open it seems to me [they] will be about the most important fruits of the campaigns yet set in motion." Halleck told Grant that "the eyes and hopes of the whole country are now directed to your army. . . . The opening of the Mississippi River will be to us of more advantage than the capture of forty Richmonds."[15]

After the repulse of Sherman's attack on Chickasaw Bluffs and the destruction of Grant's supply depot at Holly Springs in December 1862, Grant had decided to base his campaign against Vicksburg on the river itself at Milliken's Bend. He faced formidable problems of topography. A direct assault from the river against the two-hundred-foot bluff bristling with Confederate artillery would be suicidal. West of the river a maze of bayous and swamps blocked military operations except at low water — and the winter of 1862–63 was exceptionally wet. North of Vicksburg extended a 250-mile arc of hills that enclosed the Mississippi Delta, a network of swamps, rivers, and junglelike forests. Only southeast and east of Vicksburg was there dry land suitable for marching and fighting. Grant's problem was to get there with a large enough force to defeat the enemy and reestablish contact with the Union fleet, which controlled the river above Vicksburg.

Grant's Army of the Tennessee tried several methods to accomplish this purpose. Soldiers and contrabands attempted to enlarge the canal started the previous summer to rechannel the river around the fortress for a safe crossing to the east bank. The Mississippi refused to cooperate, however, and the canal was eventually abandoned. An effort to take gunboats and transports carrying troops through a series of waterways in the delta from a point opposite Helena, Arkansas, to the Yazoo River near Vicksburg was turned back by a hastily constructed fort on the Tallahatchie River a hundred miles north of Vicksburg. An attempt to cut a route through various bayous in Louisiana all the way to the Red River and then into the Mississippi looked likely to take until doomsday. Even if completed it would only have been deep enough for small boats, so it too was abandoned. Still another attempt to get Acting Rear Adm. David D. Porter's ironclad gunboats through Steele's Bayou just twenty-five miles north of Vicksburg almost trapped the flotilla when Confederate soldiers felled trees ahead of and behind the boats. General Sherman disembarked enough troops to drive the enemy away, and the gunboats backed slowly down channels scarcely wider than the vessels themselves.

While all this was going on, Northern newspapers began to criticize Grant, some of them attacking him vigorously. Exaggerated reports appeared of the demoralization of Grant's troops and of typhoid fever, dysentery, and pneumonia killing off hundreds of them. The old rumors about the general's drinking started circulating again. Still hoping to replace Grant, McClernand did his part to spread these rumors. He wrote Lincoln that "on the 13th of March, 1863, Genl. Grant I am informed was gloriously drunk and in bed sick all next day."[16]

Abraham Lincoln may have been the most photographed president before the twentieth century. Portraits by Mathew Brady, Alexander Gardner, and other photographers show a president who aged a lifetime over the four stressful years of war; in this photograph from the middle of the war, he appears much older than his age of fifty-four. LIBRARY OF CONGRESS

General-in-chief of the U.S. Army at the outbreak of the Civil War, Winfield Scott was America's most celebrated soldier since George Washington. He had fought in the War of 1812 and led the army that captured Mexico City in 1847. But by 1861 he was seventy-five years old, weighed more than three hundred pounds, suffered from edema and vertigo, and sometimes fell asleep during conferences. His physical incapacities were matched by the passiveness of his "Anaconda Plan" strategy. On November 1, 1861, he retired from the army.
LIBRARY OF CONGRESS

Few Union officers looked less like a general than Benjamin Butler. A prewar Democrat, he had actually supported Jefferson Davis for the party's presidential nomination in 1860. But the initiative and energy he showed in the occupation of Annapolis and Baltimore with Union militia at the beginning of the war earned Lincoln's gratitude and Butler's promotion to major general. His war record thereafter, however, was decidedly mixed.
LIBRARY OF CONGRESS

At the age of thirty-four, George B. McClellan was appointed commander of the Army of the Potomac in July 1861 and general-in-chief in November of that year. Newspapers extolled him as "the Young Napoleon," an image that he tried to convey in this Napoleonic pose for the photographer. Lincoln soon discovered, however, that McClellan's generalship was anything but Napoleonic.

NATIONAL ARCHIVES

A former Democrat and a close friend of General McClellan in 1861, Edwin M. Stanton shared with McClellan a contemptuous opinion of the Lincoln administration. After Lincoln appointed him secretary of war in January 1862, however, Stanton's opinions of the president and the general underwent 180-degree reversals. An efficient administrator, Stanton was also a lighting rod for hostility from McClellan and his supporters.

LIBRARY OF CONGRESS

The author and translator of books on military history and theory, mining law, and international law, Henry W. Halleck was known as "Old Brains." On the strength of his administrative ability and the success of armies under his command in the Kentucky-Tennessee theater in 1862, Lincoln appointed him general-in-chief in July of that year. Halleck's indecisiveness, however, caused Lincoln to lose faith in him.

Gen. Ambrose Burnside successfully commanded a small army that won control of key areas and cities on the North Carolina coast in 1862. Disappointed with McClellan after the Seven Days' battles and Second Bull Run, Lincoln twice offered Burnside command of the Army of the Potomac. Burnside declined and urged second and third chances for McClellan. Lincoln decided not to give that general a fourth chance, however, and appointed a reluctant Burnside to the command in November 1862.

This photograph of Lincoln and McClellan in a tent near the Antietam battlefield was taken by Alexander Gardner on October 3, 1862, during Lincoln's visit to the Army of the Potomac after the battle. Ten days later the president wrote to McClellan, reminding him of their discussion of "what I called your over-cautiousness." That conversation probably occurred in this tent. McClellan did not take Lincoln's advice to heart, and a month later the president removed him from command. LIBRARY OF CONGRESS

An obscure colonel of an Illinois regiment in 1861, Ulysses S. Grant discovered that the enemy colonel during a minor confrontation in Missouri "had been as afraid of me as I had been of him. The lesson was valuable." He demonstrated this lesson in the capture of Fort Donelson, in seizing victory from the jaws of defeat at Shiloh, in the capture of Vicksburg, and in the victory at Chattanooga. Lincoln appointed Grant general-in-chief in 1864, expecting that he would finally infuse this spirit into the officer corps of the Army of the Potomac, which was previously more afraid of Robert E. Lee than Lee was of them.

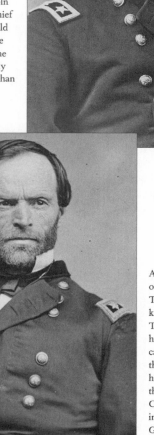

As the military campaigns of 1864 began, Gen. William T. Sherman was not widely known outside his own army. That would soon change, however, as Sherman's campaign that resulted in the capture of Atlanta and his subsequent marches through Georgia and the Carolinas brought him fame in the North second only to Grant's, and infamy in the South second to none.

Gen. John A. McClernand demonstrated a modest capacity for military leadership and an unlimited capacity for political intrigue to advance his military career. Lincoln initially shared McClernand's high opinion of his own abilities, but the president soon saw through the general's schemes to supersede Grant and supported the latter's removal of McClernand from corps command during the Vicksburg campaign.
LIBRARY OF CONGRESS

Although Lincoln complained of Gen. William S. Rosecrans's lengthy preparations, which delayed advances against the enemy in Tennessee in the fall of 1862 and again in the summer of 1863, the president was gratified by the general's success in the early stages of those campaigns. After Rosecrans's defeat at Chickamauga, however, the president described him as "confused and stunned like a duck hit on the head."
LIBRARY OF CONGRESS

Gen. George G. Meade worked his way up from brigade to corps command with solid if unspectacular performance at each level of command in the Army of the Potomac. He was the consensus choice to take over the army when Gen. Joseph Hooker faltered during the Gettysburg campaign. Despite Lincoln's disappointment with Meade's lack of aggressiveness after Gettysburg, he kept him in command of that army for the rest of the war.

LIBRARY OF CONGRESS

A former Speaker of the national House of Representatives and governor of Massachusetts, Nathaniel P. Banks could hardly be denied the commission he sought as major general of volunteers. Although he enjoyed some success as commander of the Army of the Gulf in Louisiana in 1863, he had been outfought by Stonewall Jackson in the Shenandoah Valley in 1862, and his Red River campaign of 1864 was a fiasco.

LIBRARY OF CONGRESS

A native of Virginia who had married a woman from New York, Gen. George Thomas remained loyal to the United States at the cost of ostracism by his Virginia relatives. Known as the "Rock of Chickamauga" for his unyielding defensive stand in that battle, he also earned plaudits as the "Hammer of Nashville" for his crushing offensive that virtually destroyed the Confederate Army of Tennessee in December 1864.

NATIONAL ARCHIVES

Wearing his trademark porkpie hat, Gen. Philip Sheridan strikes a cocky pose for the photographer. Equally at home commanding infantry and cavalry, the thirty-three-year-old Sheridan smashed Jubal Early's Confederate corps in the Shenandoah Valley in 1864, assuring Lincoln's reelection as president.

LIBRARY OF CONGRESS

The grim harvest of war is illustrated by these two photographs. The one on the left was taken at Gettysburg on July 5, 1863, two days after the battle, showing the bloated corpses of Union soldiers killed there. The other photograph depicts freed slaves after the war disinterring the remains of Union soldiers who had been killed at Cold Harbor, Virginia, for reburial in the national military cemetery established there. Those killed at Gettysburg were also reinterred

in one of the first such cemeteries, where on November 19, 1863, Lincoln consecrated "these honored dead" and resolved that they "shall not have died in vain." Seventy-two national cemeteries were ultimately created as the final resting places for Union soldiers who died in the Civil War—and also for later veterans of the U.S. armed forces.

Commander in Chief Lincoln spent countless hours in the War Department telegraph office next to the White House, anxiously awaiting news from the front and sending telegrams to generals in several theaters of the war. According to the memoirs of David Homer Bates, a wartime telegrapher, the president also drafted part of the Emancipation Proclamation in that office during the Seven Days' battles in Virginia. This engraving from the frontispiece of Bates's *Lincoln in the Telegraph Office* shows the commander in chief working on the proclamation as he waits for telegrams from Virginia. LIBRARY OF CONGRESS

In February 1864 the New York portrait artist Francis B. Carpenter obtained an introduction to Abraham Lincoln in the White House. Carpenter considered the Emancipation Proclamation to be the preeminent achievement of the Civil War—indeed, of all American history—and he wanted to paint a picture commensurate with that achievement. Lincoln also believed that "if my name ever goes into history, it will be for this act," so he readily consented to cooperate in Carpenter's project. The artist selected the moment that Lincoln first read a draft of the proclamation to his cabinet on July 22, 1862, as the event he wished to portray. For six months Carpenter virtually lived in the White House, making sketches of the cabinet room, commissioning photographs of Lincoln and cabinet members, and painting individual portraits of them as models for their depiction in the huge canvas of the final painting. From left to right, the figures in the painting are Secretary of War Edwin M. Stanton, Secretary of the Treasury Salmon P. Chase, Lincoln, Secretary of the Navy Gideon Welles, Secretary of the Interior Caleb Smith (who had died a month before Carpenter began the painting), Secretary of State William H. Seward, Postmaster General Montgomery Blair, and Attorney General Edward Bates. Intending a study in allegory as well as realism, Carpenter portrayed the two most radical members of the cabinet, Stanton and Chase, on the left, and the more conservative officials on the right, with Lincoln in the center. Befitting his dominant position in the cabinet, Seward sits directly across the table from Lincoln and is the only figure looking directly at the president.

An engraving of the painting, portrayed here, was a bestseller in its time at ten dollars a copy. LIBRARY OF CONGRESS

In this photograph Horace Greeley looks like everyone's favorite uncle. The image is misleading, for Greeley was the foremost journalist in America, and his slashing editorials against "the Slave Power," "Rebels," and "Copperheads" in his *New York Tribune* spearheaded the radical wing of the Republican Party. Of mercurial temperament, Greeley criticized Lincoln for slowness in moving against slavery in 1862 and for steadfastness in insisting on emancipation as a condition of peace in 1864. LIBRARY OF CONGRESS

Clement L. Vallandigham's handsome countenance did not help his reputation among Republicans and other supporters of the war. Sympathetic to the South and slavery, Vallandigham believed that the Union could be restored only by negotiations and compromise. He returned from Canadian exile to write the antiwar plank in the 1864 Democratic platform. LIBRARY OF CONGRESS

Goaded by Democratic politicians and newspapers that denounced the draft as a Republican scheme to make poor white men fight to free the slaves who would come north to take their jobs, thousands of Irish Americans rioted when conscription began in New York City on July 13, 1863. For four days the Draft Riots raged, as mobs attacked hated symbols of the war, the draft, and emancipation. Almost a dozen black people were lynched, and the Colored Orphan Asylum was burned to the ground, as depicted here. More than 105 people were killed, most of them rioters shot by police and soldiers. LIBRARY OF CONGRESS

On May 23 and 24, 1865, the Army of the Potomac and General Sherman's Army of Georgia, each one hundred thousand strong, marched down Pennsylvania Avenue in a victory lap designated as "The Grand Review." As they passed in front of reviewing stands near the White House, government officials, including the new president, Andrew Johnson, saluted the armed might of the republic—all of them, certainly, wishing that Abraham Lincoln could have been there to see the spectacle. This photo shows part of the Army of the Potomac on the march.

The president did not deign to reply. But he could not ignore letters from the two most influential Republican newspaper editors in the Midwest. In February Joseph Medill of the *Chicago Tribune* wrote to Elihu Washburne, Grant's chief congressional supporter. "Your man Grant" was a miserable failure, declared Medill. "No man's career in the army is more open to destructive criticism than Grant's. We have kept off him on your account. We could have made him stink in the nostrils of the public like an old fish had we properly criticised his military blunders. Was there ever a more weak and imbecile campaign?"[17] Several weeks later editor Murat Halstead of the *Cincinnati Commercial* wrote to Salmon P. Chase, who passed along the letter to Lincoln with an endorsement that such "reports concerning General Grant" were "too common to be safely disregarded." Grant was "a jackass in the original package," wrote Halstead. "He is a poor stick sober, and he is most of the time more than half drunk. . . . Grant will fail miserably, hopelessly, eternally." Even Elihu Washburne's brother Cadwalader, a major general, wrote to Elihu: "I fear Grant won't do. The truth is, Grant has no plan for taking Vicksburg, & is frittering away time & strength to no purpose. The truth must be told even when it hurts. You cannot make a silk purse out of a sow's ear."[18]

Lincoln was deluged with politicians demanding Grant's removal. The president resisted the pressure. The anecdote about his desire to know what brand of whiskey Grant drank so he could send some to his other generals is probably apocryphal. But Lincoln *did* say, after Grant had confounded his critics, that "I have had stronger influence brought against Grant . . . than for any other object, coming too from good men. . . . If I had done as my Washington friends, who fight battles with their tongues instead of swords far from the enemy, demanded of me, Grant . . . would never have been heard from again."[19]

But Lincoln did express some dissatisfaction with the apparent lack of progress in the Vicksburg campaign. On March 20 he told the Washington correspondent of the *New York Tribune,* off the record, that he thought "all these side expeditions through the country dangerous. . . . If the rebels can blockade us on the Mississippi, which is a mile wide, they can certainly stop us on the little streams not much wider than our gunboats and shut us up so we can't get back again." On April 2 Halleck warned

Grant that Lincoln had become "impatient" with the various abortive efforts to get at Vicksburg.[20] With the president's approval, Stanton sent the War Department trouble-shooter Charles A. Dana to the western theater, ostensibly to investigate the paymaster service but in reality to determine whether Grant deserved the administration's continued support. Dana soon began sending favorable reports by special cipher to Stanton, who shared them with Lincoln. These reports probably were a major factor in Lincoln's decision to stick with Grant.[21]

That general soon justified the president's faith in spectacular fashion. All the efforts to get at Vicksburg by tributary waterways having failed, Grant decided to have Porter's gunboats and transports run the batteries on the big river itself. The soldiers would build roads and causeways down the west bank to rendezvous with the fleet and cross to the east bank somewhere below Vicksburg. Despite Sherman's skepticism, it worked. The fleet ran the batteries on the night of April 17 with what Grant and Porter considered acceptable losses. While cavalry commander Benjamin Grierson led a diversionary raid through central Mississippi, and Sherman feinted another attack on the bluffs north of Vicksburg, Grant crossed two-thirds of his army (soon followed by Sherman's corps) forty miles downriver on April 30.

Halleck and Lincoln wanted Grant to unite his army with General Banks's Army of the Gulf for a joint attack on Port Hudson, followed by a combined attack on Vicksburg, or vice versa. In such a case Banks would outrank Grant and take command. But the two hundred river miles between the two armies and the logistical nightmare of trying to unite and supply them — plus, probably, Grant's disinclination to yield command of the enterprise to Banks — prevented any joint effort.[22] After crossing the Mississippi, Grant cut loose from the river. His troops lived mainly off the land for the next three weeks until they could fight their way back to Vicksburg and make contact again with their riverborne supplies. During those three weeks, Grant's men marched 130 miles, fought and won five battles against separate forces that, if combined, would have been nearly as large as Grant's own, and penned the Confederates up in the Vicksburg defenses.

Lincoln had finally found a general who could march his army as fast and light as the enemy. The president was delighted by a tongue-in-cheek letter he received from

Elihu Washburne, who traveled with Grant for part of the campaign. "I am afraid Grant will have to be reproved for want of style," wrote Washburne. "On this whole march for five days he has had neither a horse nor an orderly or servant, a blanket or overcoat or clean shirt, or even a sword. . . . His entire baggage consists of a tooth-brush." After driving the enemy into the Vicksburg fortifications, Grant ordered attacks on May 19 and 22. They were repulsed, but the Federals tightened their grip and Vicksburg's surrender seemed only a matter of time. "Whether Gen. Grant shall or shall not consummate the capture of Vicksburg," wrote Lincoln on May 26, "his campaign from the beginning of this month up to the twenty second day of it, is one of the most brilliant in the world."[23]

Lincoln needed this good news from Mississippi because events on other fronts — especially the political front — were not encouraging. In January 1863 the president told Senator Charles Sumner that he feared " 'the fire in the rear' — meaning the Democracy, especially at the Northwest — more than our military chances."[24] The strength of the antiwar Copperheads varied in inverse ratio to Union military fortunes.

Because military success was a scarce commodity in the first four months of 1863, Copperheads flourished as never before. Hostility to the Emancipation Proclamation fueled their opposition to the war. Enactment of a national conscription law in March 1863 gave the antiwar movement an added impulse.

The leader of the Peace Democrats (as they preferred to call themselves) was Clement L. Vallandigham of Ohio, who hoped to become governor of that third-largest Northern state in 1863. Vallandigham delivered a major antiwar address in the House of Representatives on January 14, 1863, and followed it with a speaking tour that set forth the principal Copperhead themes. The Lincoln administration was fighting not for Union, he charged, but for abolition. And what was the result? "Let the dead at Fredericksburg and Vicksburg answer." The Confederacy could never be conquered; the only trophies of this unconstitutional war were "defeat, debt, taxation, sepulchres . . . the suspension of *habeas corpus,* the violation . . . of freedom of the press and of speech . . . which have made this country one of the worst despotisms on earth for the past twenty months." What could be done? "Stop fighting. Make an armistice. . . .

Withdraw your army from the seceded States." Start negotiations for reunion on the basis of compromise with the South. Such a settlement would preserve slavery, of course, but Vallandigham had no sympathy for the "fanaticism and hypocrisy" of those who objected. "I see more of barbarism and sin, a thousand times, in the continuance of this war . . . and the enslavement of the white race by debt and taxes and arbitrary power" than in black slavery.[25]

Copperhead newspapers denounced the conscription act and urged resistance to the enrollment of those who were eligible for the draft. Enrollment officers in many localities were assaulted and several were murdered. Newspapers and some local Democratic leaders also encouraged desertion. "You perceive that it is to emancipate slaves . . . that you are used as soldiers," declared an Iowa newspaper. "Are you, as soldiers, bound by patriotism, duty or loyalty to fight in such a cause?" A father wrote to his son in the Sixteenth Illinois Infantry a letter that found its way into newspapers: "Come home, if you have to desert, you will be protected — the people are so enraged that you need not be alarmed if you hear of the whole of our Northwest killing off the abolitionists."[26]

These events provided the context for the civil liberties cause célèbre of the war. After General Burnside's departure from the Army of the Potomac, Lincoln appointed him commander of the Department of the Ohio, embracing states bordering that river. In April 1863 Burnside issued an order stating that anyone who committed "expressed or implied" treason would be subject to trial by a military tribunal (authorized by Lincoln's executive order of September 24, 1862). Courting a martyrdom to advance his quest for Ohio's governorship, Clement Vallandigham lost no time in testing Burnside's order. On May 1 he made a speech at Mount Vernon, Ohio, that rang all the changes on the unconstitutionality of the war, emancipation, the draft, suspension of habeas corpus, and the tyranny of the administration. Burnside promptly had Vallandigham arrested. A military court convicted him and sentenced him to prison for the rest of the war.

These proceedings produced cries of outrage from Northern Democrats and expressions of anxiety even among Republicans. Though surprised and embarrassed by Vallandigham's arrest, Lincoln felt he had no choice but to back Burnside. "All the cabinet regretted the necessity of arresting" the Ohio Democrat, Lincoln wired Burn-side, "some perhaps, doubting, that there was a real necessity for it — but, being done, all were for seeing you through with it."[27] In an effort to quell the uproar and tarnish Vallandigham's martyrdom, the president commuted his sentence from imprisonment to banishment to the Confederacy. Federal troops escorted Vallandigham under flag of truce to Confederate lines in Tennessee. Ohio Democrats nominated him in absentia for governor. Vallandigham slipped out of the Confederacy on a blockade-runner and settled in Windsor, Ontario, from where he conducted his campaign for governor.

Democratic leaders in Ohio and New York addressed protests to the president in the form of resolutions accusing him of upholding the conviction of Vallandigham "for no other reason than words addressed to a public meeting, in criticism of the course of the Administration." Such action was "a palpable violation of the Constitution," which "abrogates the right of the people to assemble and discuss the affairs of government, the liberty of speech and of the press, the right of trial by jury and the privilege of habeas corpus . . . aimed at the rights of every citizen of the North."[28]

These resolutions gave Lincoln an opening to take his case to the Northern people. On several occasions during the war he used the medium of public letters for this purpose, as a modern president uses a prime-time speech or news conference. On June 12 and 28 Lincoln wrote such letters to the New York and Ohio Democrats. He denied that Vallandigham had been arrested "for no other reason than words addressed to a public meeting." On the contrary, it was "because he was laboring, with some effect, to prevent the raising of troops [and] to encourage desertions. . . . He was damaging the army, upon the existence and vigor of which the life of the nation depends." As commander in chief Lincoln had the constitutional power and duty to preserve that life. Suspension of the writ of habeas corpus was a vital weapon in that effort. The commander in chief also had the authority to order military trials in war zones, he claimed. Although Vallandigham had been arrested in Ohio, not in the South, Lincoln insisted that the whole country was a war zone. Draft resistance and murders of enrollment officers took place in the North. Civil courts were "utterly incompetent" to stop these activities, said Lincoln. In some places Copperhead influence was so strong that no jury would convict those who tried to sabotage the war effort. This "clear, flagrant, and giant rebellion," wrote Lincoln, reached into all corners of the country, where "under cover of 'liberty of speech,' 'liberty of the press,' and 'habeas corpus,' " the enemy "hoped to keep on foot amongst us a most efficient corps of spies, informers, suppliers, and aiders and abettors of their cause."

A significant part of the impact of these letters came from two colloquial illustrations that demonstrated Lincoln's gift for explaining complex issues in easily understood terms. The official army punishment for desertion was death. (Lincoln spent many hours reviewing such cases and finding reasons to commute death sentences.) Referring to Vallandigham's alleged encouragement of desertion, Lincoln asked: "Must I shoot a simple-minded soldier boy who deserts, whilst I must not touch the hair of a wily agitator who induces him to desert?" Almost as widely quoted was a piquant metaphor that challenged the protesters' assertion that wartime restrictions on civil liberties would create a fatal precedent for similar restrictions in peacetime. He could no more believe this, wrote Lincoln, "than I am able to believe that a man could contract so strong an appetite for emetics during temporary illness, as to persist in feeding upon them during the remainder of his healthy life."[29]

These letters, published in hundreds of Northern newspapers, were enormously effective. Half a million copies of the letter to New York Democrats were also published as a pamphlet. The "wily agitator" image did much to discredit Vallandigham and his fellows in the court of public opinion. An official judicial body also vindicated the president. Vallandigham's lawyers had appealed to the federal circuit court in Cincinnati for his release on a writ of habeas corpus. The judge refused and endorsed Lincoln's understanding of his constitutional powers as commander in chief. "It is not claimed that in time of war the President is above the Constitution," ruled the court. "His acts in this capacity must be limited to such as are deemed essential to the protection of the Government and the Constitution." And who was to decide what was essential? "The President is guided solely by his own judgment, and is amenable only for an abuse of his authority by impeachment."[30]

The timing of Lincoln's public letters

turned out to be fortuitous. Within a few days of their publication Union victories at Gettysburg, Vicksburg, and Port Hudson lifted the pall of Northern gloom and demoralization that had fueled protests against the president's "despotism."

When Lincoln visited the Army of the Potomac in the second week of April, he discussed with General Hooker various operational options for a campaign against the Army of Northern Virginia lying across the Rappahannock River. The president wrote a memorandum embodying the main point he wanted Hooker to keep in mind: "Our prime object is the enemies' army in front of us, and is not with, or about Richmond."[31] They had not decided whether Hooker should cross the river beyond the Confederate left or right flank before Lincoln returned to Washington. On April 11, however, Hooker sent the president a detailed plan of operations. His cavalry would raid Lee's communications between Fredericksburg and Richmond. At the same time part of the infantry would feint an attack just below Fredericksburg, while the rest marched upriver to cross at fords to come in on the enemy rear. If all went well Lee would either be crushed between the two wings of Union infantry — each almost equal in number to the Confederate infantry — or have to retreat toward the raiding Union cavalry, enabling Hooker to pitch into the enemy rear as the cavalry delayed them in front.[32]

Before he had left the army on April 11, Lincoln had given Hooker one other piece of advice. Well aware that at Antietam and Fredericksburg at least two corps had scarcely fired a shot, the president said: "In your next fight, put in all your men."[33] If Hooker had done so, events in the next few weeks might have been quite different.

Hooker's operation began flawlessly. Union cavalry tore up Confederate railroads, but the damage was limited and soon repaired. The flanking infantry successfully crossed the Rappahannock and was advancing on the Confederate rear at Fredericksburg by May 1. But Lee detached Jackson's corps to block the advance, and Hooker inexplicably pulled back to a defensive position near the crossroads mansion and outbuildings called Chancellorsville. From then on he lost the initiative to Lee, who daringly sent Jackson on a flank march that crushed the Union right on May 2, drove into the center on May 3, and forced the left back across the river on May 4. Hooker gave up and recrossed the whole army to the north bank of the Rappahannock during a driving rainstorm on May 6. Although the Battle of Chancellorsville cost Lee Stonewall Jackson from a friendly fire wound that proved fatal, it was nevertheless a decisive Confederate victory — and a defeat not so much of the Army of the Potomac as of Hooker, who lost control of the battle. And contrary to Lincoln's advice, he had not put in all of his men. Two of his seven corps and part of another stood virtually idle during the fighting.[34]

Lincoln spent many anxious hours in the War Department telegraph office receiving fragmentary and contradictory information about the course of the battle. When word finally came on May 6 that the army had retreated across the river, the president's face turned "ashen," according to journalist Noah Brooks, who had become close to Lincoln. "Had a thunderbolt fallen upon the President he could not have been more overwhelmed. . . . Clasping his hands behind his back, he walked up and down the room, saying, 'My God! my God! What will the country say! What will the country say!' "[35]

Lincoln departed immediately to confer with Hooker at army headquarters. That general blamed others for his failure: Gen.

Oliver Howard and his Eleventh Corps, which had been routed by Jackson's May 2 flank attack; Gen. John Sedgwick, commander of the Sixth Corps, which Hooker said had failed to fight its way through from Fredericksburg to join the main army at Chancellorsville; and cavalry commander George Stoneman, whose raid, said Hooker, had been feeble and ineffective. Most of the corps commanders, by contrast, considered Hooker responsible, but they evidently conveyed little of their disillusionment directly to Lincoln during his May 7 visit. The president, according to Fifth Corps commander George Meade, said that while the battle's outcome was "more serious and injurious than any previous act of the war," he nevertheless added that "he did not blame anyone." Lincoln wanted Hooker to begin a new movement against the enemy as soon as possible, "to supersede the bad moral effect of the recent one." Hooker had been deeply depressed after the battle; he told Meade that he "almost wished he had never been born." But "since seeing the President . . . he seems in better spirits," wrote Meade, "and I suppose, unless some strong pressure is brought to bear from external sources, he will not be disturbed."[36]

Strong pressure, however, *was* brought

during the following week. The senior corps commander, Gen. Darius Couch, said he would no longer serve under Hooker and requested a transfer. Other generals made their dissatisfaction known indirectly to Lincoln. Pennsylvania governor Andrew Curtin talked with the three corps commanders from his state, who told him they had lost confidence in Hooker. Curtin passed this information along to Lincoln. By May 13 the president was aware that the brewing discontent might fatally undermine any new offensive by Hooker. He summoned the general to Washington and told him bluntly, in person and in writing, that "it does not now appear probable to me that you can gain any thing by an early renewal of the attempt to cross the Rappahannock. I therefore shall not complain, if you do no more, for a time, than to keep the enemy at bay." Lincoln also informed Hooker that "I have some painful intimations that some of your corps and Division Commanders are not giving you their entire confidence." If he wanted to continue commanding the army, Lincoln implied, he must rebuild that confidence.[37]

A consensus among the anti-Hooker generals favored sending a petition to Lincoln to appoint Meade as Hooker's replacement. Meade refused to go along with the idea, so it died. But the pressure on Lincoln to change the command continued. Halleck had never liked Hooker, and Stanton now apparently sided with Halleck in urging Hooker's removal. The president evidently spoke with Couch and with Gen. John Reynolds, two of Hooker's strongest critics, and asked them if they would accept the command. They declined. Lincoln seems to have been irritated by his conversations with these generals, who were free with their criticism but did not wish to follow through by accepting the responsibility of command. If that was the case, said Lincoln, he would stick with Hooker: "The President said he was not disposed to throw away a gun because it missed fire once; that he would pick the lock and try again."[38] Even more irritating to Lincoln was pressure from several quarters to restore McClellan to command. More than anything else, perhaps, this lobbying for McClellan put the president's back up and made him determined to give Hooker another chance.[39]

These were difficult days for the commander in chief. A translator in the State Department who often saw Lincoln wrote that "he looks exhausted, care-worn, spiritless, extinct." Gen. Ethan Allen Hitchcock, still serving as an aide to Stanton, wrote in his diary on May 24 that the secretary of war "complained to me this morning that the President would not listen to his advice or that of Halleck. . . . This is a bad state of things." Lincoln "has given orders to Hooker as his only senior, passing by Halleck as if he were not there. Hooker's army is not equal to the duties expected of it, and Lee may move — possibly into Pennsylvania."[40]

Lee was indeed planning to move into Pennsylvania. He began to do so in the second week of June. For the third time in thirteen months, Lincoln saw a Confederate offensive as an opportunity rather than a threat. As he had done during Jackson's Shenandoah Valley campaign in May 1862 and during Lee's invasion of Maryland the previous September, the president urged his army commander to attack or trap the enemy far from his home base. But as the Army of Northern Virginia began to march up the south bank of the Rappahannock toward the Shenandoah Valley, Hooker proposed to attack the corps Lee had left as a rear guard in the trenches near Fredericksburg. Both Lincoln and Halleck (whom the president brought into communication with Hooker) disapproved. Halleck wanted

Hooker to "fight [the enemy's] movable column first, instead of attacking his intrenchments, with your own forces separated by the Rappahannock." Lincoln put it more colorfully, using a typically pointed simile. When "you find Lee coming to the North of the Rappahannock, I would by no means cross to the South of it," advised the president. "I would not take the risk of being entangled upon the river, like an ox jumped half over a fence, and liable to be torn by dogs, front and rear, without a fair chance to gore one way or kick another."[41]

Five days later, when it became clear that Lee's whole army was leaving Fredericksburg, Hooker requested Lincoln's permission to move quickly fifty miles south to attack the lightly defended Richmond defenses. "To march to Richmond at once," he said, would be "the most speedy and certain mode of giving the rebellion a mortal blow." Lincoln must have shaken his head in frustration when he read this telegram. He immediately wired Hooker: "*Lee's* Army, and not *Richmond,* is your true objective point. If he comes toward the Upper Potomac, follow on his flank, and on the inside track, shortening your lines, whilst he lengthens his. Fight him when opportunity offers." By June 14 Union intelligence had learned that the Army of Northern Virginia was strung out almost sixty miles from Winchester back to Chancellorsville. "The animal must be very slim somewhere," the president telegraphed Hooker. "Could you not break him?"[42]

On June 15 Gen. Richard Ewell's corps captured most of the Union garrison at Winchester and his advance units began crossing the Potomac into Maryland and Pennsylvania. "The enemy's long and necessarily slim line," Lincoln wired Hooker, "gives you back the chance I thought McClellan lost last fall" to defeat the Army of Northern Virginia in detail. Lincoln also instructed Hooker and Halleck to cooperate with each other to exploit this "best opportunity we have had since the war began."[43]

The president was fast losing faith in Hooker, however. The general continued to bicker with Halleck, complained that the enemy outnumbered him, and pleaded for reinforcements. After speaking with Lincoln on June 26, Gideon Welles wrote in his diary that the president "betrayed doubts of Hooker, to whom he is quite partial." "We cannot help beating them if we have the man," said Lincoln, but he feared that "Hooker may commit the same fault as

McClellan and lose his chance." The next day Hooker forced a confrontation with Halleck over a request that the Harpers Ferry garrison be added to his army. Halleck refused; Hooker offered his resignation; and probably to his surprise, Lincoln accepted it. The president told the cabinet on June 28, according to Welles, that he had "observed in Hooker the same failings that were observed in McClellan after the battle of Antietam — a want of alacrity to obey, and a greedy call for more troops which could not, and ought not to be taken from other points."[44]

Lincoln appointed Meade to succeed Hooker. He was the obvious choice, having been supported for the position by most of the corps commanders since Chancellorsville. When the Army of Northern Virginia and the Army of the Potomac clashed at Gettysburg on July 1, Meade was in his fourth day of command. He directed a skillful defense against repeated Confederate attacks and inflicted a punishing defeat on Lee's army, which lost at least one-third of its numbers (the Army of the Potomac lost one-fourth).

When the news of Gettysburg reached Washington and the North on the Fourth of July, celebrations took place and newspapers blazoned forth with such headlines as VICTORY! WATERLOO ECLIPSED! One resident of Washington wrote: "I *never* knew such excitement." The New York diarist George Templeton Strong rejoiced that "the results of this victory are priceless. . . . The charm of Robert Lee's invincibility is broken. The Army of the Potomac has at last found a general that can handle it, and has stood nobly up to its terrible work in spite of its long disheartening list of hard-fought failures. . . . Copperheads are palsied and dumb for the moment at least. . . . Government is strengthened at home and abroad."[45]

Lincoln stood at a White House balcony on this "glorious Fourth" and told a crowd of serenaders that the "gigantic Rebellion" whose purpose was to overthrow the principle that "all men are created equal" had been dealt a severe blow. But the commander in chief wanted more; he wanted Meade to give it a death blow. As the Army of Northern Virginia began its retreat on July 4, a drenching rain began to fall and continued much of the time for the next ten days. Union cavalry destroyed the Confederate pontoon bridge over the Potomac near Williamsport, Maryland, and the rising waters made the ford there impassable.

Lee's crippled army was trapped north of the river for more than a week. Here was the best chance yet to end the war, Lincoln believed. He agreed with his friend Benjamin French, commissioner of public buildings in Washington, that "if our army does all its duty Lee's army will scarcely ever see old Virginia soil again *as an army.*"[46]

On July 4 at Gettysburg, Meade issued a congratulatory order to the army, and added: "Our task is not yet accomplished, and the commanding general looks to the army for greater efforts to drive from our soil every vestige of the presence of the invader."[47] When Lincoln read these words he burst out: "Drive the invaders from our soil! *Great God! Is that all?*" To John Hay the president exploded: "This is a dreadful reminiscence of McClellan," who had proclaimed a great victory when the enemy retreated to Virginia after Antietam. "Will our Generals never get that idea out of their heads? The whole country is *our* soil."[48]

More temperately the president told Halleck that he was a "good deal dissatisfied" with Meade's order. Along with other evidence of a lackluster pursuit of the retreating rebels, it seemed to show only a desire "to get the enemy across the river again without a further collision" instead of "a purpose to prevent his crossing and to destroy him." Halleck fired off telegrams urging Meade to "push forward and fight Lee before he can cross the Potomac. . . . You have given the enemy a stunning blow at Gettysburg, follow it up and give him another before he can cross the Potomac. . . . The President is urgent and anxious that your army should move against him by forced marches."[49]

In the midst of this flurry of telegrams came one from Cairo, Illinois, carried there by a fast dispatch boat from Vicksburg. Sent by Acting Rear Admiral Porter to Gideon Welles, it announced the surrender of Vicksburg and its thirty thousand defenders on July 4. Lincoln was ecstatic. He put his arm around the bewigged navy secretary, whom he called Father Neptune, and exclaimed "my joy at this result. It is great, Mr. Welles, it is great!" The president headed for the telegraph office. "I will myself telegraph this news to General Meade. . . . It will inspire [him]." Instead Lincoln sent a note to Halleck, who wired it verbatim to Meade: "Vicksburg surrendered to General Grant on July 4. Now, if General Meade can complete his work, so gloriously begun so far, by the literal or substantial destruction of Lee's army, the rebellion will be over."[50]

From Meade came promises to try, but also reports of supply difficulties, roads of bottomless mud, the exhaustion of his men, and a strong defensive perimeter at Williamsport established by Lee while his engineers worked feverishly to rebuild a pontoon bridge. Lincoln had heard it all before, and he must have sighed with exasperation. On July 11, however, John Hay reported the president to be in "a specially good humor today" because Meade had telegraphed "his intention of attacking them in the morning." Lincoln had been out of sorts with the general "but concluded today that Meade would yet show sufficient activity to inflict the Coup de grace upon the flying rebels."[51]

No attack occurred July 12. Instead came another telegram from Meade stating that he would attack the next morning "unless something intervenes." When Lincoln read this dispatch, his shoulders sagged and he remarked: "They will be ready to fight a magnificent battle when there is no enemy there to fight." The president was right: "Something" intervened. Meade called his seven senior generals into a council of war. A majority voted to postpone the attack and instead to reconnoiter the enemy's line for a possible weak spot. After talking with Lincoln, Halleck sent Meade an exhortative telegram: "Act upon your own judgment and make your generals execute your orders. Call no council of war. It is proverbial that councils of war never fight."[52]

The next morning — three hours after dawn — the Army of the Potomac's infantry lurched forward. As Lincoln had predicted, they found no enemy to fight. The Army of Northern Virginia had crossed on the rebuilt pontoon bridge and at a ford (the river had dropped just enough). Union cavalry captured about a thousand men of the rear guard; if the infantry had advanced earlier they might have captured more.

When the news of Lee's escape reached Washington, Lincoln was bitter. "That, my God, is the last of this Army of the Potomac," he exclaimed to Welles. "There is bad faith somewhere." Only one corps commander had voted for an attack on the thirteenth, when it might have succeeded. "What does it mean, Mr. Welles? Great God! What does it mean?" Only once or twice before, wrote Welles, "have I ever seen the President so troubled, so dejected and discouraged." Salmon P. Chase confirmed this observation: "He was more grieved and indignant than I have ever seen him." Lincoln told his son Robert that "if I had gone there I could have whipped them myself."[53]

Halleck conveyed Lincoln's mood in a telegram to Meade: "The escape of Lee's army without another battle has created great dissatisfaction in the mind of the President, and it will require an active and energetic pursuit on your part to remove the impression that it has not been sufficiently active heretofore." Famous for his short-fused temper, Meade fired back a telegram angrily tendering his resignation. Halleck consulted Lincoln, who said that the resignation of the general who was being hailed as the hero of Gettysburg could of course not be accepted. Halleck so informed Meade in a dispatch that constituted a quasi apology.[54]

Lincoln sat down to write a letter intended to mollify Meade. "I am very — *very* grateful to you for the magnificent success you gave the cause of the country at Gettysburg," he wrote to the general, "and I am sorry now to be the author of the slightest pain to you." But as his pen scratched over the paper, Lincoln's words strayed far from those of congratulations and apology. "My dear general," the president continued, "I do not believe you appreciate the magnitude of the misfortune involved in Lee's escape. He was within your easy grasp, and to have closed upon him would, in connection with our other late successes, have ended the war. As it is, the war will be prolonged indefinitely. . . . Your golden opportunity is gone, and I am distressed immeasurably because of it."[55]

As he blotted the ink and read over this letter, Lincoln realized that he could not send it unless he really did want to provoke Meade's resignation. So he filed it away unsent. Within a couple of days the president had recovered his equanimity. The "other recent successes" he referred to in his letter to Meade did much to offset his disappointment: the capture of Port Hudson as well as Vicksburg, which opened the Mississippi and split the Confederacy in twain; and an impressive advance by Rosecrans's Army of the Cumberland that promised success for Lincoln's goal of finally liberating East Tennessee. On July 17 the president told his cabinet that Meade "has committed a terrible mistake, but we will try him further." Four days later Lincoln wrote a letter to General Howard — which he *did* send, and which Howard probably showed to Meade. Lincoln acknowledged that he had perhaps been unreasonable to expect Lee's army to have been destroyed. "I had always believed — making my belief a hobby possibly —

that the main rebel army going North of the Potomac, could never return, if well attended to." In any case, "a few days having passed, I am profoundly grateful for what was done, without criticism for what was not done. Gen. Meade has my confidence as a brave and skillful officer, and a true man."[56]

Nevertheless the president continued to believe that Meade should have attacked at Williamsport. Historians will continue to debate the pros and cons of that question. A Union assault might have succeeded — or it might not have. Failure might have neutralized the success at Gettysburg. But as Lincoln said on another occasion, to McClellan: "If we never try, we shall never succeed." On the day before he wrote his unsent letter to Meade, the president sent a much different letter to a general who *did* try: "I do not remember that you and I ever met personally," Lincoln wrote to Ulysses S. Grant. "I write this now as a grateful acknowledgment for the almost inestimable service you have done the country." The president confessed that he had been impatient with the various abortive efforts to get through the bayous and swamps in February and March. And when Grant finally did run the batteries and get below Vicksburg,

"I thought you should go down the river and join Gen. Banks; and when you turned Northward Eastward of the Big Black [River], I feared it was a mistake. I now wish to make the personal acknowledgment that you were right, and I was wrong."[57]

It would be another eight months before Lincoln and Grant met personally. But from the moment the commander in chief wrote this letter, they began to forge the partnership that would win the war.

8

THE HEAVIEST
BLOW YET DEALT
TO THE REBELLION

Victory was a wondrous tonic for Lincoln.
Three weeks after John Hay had described
the president as "grieved silently but deeply
about the escape of Lee," Hay wrote to his
fellow secretary John Nicolay that "the
Tycoon [their private nickname for Lincoln]
is in fine whack. I have rarely seen him more
serene & busy. He is managing this war, the
draft, foreign relations, and planning a
reconstruction of the Union, all at once."[1]

Managing the draft was no small task after
the lethal riots in New York City on July
13–17. Governor Horatio Seymour pleaded
with the administration after the riots were
suppressed to postpone the draft lottery for
fear of sparking another eruption. Lincoln
refused to give in to what he considered
another form of rebellion.[2] Drafting resumed in New York on August 19, protected
by twenty thousand troops that the government had moved to the volatile city. This

time peace and order prevailed.

In foreign policy Lincoln's main concern in the summer of 1863 was French intervention in Mexico. The French presence not only violated the Monroe Doctrine but also presented the danger of French support for the Confederacy. Mexican political and financial instability in 1861 had provoked a joint military expedition by Britain, France, and Spain to collect debts owed by Mexico to foreign creditors. Britain and Spain withdrew their troops in 1862 after negotiating a settlement. But Emperor Napoleon III imposed impossible demands on the weak Mexican government. He sent additional French troops (thirty-five thousand by 1863), who seized Mexico City and overthrew the liberal leader Benito Juárez in June 1863. The Confederacy had formed quasi alliances with anti-Juárez chieftains in Mexico's northern provinces, which profited from the contraband trade across the Texas border. Confederate diplomats also angled for an agreement with France for recognition of the Confederacy in return for Confederate support of Napoleon's puppet regime in Mexico.[3]

The Lincoln administration regarded this situation as intolerable. A cornerstone of the administration's national strategy was prevention of foreign intervention in the war. After the capture of Vicksburg and Port Hudson, Lincoln felt that he was in a position to warn off the French. But his plans for doing so produced a conflict with the military strategy recommended by two of his principal subordinates. Now that the Mississippi River was open from Minnesota to the Gulf, Generals Grant and Banks wanted to launch a campaign against Mobile, the Confederacy's chief blockade-running port on the Gulf. This was a sound strategic goal, but Lincoln's first priority was an expedition into Texas to plant the flag there as a warning to France. A campaign against Mobile, the president told Grant, "would appear tempting to me also, were it not that in view of recent events in Mexico, I am greatly impressed with the importance of re-establishing the national authority in Western Texas as soon as possible."[4]

Lincoln's reference to western Texas is puzzling, since any Union invasion would have to be mounted from Louisiana against *eastern* Texas. General Banks did undertake such a campaign in September 1863. A naval flotilla and a division of four thousand soldiers commanded by none other than William B. Franklin, who had been transferred as far away from Virginia as possible, attacked Confederate defenses at Sabine Pass on the Gulf just west of the Louisiana border. Franklin bungled the operation, and the Texans drove the invaders away in ignominy. Banks eventually landed a force at Brownsville to control the mouth of the Rio Grande. But this was a rather feeble "occupation" of Texas and did little if anything to impress France. And the failure to launch a campaign against Mobile in 1863 may have been a major missed opportunity.

The principal strategic success after Gettysburg and Vicksburg in 1863 came in East Tennessee. Both the Union Army of the Cumberland and Confederate Army of Tennessee had been so badly cut up in the Battle of Stones River that neither could do much through the rest of the winter. Union infantry considerably exceeded the enemy's in numbers, but Gen. Braxton Bragg's Confederate cavalry carried out punishing raids against Gen. William S. Rosecrans's communications. Northern cavalry trying to counter Rebel horsemen like Nathan Bedford Forrest and John Hunt Morgan always seemed to arrive at the scene of destruction too late. In February 1863 Lincoln had addressed Rosecrans on this subject. The president recognized that "in no other way does the enemy give us so much trouble" as with these raids. To have Union cavalry always acting on the defensive did little to stop them. Thus Lincoln urged Rosecrans to "organize proper forces, and make *counter-raids*" that would accomplish the dual objectives of disrupting enemy supplies and forcing Confederate cavalry to leave off their raids to combat Union horsemen.[5]

Lincoln's suggestion bore fruit. In April one of Rosecrans's brigade commanders, Col. Abel Streight, led a raid by seventeen hundred men mounted on mules (supposedly hardier than horses and requiring less forage) against the railroad between Atlanta and Chattanooga. Forrest's troopers finally caught up with and captured most of the raiders. But Streight's effort had one beneficial if perhaps unintended consequence. Benjamin Grierson's mounted raid through Mississippi took place at the same time, providing an essential diversion in aid of Grant's movements against Vicksburg. Because Forrest was pursuing Streight, Grierson was unopposed by the Confederacy's best cavalry commander.

But cavalry raids, however spectacular, were not going to achieve Lincoln's goal of liberating East Tennessee. That was the task of Rosecrans's infantry. As the weeks of fine spring weather went by and Rosecrans did not advance against the enemy defenses twenty-five miles south of Murfreesboro, Lincoln again became impatient. In response to importunate telegrams from Halleck, Rosecrans stubbornly insisted that he could not move until everything was ready. On June 11 Halleck warned Rosecrans of the president's "great dissatisfaction" with "your inactivity." Five days later the general-in-chief demanded of Rosecrans: "Is it your intention to make an immediate movement forward? A definite answer, yes or no, is required." In reply Rosecrans bristled: "If immediate means tonight or tomorrow, no. If it means as soon as all things are ready, say five days, yes."[6]

Rosecrans was almost as good as his word. Seven days later, on June 23, he moved. Once started, he maneuvered his sixty-three thousand men with speed and skill despite incessant rain. The forty-five thousand Confederates held a strong defensive position at four gaps in the foothills of the Cumberland Mountains. Feinting with his cavalry and one infantry corps toward the western gaps, Rosecrans sent three corps through and around the other gaps with such force and swiftness that the Confederates were knocked aside or flanked almost before they knew what had hit them. Driven back fifteen miles to Tullahoma, Bragg received another rude surprise when a Union brigade of mounted infantry, armed with new seven-shot Spencer rifles, which had led the advance through Hoover's Gap, got around to the Confederate rear and threatened their rail lifeline. Once again Bragg fell back, this time all the way to Chattanooga.

Lincoln could take some credit for the success of the brigade armed with Spencer repeaters. He had always been interested in new technologies. In 1849 Lincoln had patented a device for lifting steamboats over shoals.[7] (He is the only president of the United States to have held a patent.) In the 1850s he occasionally delivered a lecture called "Discoveries and Inventions." During the war Lincoln functioned at times as chief of ordnance, ordering the hidebound Brig. Gen. James Ripley, who officially held that position until the president forced his retirement in September 1863, to test new weapons offered by inventors. Some of the latter were crackpots, and some of Lincoln's subordinates complained that he wasted too much time with these men. On the other hand the president helped pave the way for the navy's contract with John Ericsson to build the *Monitor* and for the army to try Thaddeus Lowe's observation balloons. Lincoln personally test-fired breech loading and repeating rifles on the open ground south of the White House. On more than one occasion he overrode General Ripley and ordered the Ordnance Bureau to purchase the best of these — especially the seven-shot repeating rifles and carbines invented by Connecticut Yankee Christopher Spencer. These guns turned out to be the best shoulder weapons of the war. The carbines gave Union cavalry a significant advantage in the last fifteen months of the war. Infantry regiments armed with Spencer rifles gained a fearsome reputation among enemy units.[8]

The brigade of mounted infantry that rendered such good service in Rosecrans's Tullahoma campaign was commanded by Col. John T. Wilder, a young iron manufacturer from Indiana who had used his personal credit to buy the Spencers for his brigade. (The government later reimbursed Wilder and his men.) They earned the name "the Lightning Brigade" in this campaign, and pioneered new tactics to make the best use of their new weapons. Without Lincoln's earlier personal support for Spencer, however, there might not have been a Lightning Brigade and 85,000 Union soldiers equipped with Spencer carbines or rifles by the end of the war.

In little more than a week the Army of the Cumberland forced Bragg's Army of Tennessee back seventy miles almost into Georgia at the cost of only 560 Union casualties. On July 7 Secretary of War Stanton telegraphed Rosecrans news of the great victories at Gettysburg and Vicksburg, and added: "You and your noble army now have the chance to give the finishing blow to the rebellion. Will you neglect the chance?" A piqued Rosecrans wired back: "You do not appear to observe the fact that this noble army has driven the rebels from Middle Tennessee. . . . I beg in behalf of this army that the War Department may not overlook so great an event because it is not written in showers of blood."[9]

The Rebels had been driven from Middle Tennessee, to be sure. But the enemy still controlled East Tennessee. Lincoln urged the victorious Rosecrans to keep going. But the methodical general insisted that he must secure his communications back through Nashville to Louisville and bring up enough supplies to sustain a further advance over difficult terrain. Rosecrans also wanted his left flank protected by a simultaneous advance toward Knoxville by Ambrose Burnside's small Army of the Ohio. These reasons for not moving immediately gave Lincoln another case of déjà vu. The second half of July and the first half of August went by as increasingly urgent orders from Halleck flew over the wires to Rosecrans and testy replies flew back. "The patience of the authorities here has been completely exhausted," Halleck told the general. "It has been said that you are as inactive as was General Buell, and the pressure for your removal has been almost as strong."[10]

Rosecrans did not have to be a mind reader to know who was the principal one of "the authorities here" or where the pressure was coming from. On August 1 the general wrote directly to Lincoln explaining the necessity for his prolonged preparations. In reply Lincoln assured him of his continued "kind feeling and confidence in you." The president said that Halleck had probably overstated his "dissatisfaction." Nevertheless Lincoln asked Rosecrans a couple of pointed questions in response to the general's explanations about getting up supplies and his shortage of horses. "Do you not consume supplies as fast as you get them forward" even when you are sitting still? And what happened to all those thousands of horses the quartermaster general sent you? "Do not misunderstand," the president concluded. "I am not casting blame on you. . . . I am not watching you with an evil eye."[11]

Rosecrans was probably not convinced. He delayed another week but finally moved on August 16. As before, he advanced quickly and cleverly once he got started. He feinted with three brigades toward the Tennessee River crossings above Chattanooga, and then crossed most of the army at several places below the city. Bewildered by "the popping out of rats from so many holes," Bragg discovered that his defenses at Chattanooga had been turned by the appearance of Union divisions south of the city.[12] As these divisions began to traverse the rugged mountains toward Bragg's lifeline, the Western and Atlantic Railroad, the Confederates evacuated Chattanooga on September 9. Burnside's army had advanced in tandem with Rosecrans and had captured Knoxville a week earlier. Two years after he had hoped his armies would come to the rescue of East Tennessee Unionists, Lincoln finally saw that hope fulfilled.

It was one thing for Union armies to get

there; it was quite another to stay there in the face of a determined Confederate counterattack. Jefferson Davis decided to reinforce Bragg with two of Longstreet's divisions from the Army of Northern Virginia. Part of these troops arrived over the South's worn-out railroad system in time to take part in the crucial second day of the Battle of Chickamauga, September 20. Longstreet personally directed an attack through a gap in the Union line caused by a mistaken order. Wilder's Lightning Brigade punished the attackers with its rapid-firing Spencers. The Confederate assault nevertheless burst through the Union right and sent one-third of the Army of the Cumberland — including Rosecrans — flying back to Chattanooga in an apparent rout. But Gen. George Thomas stayed on the field with the rest of the army, organized a new defense, and stopped the Confederate advance. For his superb battlefield leadership Thomas earned fame as "the Rock of Chickamauga."

Nevertheless it was a serious Union defeat. The army was virtually besieged in Chattanooga by the Confederates, who occupied Missionary Ridge on the east and Lookout Mountain to the southwest. The only supply route open to Rosecrans was an almost impassable road over rugged Walden's

Ridge to the north.

On the morning of September 21 Lincoln walked into John Hay's bedroom before the secretary was up, "& sitting down on my bed said 'Well, Rosecrans has been whipped, as I feared. I have feared it for several days. I believe I feel trouble in the air before it comes.' "[13] The question was what to do about it. Lincoln again haunted the telegraph office and fired off dispatches taking direct control of the situation. To Burnside at Knoxville he sent orders to reinforce Rosecrans in Chattanooga. When he learned that Burnside had earlier sent most of his force in the opposite direction to attack guerrillas at Jonesboro, Lincoln lost his temper. "Damn Jonesboro!" he exclaimed. He sent another telegram ordering Burnside to forget Jonesboro and go to Rosecrans. When he learned that Burnside had moved farther in the wrong direction on the twenty-third, the president composed an angry telegram to Burnside stating that the general's "incomprehensible" action "makes me doubt whether I am awake or dreaming."[14]

After getting this outburst off his chest, Lincoln decided not to send the telegram. And when it became clear that Burnside could not take his whole force to Chattanooga without giving up Knoxville, Lincoln ordered him to hold Knoxville without fail and to send Rosecrans whatever troops he could spare. As matters turned out, Burnside could spare none, so reinforcements for Rosecrans would have to come from elsewhere.[15]

On the evening of September 23 Lincoln rode out to his summer cottage at the Soldiers' Home hoping for his first good sleep in several nights. After he went to bed he was awakened by John Hay, who had ridden out "through a splendid moonlight" with a message from Stanton asking Lincoln to come back to the War Department for an emergency midnight conference. A "considerably disturbed" president hurriedly dressed and returned with Hay.[16] Attending the meeting were Lincoln, Stanton, Halleck, Seward, Chase, and two War Department officials. Stanton proposed that two corps be detached from the Army of the Potomac and sent by rail to reinforce Rosecrans. They were not doing anything worthwhile in Virginia, said Stanton, and might as well go where they would be useful. It would be a trip of 1,200 miles by the routes they would have to take. Stanton had consulted railroad officials and said that twenty thousand men could reach Nashville in five days and Chattanooga in a few more.

Mindful of previous movements by the sluggish Army of the Potomac, Lincoln responded skeptically that they could hardly get from Culpeper to Washington in five days!

In the end Stanton prevailed. The movement began September 24. It went like clockwork, a marvel of organization and coordination between the War Department and several railroads. Eleven days after the start, more than twenty thousand men of the Eleventh and Twelfth Corps arrived at the railhead near Chattanooga with their equipment, artillery, and horses after a trip of 1,233 miles through the Appalachians and across the unbridged Ohio River twice. It was the longest and fastest movement of such a large body of troops before the twentieth century.[17]

Sherman was also heading toward Chattanooga from Vicksburg with four divisions, repairing the railroad as they went. But there was no point in putting these troops into Chattanooga when the soldiers and horses already there were on starvation rations. Rosecrans seemed incapable of coping with the situation. After reading Charles Dana's dispatches from Chattanooga reporting Rosecrans's erratic and apathetic behavior, Lincoln commented that the general was "confused and stunned like a duck hit on the head."[18]

Rosecrans would have to go. The commander in chief, however, did not want to remove him before the Ohio gubernatorial election on October 13. Rosecrans remained popular in his home state, especially among War Democrats, whose support for the Union candidate against Clement L. Vallandigham Lincoln considered essential. The president was nervous about this election and a similar contest in Pennsylvania, where a Peace Democrat also challenged the Republican incumbent. Military strategy for dealing with the crisis in Chattanooga would have to take a temporary backseat to the national strategy of electing war candidates in two of the nation's three largest states. Lincoln told Gideon Welles that "he had more anxiety in regard to the election results" than "he had in 1860 when he was elected."[19] He need not have worried. The Union/Republican candidates in both states were elected, though the outcome in Pennsylvania was close. In Ohio, however, Vallandigham was buried by a one-hundred-thousand-vote majority for his opponent, who won 94 percent of the soldier vote.

Three days later Lincoln took decisive action. He combined all military departments between the Appalachians and the Mississippi River into a new Military Division of the Mississippi and placed Grant in command of it. He ordered Grant to Chattanooga to sort out the situation there and authorized him to replace Rosecrans with George Thomas if he judged it necessary. Grant did; Thomas became commander of the Army of the Cumberland on October 18 and vowed to "hold the town until we starve."[20] It did not come to that, however. Five days later Grant arrived in Chattanooga and put in motion an operation planned by Thomas to open a supply line from a secure railhead and steamboat landing west of Chattanooga across a pontoon bridge out of range of Confederate artillery on Lookout Mountain.

Lincoln dealt with the potential political fallout from Rosecrans's removal with a deftness that demonstrated the benefits of having a commander in chief who was also a canny politician. The Union commander in Missouri, Brig. Gen. John Schofield, had made himself persona non grata with the radical faction in the savage internecine political conflicts in that state. Lincoln worked out a deal with Missouri's two senators whereby they would support Senate confirmation of Schofield's promotion to major general and corps command in a different theater to make room for Rosecrans as department commander in Missouri. This move "will go far to heal the Missouri difficulty," said Lincoln. Equally important, "I find it scarcely less than indispensable for me to do something for Gen. Rosecrans. . . . In a purely military point of view it may be that none of these things is indispensable; but in another aspect, scarcely less important, they would give great relief."[21]

During the month after Grant's arrival in Chattanooga on October 23, the rejuvenated Army of the Cumberland was reinforced by the twenty thousand soldiers transferred from the Army of the Potomac and by seventeen thousand with Sherman from the Army of the Tennessee. For the first time in the war, troops from the three principal Union armies fought together. In a notable series of attacks on November 23–25 in which the Army of the Cumberland avenged Chickamauga, Grant's army group routed the Army of Tennessee and drove it twenty miles into Georgia. Four days later Burnside's Army of the Ohio decisively beat back a Confederate effort to recapture Knoxville. East Tennessee remained secure for the Union. "I wish to tender you," Lincoln wrote to Grant, "and all under your command, my more than thanks — my profoundest gratitude — for the skill, courage, and perseverance, with which you and they, over so great difficulties, have effected that important object. God bless you all."[22]

While Grant, Thomas, and Burnside were achieving this "important object," the Army of the Potomac had accomplished little since Gettysburg. By the last week of July, Meade and Lee confronted each other across the Rappahannock River not far from where the Army of Northern Virginia had started north seven weeks earlier. Despite Lincoln's statement to Gen. Oliver O. Howard on July 21 that Meade "has my confidence as a brave and skillful officer," the president unburdened himself to Gideon Welles only five days later: "I have no faith that Meade will attack Lee. . . . I believe he can never have another as good opportunity as he has trifled away. Everything since has dragged with him. No I don't believe he is going to fight." Lincoln even considered appointing Grant to command the Army of the Potomac, but was dissuaded by Halleck and Charles A. Dana — with an assist from Grant, who did not want the job. "It would cause me more sadness than satisfaction to be ordered to the command of the Army of the Potomac," wrote Grant on August 5. "Dissatisfaction would necessarily be produced by importing a General to Command an Army already supplied with those who have grown up, and been promoted, with it. . . . While I would disobey no order I should beg very hard to be excused before accepting that command."[23]

Another eight weeks went by, and all remained essentially quiet along the Rappahannock. Again Lincoln vented his frustration to Welles: "It is the same old story of the Army of the Potomac. Imbecility, inefficiency, — don't want to *do* — is defending the Capital. . . . Oh, it is terrible, terrible, this weakness, this indifference of our Potomac generals, with such armies of good and brave men." Why not replace Meade? Welles asked. "What can I do with such generals as we have?" Lincoln replied. "Who among them is any better than Meade? To sweep away the whole of them from the chief command and substitute a new man would cause a shock, and be likely to lead to combinations and troubles greater than we now have."[24]

Lincoln recognized that the Army of the

Potomac had not yet shed the McClellan legacy of risk aversion and a defensive mentality. Many of its high-ranking officers, including Meade, had come up under McClellan. Even though Lincoln had gotten rid of the principal McClellanites — most notably Fitz-John Porter and William Franklin — McClellan still seemed to cast a shadow over the army. To be fair, Meade and other commanders, including McClellan, operated with the government in Washington and the major newspapers of the country looking over their shoulders. Expectations of the army were high, and expressions of disappointment with its failures correspondingly harsh. Grant, Sherman, and other Western commanders had enjoyed the luxury of distance from Washington and less of the glare of publicity and high expectations that seemed to paralyze many Eastern generals.

In mid-September Meade's scouts detected the disappearance of Longstreet's two divisions, which soon turned up on the Chickamauga battlefield. Meade proposed to maneuver against Lee's weakened army to force him back toward Richmond. Lincoln expressed exasperation. "To attempt to fight the enemy slowly back to his intrenchments at Richmond . . . is an idea I have been trying to repudiate for quite a year. . . . I have constantly desired the Army of the Potomac, to make Lee's army, and not Richmond, it's objective point. If our army can not fall upon the enemy and hurt him where he is, it is plain to me it can gain nothing by attempting to follow him over a succession of intrenched lines into a fortified city."[25]

Meade's apparent unwillingness to attack helped persuade Lincoln to acquiesce in Stanton's proposal to send the Eleventh and Twelfth Corps to Chattanooga. Meade's army would still be more than strong enough for the defensive stance the general seemed to prefer. When Lee learned of the Eleventh and Twelfth Corps' departure, he seized the initiative and moved around Meade's right toward Manassas. Meade retreated, remaining between the Army of Northern Virginia and Washington. On October 14 the Union Second Corps shattered a reckless attack by A. P. Hill's corps at Bristoe Station, five miles south of Manassas.

This reverse took the steam out of Lee's advance. Lincoln thought it provided Meade with an opportunity for a counterattack. The president had Halleck send Meade a telegram stating that if he attacked "the honor will be his if he succeeds, and the blame may be mine if he fails." This remarkable offer to absolve Meade of any responsibility for failure did not work. Lee began to retreat without further harassment by the Army of the Potomac. Since Meade was close to Washington, Lincoln asked him to come up for a talk. "The president was, as he always is, very kind and considerate," Meade wrote to his wife. "He found no fault with my operations, though it was very evident he was disappointed that I had not gotten a battle out of Lee."[26]

The general misread Lincoln's affability for lack of censure. Meade seems to have had second thoughts, however, for two weeks later he told Gen. Winfield Scott Hancock that he expected to be relieved of command "at any moment."[27] But no removal order came, and in November, Meade began an offensive that drove Lee across the Rapidan River and promised to maneuver him into a position where Meade could attack to advantage. But Lee foiled this effort when one of the Union corps moved too slowly to catch the Army of Northern Virginia in the open before it could entrench a formidable position behind Mine Run. On November 30 Meade canceled a planned attack on this position because he was afraid it would turn into another Fredericksburg. Campaigning was over for the season as both armies went into winter quarters with the Rapidan between them.

In the months after Lincoln's vigorous endorsement of the recruitment of black troops in March 1863, that policy went forward with energy and success. The War Department created the Bureau of Colored Troops and sent Adj. Gen. Lorenzo Thomas to the Mississippi Valley to organize black regiments. Two regiments of General Banks's Corps d'Afrique participated in an assault at Port Hudson on May 27. They were unsuccessful, but their courage and determination impressed many previously skeptical white soldiers. And after the fall of Port Hudson on July 9, Banks wrote to Lincoln praising the part that the Corps d'Afrique had played in the siege: "Our victory at Port Hudson could not have been accomplished at the time it was but for their assistance."[28]

During Grant's siege of Vicksburg, a new regiment of former slaves helped beat off a Confederate attack on the Union supply depot at Milliken's Bend on June 7. "The bravery of the blacks" in this battle, wrote

Charles A. Dana, who was with Grant's army, "completely revolutionized the sentiment of the army with regard to the employment of negro troops. I heard prominent officers who formerly in private had sneered at the idea of negroes fighting express themselves after that as heartily in favor of it."[29]

After the capture of Vicksburg, Lincoln wrote Grant urging him to help expand Lorenzo Thomas's recruitment efforts among the freed slaves in the region. These potential soldiers were "a resource which, if vigorously applied now, will soon close the contest," wrote the president. "It works doubly, weakening the enemy and strengthening us." Grant assured Lincoln of his "hearty support" for the policy of "arming the negro. This, with the emancipation of the negro, is the heavyest blow yet given the Confederacy. . . . By arming the negro we have added a powerful ally."[30]

The most widely publicized feat of black soldiers was the assault by the Fifty-fourth Massachusetts on Fort Wagner, a Confederate earthwork guarding the entrance to Charleston Bay. This attack took place July 18, just three days after the draft rioters in New York had lynched several black people, including the nephew of a sergeant in the

Fifty-fourth who was killed in the attack on Fort Wagner. Few Republican commentators failed to compare the cowardly white murderers in New York with the heroes of the Fifty-fourth, and to point out the moral: Black men who fought for the Union deserved more respect than white men who rioted against it.

Lincoln made the same point in one of his public letters, which was read aloud at a political rally in Illinois on September 3 and published in many Northern newspapers. Addressing himself to anti-emancipation Democrats (few of whom, however, attended this rally), Lincoln said that "some of the commanders of our armies in the field who have given us our most important successes, believe the emancipation policy, and the use of colored troops, constitute the heaviest blow yet dealt to the rebellion." After this allusion to Grant and Banks (whom he did not name), Lincoln added: "You say you will not fight to free negroes. Some of them seem willing to fight for you," that is, for the Union. In an obvious reference to the Fifty-fourth Massachusetts at Fort Wagner, the president predicted that when victory finally crowned Union arms, "there will be some black men who can remember that, with silent tongue, and clenched teeth, and steady eye, and well-poised bayonet, they have helped mankind on to this great consummation; while, I fear, there will be some white ones, unable to forget that, with malignant heart, and deceitful speech, they have strove to hinder it."[31]

Two weeks before writing this letter, Lincoln had met with the black abolitionist Frederick Douglass at the White House. Douglass asked the president to do what he could to rectify some of the discriminations against black soldiers — especially the inequality of pay between them and white soldiers. Lincoln sympathized with Douglass's request but pointed out that there was nothing he could do about it immediately. The legal authority for paying black soldiers was the Militia Act of 1862, which had specified that any black men recruited by the army should receive ten dollars per month as "laborers" — even if they were actually armed as soldiers (white privates received thirteen dollars per month plus a clothing allowance). Only Congress could change this policy, and the next session would not meet until December.

Lincoln went on to note, as Douglass recalled nearly twenty years later, that "the employment of colored troops at all was a great gain to the colored people — that the measure could not have been successfully adopted at the beginning of the war . . . that their enlistment was a serious offense to popular prejudice . . . that they were not to receive the same pay as white soldiers seemed a necessary concession to smooth the way to their employment at all as soldiers. . . . But I assure you, Mr. Douglass, that in the end they shall have the same pay as white soldiers."[32]

Another subject that Lincoln and Douglass discussed was the Confederate threat to reenslave captured black soldiers or even to execute them and their white officers. After Lincoln had announced in the Emancipation Proclamation that black recruits would be accepted as soldiers, Jefferson Davis had retaliated with an order that captured officers would be turned over to state governments for punishment as "criminals engaged in inciting servile insurrection." The punishment for that crime in slave states was death. Captured enlisted men were to be remanded to "the respective States to which they belong to be dealt with according to the laws of said States" — which meant, in effect, reenslavement. The Confederate Congress on May 30 enacted these policies into law, except that the captured officers were to be tried by military courts rather than by states.[33]

To prevent the Confederacy from carrying out such draconian policies, Secretary of War Stanton suspended the exchanges of Confederate officers so that these captives could be held as hostages against the Southern threat to execute Union prisoners.[34] The Confederacy did not officially carry out any executions. But individual Southern officers and enlisted men did sometimes shoot captured black soldiers or their officers in the field even before the infamous Fort Pillow and Poison Springs massacres in 1864. On July 30, 1863, Lincoln issued an order that "for every soldier of the United States killed in violation of the laws of war, a rebel soldier shall be executed; and for every one enslaved by the enemy or sold into slavery, a rebel soldier shall be placed at hard labor on the public works." Douglass praised this order at his meeting with Lincoln on August 10, but the president expressed reservations about enforcing it. "Retaliation was a terrible remedy," Douglass paraphrased Lincoln's words, "and one which was very difficult to apply — that, if once begun, there was no telling where it would end — that if he could get hold of the Confederate soldiers who had been guilty of treating colored soldiers as felons he could easily retaliate, but the thought of hanging men for a crime perpetrated by others was revolting to his feelings."[35]

The Lincoln administration never did execute a Confederate soldier or place any of them at hard labor. Reports trickled in, however, that some captured Union soldiers had been reenslaved. As Confederate officials made clear that they would not exchange black captives under the exchange cartel that had been in effect since July 1862, the Lincoln administration suspended exchanges until the Confederacy treated alike all prisoners wearing the uniform of the U.S. Army. By the end of 1863 the Confederates offered to exchange black prisoners who had been legally free when they enlisted (mostly from the Fifty-fourth Massachusetts). But the South would "die in the last ditch," said the Confederate exchange commissioner, before "giving up the right to send slaves back as property recaptured." If that was their policy, said Stanton, the twenty-six thousand Confederate soldiers in POW camps could stay there. To accept Confederate conditions would be "a shameful dishonor. . . . When they agree to exchange all alike there will be no difficulty." The journalist Noah Brooks, who discussed this matter with Lincoln, condemned the Confederacy's "insane pertinacity upon this subject. . . . Uncle Sam is firm, and will not give up his protection of his soldiers."[36]

Despite his disappointment with Meade and the Army of the Potomac, Lincoln was far more optimistic as the year 1863 approached its end than he had been during the previous two Decembers. The off-year elections had brought solid Republican victories almost everywhere, in contrast to the 1862 political contests. Observers (including Lincoln) interpreted these elections as a ringing endorsement of emancipation as a war policy. In his address at the dedication of the soldiers' cemetery at Gettysburg on November 19, Lincoln declared that those men gave "the last full measure of devotion" so that the nation founded four score and seven years earlier not only "shall not perish from the earth," but also "shall have a new birth of freedom."[37]

In his annual message to Congress on December 8, Lincoln acknowledged that the Emancipation Proclamation had been "followed by dark and doubtful days." But now, he said hopefully, "the crisis which threatened to divide the friends of the Union is past." Black soldiers had proved that they were "as good soldiers as any" and had helped convert many opponents to supporters of emancipation. Referring to indigenous movements for the abolition of slavery in Maryland and Missouri (which were exempted from the Emancipation Proclamation), Lincoln noted that neither state "three years ago would tolerate any restraint upon the extension of slavery into new territories," but they "only dispute now as to the best mode of removing it within their own limits." Commenting on these developments, an Illinois newspaper maintained that if the Emancipation Proclamation had been submitted to a referendum a year earlier, "there is little doubt that the voice of a majority would have been against it. And yet not a year has passed before it is approved by an overwhelming majority."[38]

With the war going well and large parts of several Confederate states controlled by Northern troops, Lincoln turned his attention to further steps to bring them back into the Union. Accompanying his message to Congress, the president issued a "Proclamation of Amnesty and Reconstruction." Under his constitutional authority to grant pardons for offenses against the United States, he offered "full pardon" and restoration of property "except as to slaves" to former participants in rebellion who would swear an oath of allegiance to the United States and to all laws and proclamations concerning emancipation. (Certain classes of high-ranking Confederate civil and military officials were exempted from this offer.) When the number of voters taking the oath in any state equaled 10 percent of the number who had voted in 1860, this loyal nucleus could reestablish a state government to which Lincoln promised executive recognition.[39]

This proclamation looked to the future readmission of former Confederate states to the Union as free states. But Lincoln envisaged its main short-term purpose as a war measure to weaken the Confederacy by attracting whites to the side of the Union. In that respect it was a sort of emancipation proclamation for free white men — to "emancipate" them from their Confederate allegiance. It was part of Lincoln's national strategy to weaken the Confederacy and to mobilize maximum support for the Union cause. The president had been nursing along this effort in occupied portions of Tennessee and Louisiana for more than a year. The Proclamation of Amnesty and Reconstruction codified the process.

Abolitionists and some radical Republicans objected to parts of this policy because, while it made freedom the basis of restoration, it did not enfranchise any black men nor did it strip the planter class of land or of political power if they took the oath of allegiance. In Louisiana particularly, many of the whites who took the oath were former Whigs of wealth and conservative inclinations, while the educated *gens de couleur libre* (free people of color) class in New Orleans remained disfranchised. Congressional Republicans wanted to raise the bar for white participation and to postpone reconstruction until the war was over, in order to carry out a more radical transformation of Southern society.

Lincoln was not necessarily averse to a more thorough postwar policy. But he insisted on his 10 percent plan as a *wartime* measure to weaken the rebellion by weaning away as many of its former supporters as possible. In Louisiana he wanted "a tangible nucleus which the remainder of the State may rally around as fast as it can." The purpose of his policy, Lincoln reiterated in March 1864, was "to suppress the insurrection and to restore the authority of the United States."[40] He ordered the Union commander in the occupied portion of Arkansas to support the newly elected state government as "the best you can do to suppress the rebellion." In July 1864 the president killed the Wade-Davis reconstruction bill by a pocket veto (by which a president can veto a bill passed at the end of a congressional session simply by not signing it). He explained that he was not "inflexibly committed to any single plan of restoration" and might be willing to carry out the more radical Wade-Davis plan once the war was over. But he was unwilling "that the free-state constitutions and governments, already adopted and installed in Arkansas and Louisiana, shall be set aside and held for nought, thereby repelling and discouraging the loyal citizens who have set up the same."[41]

Tensions between the president and Congress over reconstruction policy gave Lincoln some difficult moments in the election year of 1864. His main preoccupation, however, remained the war itself. Starting with promises of success following the great military victories in the second half of 1863, prospects for 1864 dimmed by the summer as failures and stalemates on several fronts brought a plunge in Northern morale and even threatened Lincoln's reelection.

9
IF IT TAKES
THREE YEARS MORE

During the first two months of 1864 a long-range epistolary discussion of military strategy took place among Lincoln and Halleck in Washington and Grant at his new headquarters in Nashville. Grant had renewed his recommendation for a campaign to capture Mobile and then to use that city as a base for a strike northeast through Alabama into Georgia. Lincoln vetoed this plan. The same foreign-policy goals that had favored a campaign to plant the flag in Texas instead of Mobile still prevailed. The French emperor Napoleon III had created a puppet Mexican government headed by Ferdinand Maximilian, archduke of Austria and now also emperor of Mexico. The small Union presence at Brownsville did nothing to deter the French from moving to consolidate their control of Mexico right up to the Texas border. Lincoln and Halleck wanted Gen. Nathaniel Banks to undertake a major campaign to invade Texas via the Red River valley through northwest Louisiana. If successful, this enterprise would have the added benefit of gaining control of more of Louisiana and bringing out thousands of bales of cotton supposedly stored there. If it were purely a matter of military strategy, Halleck informed Grant, a thrust against Mobile might make more sense, but as "a matter of political or State policy, connected with our foreign relations," the president considered it more important to "occupy and hold at least a portion of Texas." So Banks began preparing his Red River campaign.[1]

Without Banks's Army of the Gulf, troops for a Mobile expedition would have to come mainly from the army occupying East Tennessee. Grant proposed to divide that army and send part of it against the Confederates in northern Georgia and transfer the rest to New Orleans to advance against Mobile from there. Both Lincoln and Halleck opposed this division of forces. It might jeopardize the hard-won conquest of East Tennessee by creating an opportunity for a counter-offensive by Longstreet's two divisions, wintering near the Virginia-Tennessee border, in cooperation with the Army of Tennessee in northern Georgia, now commanded by Joseph E. Johnston. Lincoln was anxious about holding East Tennessee, considering it a top priority "both [from] a political and military point of view," Halleck told Grant. And when Union forces went on the offensive in the spring, a single concentrated thrust from Chattanooga into Georgia would be better than a complicated two-pronged campaign.[2]

Despite these rebuffs of his strategic recommendations, Grant was the hero of the hour and it was clear that he would soon become the top Union commander. A bill introduced by Elihu Washburne to revive the rank of lieutenant general (three stars), last held by George Washington, was making its way through Congress. Everyone knew that Grant would be the man, and that he would thus outrank everyone else. So Halleck, acting for Lincoln, invited Grant to submit his ideas on the best strategy to be pursued in Virginia.

If Grant had been more aware of the relations between Lincoln and his commanders in that theater during the past two years, he might have avoided another rebuff. He suggested that instead of moving against Lee in northern Virginia, the Army of the Potomac should be reduced to the minimum necessary for defensive purposes. The rest of it along with other troops should launch a campaign from Norfolk against Raleigh, North Carolina. This thrust, said Grant, would cut Lee's rail communications with the lower South and force him to come south to meet the threat, leaving Richmond to fall easily into Union hands.

Halleck promised to submit this plan to Lincoln but warned Grant that the president would not like it. Lincoln had made clear that Richmond was not the main objective; "that point is Lee's army." And the best way to defeat that army was to go at it directly. "Our main efforts in the next campaign should unquestionably be against the armies of Lee and Johnston," Halleck insisted. "All our available forces in the east should be concentrated against Lee's army." If Grant had any doubts about who was calling the strategic shots in this discussion, Halleck cleared them up in a letter to Sherman, who was certain to share it with his close friend Grant. Halleck considered himself "simply a military advisor" to Lincoln who "must obey and carry out" his decisions. "It is my duty to strengthen the hands of the President as Commander-in-Chief."[3]

Grant got the message. He also picked up, indirectly, another message from Lincoln. The president was concerned about a Grant boomlet for the presidency launched by some Democrats — even a few Republicans — and supported by a number of newspapers, especially the large-circulation *New York Herald.* Before promoting Grant to lieutenant general, Lincoln wanted assurance that he had no presidential ambitions. Lincoln could scarcely work with a general-in-chief who wanted to become commander in chief. Upset by the bandying of his name as a candidate, Grant wrote letters to several people declaring that "this is the last thing I desire. I would regard such a consummation unfortunate for myself if not for the country. . . . Nobody could induce me to think of being a presidential candidate, particularly so long as there is a possibility of having Mr. Lincoln reelected."[4]

Grant's disavowals were passed along to Lincoln, as the general intended. The president nominated Grant for lieutenant general, the Senate promptly confirmed him, and Lincoln summoned Grant to Washington to receive his commission. Through some mix-up, nobody was at the station to meet the general and his son Fred. They made their way to Willard's Hotel, where Grant asked for a room. Looking down his nose at the travel-worn, unimpressive figure in a dusty uniform, the desk clerk said he had a small room at the back of the top floor. All right, said Grant. As he signed the register "U. S. Grant and son," the clerk did a double take and fell all over himself to assign Grant the best suite in the house. From there the general went to the White House, where a public reception happened to be in progress. Lincoln welcomed him, and the guests nearly smothered Grant with their attentions until he climbed onto a sofa to escape that fate. The next day Grant became the highest-ranking officer in the army, and the day after that he replaced Halleck as general-in-chief. Halleck stepped down to fill a new position as chief of staff.[5]

Grant initially hoped to maintain his headquarters in the West. But Lincoln made it clear that he wanted him to come east "to see whether he cannot do something with the unfortunate Army of the Potomac."[6] Upon reflection Grant agreed, and decided to make his headquarters in the field with that army while Halleck remained in Washington to function as a clearinghouse for communications between Grant and other field commanders. Two of the first decisions Grant made as general-in-chief were to put Sherman in command of the West and to keep Meade as commander of the Army of the Potomac. Meade's position would be difficult, with Grant looking over his shoulder and making the strategic decisions. But the two generals took a liking to each other and discovered that they could work together.

In his memoirs, written two decades later, Grant described his first substantive discussion with Lincoln. The president, according to Grant, said that "he had never professed to be a military man or to know how campaigns should be conducted, and never wanted to interfere with them; but that procrastination on the part of commanders" had compelled him to take a more active part. "All he wanted or had ever wanted was someone who would take the responsibility and act." Grant, of course, was that someone. "He did not want to know what I proposed to do."[7]

Grant's account does not ring quite true. After all, the president had vetoed three of his suggestions several weeks earlier. And Lincoln *did* want to know what Grant was going to do, at least in a broad strategic sense. Over the next few weeks Grant worked out a coordinated strategy for all major fronts, and kept the president informed. Grant noted that in the past the various Union armies in different theaters had "acted independently, and without concert, like a balky team, no two ever pulling together."[8] Employing concentration in time, Grant ordered five separate armies to advance simultaneously from exterior lines against as many smaller Confederate armies to prevent them from using their interior lines to reinforce one or another of them.

The two principal Union forces were the Army of the Potomac and Sherman's army group in northern Georgia. "Lee's army will be your objective point," Grant told Meade, having absorbed Lincoln's dictum on that issue. "Wherever Lee goes, there you will go also." Grant directed Sherman "to move against Johnston's army, to break it up and to get into the interior of the enemy's country as far as you can, inflicting all the damage you can against their war resources."[9]

Three smaller Union armies were to coordinate their operations with Meade and Sherman. Benjamin Butler's Army of the James would advance up that river to threaten Richmond from the south and cut the vital rail line between Petersburg and Richmond. Franz Sigel would lead a small force south up the Shenandoah Valley to pin down Confederate units there. And after finishing the Red River campaign, Nathaniel Banks's Army of the Gulf would finally attack Mobile and move inland toward Georgia to prevent Confederate forces in Alabama from reinforcing Johnston.

Lincoln was impressed. Grant's coordinated strategy reminded him of his own "suggestions so constantly made and as constantly neglected, to Buell & Halleck et al to move at once upon the enemy's whole line so as to bring into action our great superiority in numbers." The president also offered one of his inimitable metaphors to describe the pinning-down task of the three smaller Union armies: "Those not skinning can hold a leg." Grant liked this expression so much that he used it himself in one of his dispatches to Sherman.[10]

Before these major spring campaigns began, a number of peripheral operations had taken place. Most of them turned out to be Confederate victories. With one exception (the Red River campaign) they were of little strategic consequence, but they did much to restore sagging Southern morale. And perhaps overconfident Northerners who expected Grant and Sherman to win the war by the Fourth of July should have taken notice of these Confederate successes as a possible omen. In February a small Union force invaded the interior of northern Florida from Jacksonville. One of its goals was to secure control of enough of Florida to begin the process of reconstruction there under Lincoln's 10 percent plan. But the invaders were routed at the Battle of Olustee on February 20. In March, Nathan Bedford Forrest's cavalry raided through western Tennessee, destroying Union communications and capturing garrisons, culminating in the notorious massacre of black troops and white Tennessee Unionists at Fort Pillow on April 12. A few days later a Confederate force under Brig. Gen. John Marmaduke routed a Federal foraging party at Poison Springs, Arkansas, and killed more than a hundred soldiers of the First Kansas Colored Infantry after they had been captured. At the same time, half a continent away, Brig. Gen. Robert F. Hoke's Southern infantry, aided by the ironclad CSS *Albemarle,* recaptured Plymouth, North Carolina, from the Federals.

One thing all of these Union defeats — Olustee, Fort Pillow, Poison Springs, and Plymouth — had in common was the deliberate murder of black Union soldiers who were wounded or had tried to surrender.[11] The most thoroughly documented of these atrocities was Fort Pillow, which presented the Lincoln administration with a dilemma. The president had threatened retaliation in his proclamation of July 30, 1863. "The difficulty is not in stating the principle," said Lincoln as reports about Fort Pillow were being investigated, "but in practically applying it."[12] On May 4 the president called a special cabinet meeting to discuss what to do about this matter. Gideon Welles stated the dilemma concisely: "The idea of retaliation — killing man for man — which is the popular noisy demand is barbarous." We "cannot yield to any [such] inhuman scheme of retaliation." Lincoln agreed that "blood cannot restore blood, and government should not act for revenge." The cabinet decided to have Forrest's officers and soldiers tried for murder if they managed to capture any of them, and to warn the Confederate government that a certain number of Southern officers in Northern prisons would be set aside as hostages against such occurrences in the future.[13]

There is no evidence that either decision was ever carried out. Nor were these the last occasions when black Union soldiers were executed in cold blood after capture. The whole controversy further strengthened the administration's determination to continue the refusal to exchange prisoners until the Confederates guaranteed equal treatment and exchange of black prisoners. The

Confederates continued to refuse. Lincoln undoubtedly agreed with the Union exchange commissioner who said that these cases "can only be effectually reached by a successful prosecution of the war." After all, "the rebellion exists on a question connected with the right or power of the South to hold the colored race in slavery; and the South will only yield this right under military compulsion." Thus "the loyal people of the United States [must] prosecute this war with all the energy that God has given them."[14]

That is what Grant and Lincoln wanted to do. But one part of Grant's plan for simultaneous advances on five fronts fell victim to another Union defeat before the big push was scheduled to begin in the first week of May. Grant had from the outset considered Banks's drive up the Red River toward Texas a wasteful diversion. He ordered Banks to get it over with as quickly as possible, leave an occupation force to secure northwestern Louisiana and show the flag in Texas, and take the main body of his troops to attack Mobile. But it was not to be. Banks started late, conducted the campaign poorly, and decided to retreat after his advance divisions were defeated at Mansfield, forty miles south of Shreveport, on April 8. The retreat was also disorderly and encumbered by the cotton and other plunder that poorly disciplined Union troops tried to carry with them. The only bright spot in the campaign was the remarkable exploit by a Wisconsin colonel with a lumbering background. When Adm. David D. Porter's gunboat fleet was stranded by low water and rapids in the Red River at Alexandria, Col. Joseph Bailey supervised the construction of wing dams that enabled the gunboats to shoot the rapids and saved the fleet from capture or destruction. The Army of the Gulf did not get back to southern Louisiana until May 26, a month too late to begin the aborted Mobile campaign.[15]

Grant was exasperated by this failure. He told Halleck he wanted Banks removed from command. Halleck found it necessary to tutor Grant on the political realities in Washington, which Halleck had been painfully learning to negotiate for almost two years. He informed Grant that the president wanted to delay acting on the request for Banks's removal until he could get more information on that general's conduct of the campaign. "General Banks is a personal friend of the President, and has strong supporters in and out of Congress," Halleck told Grant. "There will undoubtedly be a very strong opposition to his being removed or superseded." Lincoln would do it "very reluctantly, as it would give offense to many of his friends," and only if Grant took the responsibility of insisting on it as "a military necessity." The president "must have something, in a definite shape, to fall back on, as his justification."

Grant suggested a compromise that would leave Banks in administrative command of the Department of the Gulf but would place Maj. Gen. Edward R. S. Canby in field command of the army. Lincoln was agreeable — especially since he needed Banks to carry out his reconstruction policy in Louisiana. The change was made on May 7, 1864, and Canby began planning a campaign against Mobile. It would eventually begin in July, a year after Grant had first suggested it.[16]

This affair actually strengthened the bonds of understanding between Lincoln and Grant. The president deferred to Grant on a military matter that fell within his province as general-in-chief. But Grant learned that Lincoln's responsibilities as commander in chief included important political considerations that could never be fully divorced from questions of military command in a democracy — especially in an election year. This potentially divisive question was amicably settled just in time, for Grant was about to take the field with the Army of the Potomac in what came to be called the Overland campaign.

Despite military setbacks in marginal theaters during the early months of 1864, the Northern people had high expectations for main campaigns in Virginia and Georgia. Media attention focused overwhelmingly on the titanic contest of Grant versus Lee in Virginia. People crowded around newspaper and telegraph offices eager for news. These were "fearfully critical, anxious days," wrote a New York diarist, in which "the destinies of the continent for centuries" would be decided.[17]

The mood in Washington was also one of "painful suspense" that "almost unfits the mind for mental activity," reported Gideon Welles. No one was more anxious than the president. He told Welles on May 7 that he had not slept the previous night. Francis Carpenter, the artist staying in the White House while he worked on his famous painting of Lincoln reading the Emancipation Proclamation to the cabinet, wrote that during the first week of Grant's campaign, the president "scarcely slept at all." On one of those days Carpenter met Lincoln "clad in a long morning wrapper, pacing back and forth [along] a narrow passage leading to one of the windows, his hands behind him, great black rings under his eyes, his head bent forward on his breast."[18]

The Army of the Potomac crossed the Rapidan River on May 4 and began moving south through the "Wilderness" of Virginia, a thick second-growth forest of scrub oak and pine where the Battle of Chancellorsville had taken place exactly a year earlier. Lee decided to hit Grant in the flank in this difficult terrain that neutralized the Union advantage in numbers and artillery. Lee's initiative brought on two days of the most confused, frenzied fighting the war had yet seen. Although the toll of casualties — almost eighteen thousand Union and at least eleven thousand Confederate — suggested a Confederate victory, Grant refused to recognize it as such. He did not think in terms of victory or defeat in single set-piece battles, which had been the previous pattern in this theater, but rather in terms of a particular stage in a long campaign. Instead of retreating north of the river as Joe Hooker had done after a similar pounding at Chancellorsville, Grant headed south toward the crucial crossroads hamlet of Spotsylvania, where almost two weeks of heavy fighting exacted another eighteen thousand and twelve thousand casualties in the two armies.

After the two days of combat in the Wilderness, Grant had sent word to Lincoln by a newspaper reporter that whatever happened in the campaign, "there is to be no turning back." Two days later came a dispatch from Grant declaring that "I propose to fight it out on this line if it takes all summer."[19] Lincoln expressed deep satisfaction. "How near we have been to this thing before and failed," he said to John Hay and Francis Carpenter. "I believe if any other General had been at the Head of that army it would now have been on this side of the Rapidan. . . . The great thing about Grant . . . is his perfect coolness and persistency of purpose. . . . He has the *grit* of a bull-dog! Once let him get his 'teeth' *in,* and nothing can shake him off. . . . It is the dogged pertinacity of Grant that wins."[20]

Initial news reports in the North conveyed an impression of great Union victories, especially after a breakthrough at the Confederate "mule shoe" salient at Spotsylvania and the capture of three thousand men of Stonewall Jackson's old division on May 12.

GLORIOUS NEWS . . . IMMENSE REBEL LOSSES, blared headlines in the usually restrained *New York Times*. "The Virginia campaign approaches a Glorious consummation," added the *New York Herald*. The *New York Tribune* proclaimed that "Lee's Army as an effective force has practically ceased to exist" and LIBERTY — UNION — PEACE were nigh.[21]

Lincoln feared that such extravagant claims would boomerang if the news turned out to be too good to be true — which it soon did. "The people are too sanguine," he told Noah Brooks, who had become a quasi-official presidential spokesman. "They expect too much at once. . . . I wish when you write and speak to people you would do all you can to correct the impression that the war in Virginia will end right off victoriously."[22]

Sure enough, in the third week of May both the news and the public mood began to turn sour. The two auxiliary campaigns in Virginia that Grant had designed to "hold a leg" while the Army of the Potomac did the skinning had failed. Advancing up the Shenandoah Valley, Franz Sigel's small army was defeated by an even smaller Confederate force at New Market on May 15; some of those Confederate troops were then able to reinforce Lee. The advance of Benjamin Butler's Army of the James against Petersburg and the railroad north to Richmond was also frustrated by Butler's tentativeness and quarrels with his subordinates, and the effective fighting of a Confederate force commanded by Pierre G. T. Beauregard that defeated Butler on May 16 in the Battle of Drewry's Bluff, seven miles south of Richmond. The Federals retreated to a defensive position across the narrow neck of land between the James and Appomattox Rivers just north of Petersburg. The Confederates constructed their own entrenchments across the neck where the Army of the James, in Grant's words, was "as completely shut off from further operations directly against Richmond as if it had been in a bottle strongly corked."[23] Beauregard sent several thousand men to reinforce Lee.

While this was going on, Union wounded from the Wilderness and Spotsylvania arrived by the thousands daily at military hospitals in Washington. The shock of these casualties — thirty thousand killed and wounded in two weeks — brought home the cost of the war more than ever before. "The carnage has been unexampled," wrote Attorney General Edward Bates in his diary. Elizabeth Blair Lee, whose husband was an acting rear admiral, one brother a major general with Sherman and the other postmaster general, wrote that "the lines [of] ambulances & the moans of the poor suffering men were too much for my nerves."[24]

As anxious relatives scanned the casualty lists in Northern newspapers and read about Butler's and Sigel's defeats, the Northern mood grew "despondent and bad."[25] It grew worse as Grant's attack at Cold Harbor on June 3 achieved nothing but seven thousand Union casualties in an hour. A series of assaults on Confederate defenses at Petersburg on June 15–18 cost another twelve thousand Union losses with apparently nothing to show for them except the prospect of a long siege. Even in Georgia the advance of Sherman some seventy miles during May also stalled twenty miles short of Atlanta in June.

Lincoln's concern changed from one of dampening excessive Northern optimism in May to one of stemming the steep decline of morale in June. In a speech on June 16 at the fair in Philadelphia to raise money for the United States Sanitary Commission, the president acknowledged that "war, at best, is terrible, and this war of ours, in its magnitude and duration, is one of the most terrible. . . . It has carried mourning to almost every home, until it can almost be said that the 'heavens are hung in black.' " Many were asking, "When is the war to end?" Lincoln wished he could answer, "Soon." But it must and would end only in victory. "We accepted this war for an object, a worthy object, and the war will end when that object is attained. Under God, I hope it never will until that time. [Great cheering] General Grant said, I am going through on this line if it takes all summer [Cheers] . . . I say we are going through on this line if it takes three years more. [Cheers]"[26]

The Republican national convention renominated Lincoln almost unanimously on June 7. He had staved off an early challenge from Chase, who was the favorite of radical Republicans dissatisfied with the president's reconstruction policy. But even after his renomination, Lincoln knew that his support from the radical wing of the party remained tenuous. On May 31 a splinter group of abolitionists and radical German Americans had nominated John C. Frémont for president. Frémont remained bitter toward Lincoln for removing him from his first command in 1861 and not giving him a third chance after he had resigned from his second in June 1862. Frémont's challenge was a marginal one, however; the main danger to Lincoln's standing in the party came from within it. If the war continued to go badly, portents of a movement for a new convention to nominate someone else might become a reality.

This murky political situation impinged on a thorny command problem in the Army of the James. It concerned Benjamin Butler. This former Democrat, who had supported Jefferson Davis for the Democratic presidential nomination in 1860, was one of the most remarkable political chameleons of the age. Having been commissioned a major general of volunteers so early in the war, as a way of mobilizing Democrats for the war effort, Butler outranked almost all other generals still in the army in 1864. More than once Lincoln must have rued that early appointment. But in 1861 Butler's success in getting troops to Washington and his initiative in securing Baltimore seemed to have justified it. His invention of the "contraband" designation for Confederate-owned slaves made him something of a hero to antislavery Republicans and began Butler's migration toward the radical wing of that party. His efficient but heavy-handed administration of occupied Louisiana in 1862 — and especially his organization of black regiments there before the administration sanctioned this policy — expanded his radical credentials.

But reports of corruption, of trading with the enemy, and of harassing foreign consuls in New Orleans caused Lincoln to replace Butler with General Banks in December 1862. The president was surprised, and perhaps dismayed, by the political fallout from Butler's removal. The paunchy, squint-eyed general had built a strong constituency among Republicans while retaining support from the prowar wing of the Democratic Party. Lincoln felt compelled to find a new command for him. In the fall of 1863 the president appointed him head of the Department of Virginia and North Carolina, where he also became commander of the newly formed Army of the James.[27]

The "bottling up" of that army after its defeat in the Battle of Drewry's Bluff led to recriminations between Butler and his two corps commanders, Quincy Gillmore and William F. Smith. The latter was the same Smith who had worked to undermine Burnside in December 1862 and whom Lincoln had transferred to the Western theater. There he had come under Grant's command at Chattanooga and had impressed Grant with his ability. Gillmore was an artillery expert whose guns had compelled the surrender of Fort Pulaski in 1862 and had pulverized Fort Sumter to rubble in 1863. Grant put these two professionals in command of the two corps of the Army of the James in the hope that they would provide the necessary leadership to compensate for Butler's lack of combat experience — but it did not work out that way. There was plenty of blame to share among the three generals for their failure, and they soon began quarreling with one another.

Grant had to intervene. When the Army of the Potomac invested Petersburg in June 1864, the Army of the James was in effect integrated with it under Grant's overall leadership. Because of Butler's seniority, however, he would command the whole if Grant was absent. Considering this possibility unacceptable, Grant asked Halleck on July 1 to have the president transfer Butler to another theater. That would be easier said than done, Halleck told Grant. He proposed an alternative that might be described as the Banks solution: Kick Butler upstairs as a department administrator, as with Banks in Louisiana, and put Smith in field command of the troops. Grant initially liked the idea, and Lincoln reluctantly approved the order on July 7.

At some point in the next few days, however, Grant changed his mind and had the order quashed. He had become disillusioned with Smith, who possessed an unfortunate tendency to criticize everyone, including Meade and even Grant himself. Having learned about the political sensitivity of shelving Banks, Grant may have realized that doing the same with Butler was even more problematic. Some of Salmon P. Chase's former supporters had turned their attention to Butler as a possible presidential nominee who could attract War Democrats as well as disaffected Republicans if the deteriorating military situation caused Lincoln's candidacy to collapse. The president may have conveyed to Grant the political danger of alienating Butler (if so, documentation is lacking). Or Grant may have figured it out on his own. In any event Butler and Smith could not get along. One of them would have to go, and Grant decided to send Smith packing. An amused officer on General Meade's staff commented: "Thus did Smith the Bald try the Macchiavelli against Butler the cross-eyed, and got floored in the first round."[28]

Lincoln had plenty of other worries besides Butler in that ill-starred month of July 1864.

Despite the behind-the-scenes intrigues among Republicans, the greater threat to his reelection — and to the war effort — was the surging strength of the Democratic Party. The peace wing of that party thrived on the growing public conviction that the war was a failure. And more than anything else, Gen. Jubal Early's raid to the outskirts of Washington in mid-July fed that conviction.

Early's raid had begun when Lee detached his corps from the Army of Northern Virginia in mid-June to drive away a Union force threatening Lynchburg. Gen. David Hunter had replaced Franz Sigel as commander of Union troops in the Shenandoah Valley. Hunter advanced toward Lynchburg but retreated into West Virginia when confronted by Early's corps. Seeing an open road north to the Potomac, Early seized it, crossed into Maryland, and marched on Washington after pushing aside a cobbled-together Union blocking force in the Battle of Monocacy, near Frederick, on July 9.

Here a stunning reversal of the fortunes of war. Instead of capturing Richmond by the Fourth of July, as many optimistic Northerners had anticipated two months earlier, they saw a Confederate force of fifteen thousand men threatening

Washington. Grant had combed most of the heavy artillery regiments out of the Washington defenses and converted them into infantry to make up the large losses in the Army of the Potomac. As Early approached the capital on July 10, therefore, almost the only soldiers in the extensive fortifications that ringed the city were convalescents from army hospitals and hastily mobilized emergency militia.

Grant and Halleck had initially discounted Early's threat. Grant even denied for several days that Early's corps had been detached from the main army. Not until July 6 did Halleck acknowledge that "the invasion is of a pretty formidable character." In response Grant sent from Petersburg a division of the Sixth Corps and some cavalry, which fought at Monocacy on July 9. They slowed Early by a day. On July 10 Lincoln asked Grant to leave enough troops to hold the siege lines on the Richmond/Petersburg front and to bring the rest to Washington. The president's purpose was not only the defense of the capital. Once again he saw in a Confederate invasion an opportunity to trap the invaders before they could get back home. He wanted Grant to "make a vigorous effort to destroy the enemy's force in this vicinity. I think there is really a fair chance to do this if the movement is prompt."[29]

Grant replied that he could not come himself but would send the rest of the Sixth Corps plus a division of the Army of the Gulf (Nineteenth Corps) that was already on its way from Louisiana. As advance units of the Sixth Corps began arriving on July 11, Lincoln went personally to Fort Stevens north of the city, where they were skirmishing with Early's troops. The six-foot-four-inch president wearing his top hat made a large target as he peered over the parapet at enemy sharpshooters. As John Hay recorded the incident, "A soldier roughly ordered him to get down or he would have his head knocked off."[30]

By tradition this soldier was Capt. Oliver Wendell Holmes, Jr., a thrice-wounded veteran who was serving as a staff officer for Sixth Corps commander Gen. Horatio Wright. "Get down, you fool," Holmes reportedly said, not realizing in the excitement of the moment that he was speaking to the president. There is no definitive evidence either for or against the story that Holmes was the man who ordered Lincoln to get down. The next day, as the Sixth Corps was preparing to drive Early away, Lincoln returned to Fort Stevens. A Union officer was shot while standing close to the president. This time General Wright himself ordered Lincoln to take cover (more politely than Holmes).[31]

Even as Early was probing the Washington defenses, Lincoln's "only concern," according to John Hay, was "whether we can bag or destroy this force in our front." The president urged General Wright to pursue the retreating enemy and cut them off before they could retreat across the Potomac. But it did not happen. Wright's pursuit was too slow, and on July 14 Lincoln sarcastically told Hay: "Wright telegraphs that he thinks the enemy are all across the Potomac but that he has halted & sent out an infantry reconnaissance, for fear he might come across the rebels & catch some of them."[32] By coincidence it was exactly a year earlier that Lincoln had written his unsent letter to General Meade deploring the escape of the Army of Northern Virginia across the same river after Gettysburg.

Responsibility for the Union forces pursuing Early was fragmented among Wright, Hunter (whose Eighth Corps had returned from West Virginia), and the commanders of the Washington and Baltimore defenses. The logical person to take charge and coordinate these forces was General Halleck. But as Hay accurately noted, "There seems to be no head about this whole affair. Halleck hates responsibility: hates to give orders." The usually mild-mannered Edward Bates undoubtedly expressed Lincoln's sentiments also when he lamented: "Alas! for the impotence or treachery of our military leaders! The raiders have retired across the Potomac, with all their booty safe! Nobody seems disposed to hinder them." On July 15 Bates recorded that "I spoke my mind, very plainly," to Lincoln and three other cabinet members "about the ignorant imbecility of the late military operations, and my contempt for Genl. Halleck." Nobody disagreed with him.[33]

Lincoln tried to cut through this military red tape by combining the four military departments under a single commander. Grant suggested Gen. William B. Franklin for the position, but Halleck knew that the president would never accept this McClellan protégé who had done so much to undermine Burnside. Grant then suggested Meade, who seemed to have outlived his usefulness as commander of the Army of the Potomac. Lincoln undoubtedly agreed — in principle at least. But as a practical matter he vetoed this idea because in the current depression of public opinion the transfer of Meade would only intensify the demoralization. Recalling the post-Gettysburg Meade, Lincoln also doubted whether he was the right man to chase down and destroy Early. So on July 27 Lincoln issued an order placing Halleck himself temporarily in charge of the merged departments. Aware of Halleck's shortcomings, however, the president telegraphed Grant to meet him at Fort Monroe on July 31 for a personal conference to decide on a long-term solution of the mess.[34]

Before this meeting took place, two more disasters occurred, both on July 30, that caused a further plunge in Northern morale. On that date Jubal Early's cavalry rode into Chambersburg, Pennsylvania, demanded a ransom of five hundred thousand dollars, and burned down the town when its residents could not comply. Two hundred miles away near Petersburg, soldiers of the Forty-eighth Pennsylvania set off a gunpowder mine that blew a huge hole in the Confederate line. But Union commanders bungled the subsequent assault through the gap. The Confederates sealed it off with a counterattack that inflicted four thousand casualties on the Union forces (including several dozen black soldiers who were shot after they had surrendered). Grant watched the fiasco of this failed attack, and reported disconsolately to Washington: "It was the saddest affair I have witnessed in the war. Such opportunity for carrying fortifications I have never seen and do not expect again to have."[35]

Neither Lincoln nor Grant could have been in a good mood when they met on July 31 for a discussion that lasted five hours. No record was made of their conversation. Lincoln may have come as close as he ever did to chewing out Grant for all the failures that had occurred during the past six weeks.[36] Whatever else happened at this meeting, one thing is clear: The commander in chief and general-in-chief agreed to put the young but hard-driving commander of the Army of the Potomac's cavalry, Gen. Philip H. Sheridan, in charge of the newly created Middle Military Division (later called the Army of the Shenandoah). The day after this meeting Grant telegraphed Halleck that he was sending Sheridan for "temporary duty whilst the enemy is being expelled from the border. . . . I want Sheridan put in command of all the troops in the field, with instructions to put himself south of the enemy [Early had given signs of moving north across the Potomac again] and follow him to the death."[37]

Because General Hunter outranked Sheridan and Grant had not clarified their relationship, Halleck quibbled and delayed in carrying out this order. An exasperated Lincoln telegraphed Grant on August 3: "I have seen your despatch in which you say 'I want Sheridan put in command of all the troops in the field . . . to put himself South of the enemy, and follow him to the death.' " Lincoln liked the sound of this. "But please look over the despatches you may have received from here, even since you made that order, and discover, if you can, that there is any idea in the head of anyone here, of 'putting our army South of the enemy' or of 'following him to the *death*' in any direction. I repeat to you it will neither be done or attempted unless you watch it every day, and hour, and force it."[38]

This thinly veiled rebuke of both Grant and Halleck brought Grant to Washington on two hours' notice. From there he went on to western Maryland to sort out the command relationship between Sheridan and Hunter. The latter resigned his post (whether with good or ill grace is not clear) in favor of Sheridan. That small, bandy-legged major general with his trademark porkpie hat thus became the sole commander of a powerful new army consisting of the Sixth Corps, Hunter's Eighth Corps, two divisions of the Nineteenth Corps lately from Louisiana, and three divisions of cavalry. It was an imposing command for the thirty-three-year-old Sheridan, and many wondered whether he was equal to it. Lincoln shared that concern. Sheridan would soon assuage those doubts in spectacular fashion. Until then, however, the Union cause would endure a long night of despair before dawn finally came.

10
NO PEACE
WITHOUT VICTORY

The Northern people and their president had endured other times of despondency during the war: the early winter of 1861–62, the summer of 1862, and the winter and spring of 1862–63. But at no time did their morale sink lower than in the summer of 1864. By the Fourth of July the two main Union armies seemed to be bogged down in front of Richmond/Petersburg and Atlanta after suffering a combined total of ninety-five thousand casualties in the worst carnage of the war. In the Army of the Potomac the number of battle casualties for the two months from May 5 to July 4 was nearly two-thirds of the total in *the previous three years.* Some people in the North — including Mary Lincoln — began calling Grant a "butcher."

"Who shall revive the withered hopes that bloomed at the beginning of General Grant's campaign?" asked an editorial in the *New York World* on July 12. The bloody stalemate had become "a national humiliation," declared the *World*. "This war, as now conducted, is a failure without hope of other issue than the success of the rebellion."[1] With unfortunate timing Lincoln on July 18 issued a call for five hundred thousand more volunteers, with deficiencies in meeting quotas to be filled by a new draft. This call was "a cry of distress," lamented the *World*. "Who is responsible for the terrible and unavailing loss of life which renders five hundred thousand new men necessary so soon after the opening of a campaign that promised to be triumphant?"[2]

The *World* was a Democratic newspaper; with the presidential election approaching, it left readers with no doubts that it considered the Republican commander in chief responsible for this humiliating failure. Many Republicans were dejected. "The immense slaughter of our brave men chills and sickens us all," wrote Gideon Welles. "It is impossible for the country to bear up under these monstrous errors and wrongs." A State Department translator visited Philadelphia in early August. "What a difference between now and last year!" he wrote in his diary. "No signs of any enthusiasm, no flags; most of the best men gloomy and despair-

ing."[3] From New York City, George Templeton Strong could "see no bright spot anywhere." Even Benjamin Butler's wife, Sarah,
wondered, "What is all this struggling and
fighting for? This ruin and death to thousands of families? . . . What advancement of
mankind to compensate for the present hor-
rible calamities?"[4]

Sarah Butler's plaintive question has
surfaced in all wars, but it had a special
force in that summer of discontent. As
before in the war, the peace wing of the
Democratic Party gained strength in propor-
tion to the public perception of the war as a
failure. The Copperheads looked forward to
victory on a peace platform in the presidential election. "Stop the War!" demanded
editorials in Copperhead newspapers. "If
nothing else would impress upon the people
the absolute necessity of stopping this war,
its utter failure to accomplish any results . . .
would be sufficient." A Boston Democrat
believed Northerners were coming to the
conclusion that "the Confederacy perhaps
can never really be beaten, that the attempts
to win might after all be too heavy a load to
carry, and that perhaps it is time to agree to
a peace without victory."[5]

Several Democratic district conventions
passed resolutions calling for a cease-fire

and peace negotiations. Confederate agents in Canada, who were subsidizing several Democratic newspapers and politicians across the border, encouraged the idea that such negotiations might pave the way to eventual reunion. First might come "a treaty of amity and commerce," suggested one of the Confederate agents, Clement C. Clay, followed "possibly" by "an alliance defensive, or even, for some purposes, both defensive and offensive." If Peace Democrats were taken in by such double-talk, wrote Clay to Confederate secretary of state Judah Benjamin, who oversaw these Canadian operations, he was careful not to dispel their "fond delusion."[6]

Confederate hopes in 1864 were based on a military strategy of holding out until the Northern elections and inflicting heavy casualties on attacking Union forces to turn the electorate against Lincoln. A War Department official in Richmond said that "if we can only *subsist*" until the Northern elections, "giving an opportunity for the Democrats to elect a President . . . we may have peace." Gen. James Longstreet predicted that "if we can break up the enemy's arrangements early, and throw him back, he will not be able to recover his position or his morale until the Presidential election is over, and then we shall have a new President to treat with."[7]

By July 1864 that strategy seemed to be working. The peace contagion had spread well beyond the Copperheads. The observation by the *Richmond Dispatch,* the Confederacy's largest newspaper, that a majority of Northerners would accept peace even at the price of Confederate independence may not have been far wrong. "They are sick at heart of the senseless waste of life," declared the *Dispatch.* In New York, George Templeton Strong was "most seriously perturbed" by the "increasing prevalence" of "aspirations for 'peace at any price.' " The astute Republican politico Thurlow Weed wrote to William H. Seward in August that Lincoln's reelection was "an impossibility" because "the people are wild for peace."[8]

Horace Greeley agreed with this assessment. In early July he set in motion a bizarre, failed peace initiative that nevertheless had important consequences. From a self-styled "intermediary" Greeley received word that two of the Confederate agents in Canada were accredited by Jefferson Davis to negotiate a peace settlement. The credulous editor enclosed this information in a letter to Lincoln on July 7. "Our bleeding, bankrupt, almost dying country," Greeley declaimed, "longs for peace — shudders at the prospect of fresh conscriptions, of further wholesale devastations, and of new rivers of human blood." Therefore "I entreat you to submit overtures for pacification to the Southern insurgents."[9]

Lincoln did not believe for a moment that the Confederate agents had genuine negotiating powers. And even if they did, the president knew that Jefferson Davis's inflexible condition for peace was Confederate independence. Yet, given the political context in July, Lincoln could not appear to rebuff any peace overture, however spurious. He also understood that the job of commander in chief was not only to conduct the war but also to shape the conditions for peace. In this case, moreover, he thought he saw a chance to rally flagging Northern spirits by demonstrating that any peace short of military victory was unacceptable. So Lincoln immediately sent Greeley a telegram authorizing him to bring to Washington under a safe-conduct pass "any person anywhere professing to have any proposition of Jefferson Davis in writing, for peace, embracing the restoration of the Union and abandonment of slavery."[10]

Lincoln's response put Greeley on the spot by making him a guarantor of the agents' credentials and a witness to the president's apparent willingness to negotiate. Greeley balked, but Lincoln prodded him into action by sending John Hay to join Greeley at Niagara Falls, Canada, to meet with the Confederates. The president was willing to compromise his principle of refusing to acknowledge officially the existence of the Confederate government by insisting on the agents' acceptance of restoration of the Union as a prerequisite for negotiations. Hay carried to Niagara Falls a letter from Lincoln addressed "To Whom It May Concern," stating that "any proposition which embraces the restoration of peace, the integrity of the whole Union, and the abandonment of slavery, and which comes by and with an authority that can control the armies now at war with the United States will be received and considered by the Executive government of the United States, and will be met by liberal terms on other substantial and collateral points."[11]

This letter was a crucial document that framed all discussions of peace from then on. Lincoln intended it not only to lay out his own conditions for peace but also to elicit the Confederacy's unacceptable counteroffer. On this occasion, however, the Southern agents outmaneuvered Lincoln.

They admitted to Greeley and Hay that they had no authority to negotiate peace. Then they released to the press a letter addressed to Greeley that accused Lincoln of sabotaging the possibility of negotiations by prescribing conditions he knew to be unacceptable to the Confederacy. Shedding crocodile tears, they expressed "profound regret" that the South's genuine desire for a peace "mutually just, honorable, and advantageous to the North and South" had not been met with equal "moderation and equity" by Lincoln. Instead, his "To Whom It May Concern" letter meant "no bargaining, no negotiations, no truces with rebels except to bury their dead. . . . If there be any citizen of the Confederate States who has clung to the hope that peace is possible," Lincoln's draconian terms "will strip from their eyes the last film of such delusion." The Confederate agents urged "patriots and Christians" in the North "who shrink appalled from the illimitable vistas of private misery and public calamity" presented by Lincoln's policy of perpetual war to "recall the abused authority and vindicate the outraged civilization of their country" by voting Lincoln out of office in November.[12]

This letter was, as the *New York Times*

recognized, "an electioneering dodge on a grand scale" to damage Lincoln "by making him figure as an obstacle to peace." It worked. As Clement C. Clay reported with satisfaction to Judah Benjamin, Northern Democratic newspapers "denounce Mr. Lincoln's manifesto in strong terms, and many Republican presses (among them the New York Tribune) admit it was a blunder. . . . From all I can see or hear, I am satisfied that this correspondence has tended strongly toward consolidating the Democracy and dividing the Republicans."[13]

Greeley did indeed criticize Lincoln both publicly and privately. The president, he wrote in an editorial, made "a very grave mistake" by announcing his own terms instead of asking the rebels to state *their* terms first. In a remarkable letter to Lincoln on August 9, Greeley chastised the commander in chief for giving the impression that his policy was "No truce! No armistice! No negotiation! No mediation! Nothing but [Confederate] surrender at discretion! I never heard of such fatuity before."[14]

Greeley may have had in mind an editorial in the *New York Times,* which spoke for the administration. "Peace is a consummation devoutly to be wished," declared the *Times,* but not peace at the price of the Union. "War alone can save the Republic. . . . If the Southern people will not give us peace as their fellow-countrymen, we shall secure it as their conquerors. We know this is not gracious language. But it is native fact." Greeley deplored such language, he told Lincoln, because "to the general eye, it now seems the rebels are anxious to negotiate and that we repulse their advances. . . . If this impression be not removed we shall be beaten out of sight next November."[15]

Greeley was right about the potential political consequences of this affair. The Confederates had scored a propaganda triumph and given the Democrats a boost. Lincoln sought to neutralize the setback by sanctioning the publicizing of another and almost simultaneous peace contact. On July 17 two Northerners met under flag of truce with Jefferson Davis and Judah Benjamin in Richmond. They were James R. Gilmore, a journalist, and Col. James Jaquess of the Seventy-third Illinois, on furlough and temporarily resuming his peacetime vocation as a Methodist clergyman who wished to stop fellow Christians from slaughtering one another. Lincoln had given them a pass through Union lines in Virginia with the understanding that their mission was strictly unofficial — although they were well acquainted with Lincoln's conditions for peace. Davis decided to meet with them because, like Lincoln, he had to consider the desire for peace among his own people and could not afford to spurn any apparent opportunity for negotiations.

Gilmore and Jaquess informally repeated the terms Lincoln had offered in his Proclamation of Amnesty and Reconstruction the previous December: reunion, emancipation, and amnesty. According to Gilmore's account, Davis responded angrily: "Amnesty, Sir, applies to criminals. We have committed no crime. At your door lies all the misery and crime of this war. . . . We are fighting for Independence — and that, or extermination, we *will* have. . . . You may 'emancipate' every negro in the Confederacy, but *we will be free.* We will govern ourselves . . . if we have to see every Southern plantation sacked, and every Southern city in flames."[16]

Upon his return north, Gilmore published a brief account of the meeting in a Boston newspaper and a subsequent detailed narrative in *Atlantic Monthly.* Lincoln approved these articles because they shifted part of the burden of refusing to negotiate from his shoulders to Davis's. The *New York Times* immediately grasped this point. The Gilmore-Jaquess mission, declared the *Times,* "proved of extreme service . . . because it established that Jeff. Davis will listen to no proposals of peace that do not embrace disunion. . . . In view of the efforts now being made by the Peace Party of the North to delude our people into a belief that peace is now practicable without disunion," Davis's words were "peculiarly timely and valuable."[17]

The publicity surrounding these peace overtures should have put to rest the Copperhead argument that the nation could have peace *and* reunion without military victory. But it did not. At the rock-bottom point of Northern morale in August 1864 — when, as Thurlow Weed said, "the people are wild for peace" — Democrats were able to slide around the awkward problem of Davis's conditions by pointing to Lincoln's second condition — "abandonment of slavery" — as the real stumbling block to peace. From across the political spectrum, from Copperheads to War Democrats — and even beyond to some Republicans — came denunciations of the president for his "prostitution of the war into an abolition crusade." Democratic newspapers proclaimed that "tens of thousands of white men must bite the dust to allay the negro mania of the President." For that purpose "our soil is drenched in blood . . . the widows wail and the children hunger." Emancipation was now Lincoln's war aim; "the idea of restoring the Union no longer troubles the Executive brain."[18]

The *New York World* was closely affiliated with Gen. George B. McClellan, the leading contender for the Democratic presidential nomination. The *World* claimed that Lincoln "prefers to tear a half million more white men from their homes . . . to continue a war for the abolition of slavery rather than entertain a proposition for the return of the seceded states with their old rights." No such proposition existed, of course, but Democratic newspapers convinced thousands of Northern voters that the Confederate government *would have made* such a proposition if Lincoln had not required abandonment of slavery as "a *ne plus ultra* in the terms of peace," as the *New York Herald* put it.[19]

Even some Republican editors expressed "painful and perplexing surprise" that Lincoln had made "the abolition of slavery the principal object of prosecuting the war."[20] Horace Greeley, who two years earlier had criticized Lincoln's slowness to act against slavery, now condemned him for insisting on what Greeley had then demanded. "We do not contend," wrote Greeley in a widely reprinted *Tribune* editorial, "that reunion is possible or endurable only on the basis of Universal Freedom. . . . War has its exigencies which cannot be foreseen . . . and Peace is often desirable on other terms than those of our own choice." George Templeton Strong sadly concluded that Lincoln's emancipation condition was a "blunder" that "may cost him his election. . . . [It has] given the disaffected and discontented a weapon that doubles their power of mischief."[21]

The enormous pressure on Lincoln to drop his "abandonment of slavery" condition for peace negotiations almost caused him to succumb. On August 17 he drafted a letter to a Wisconsin newspaper editor who had previously supported the administration but said he could no longer do so if the president intended the war to continue until slavery was abolished. "To me," Lincoln began his letter, "it seems plain that saying re-union and abandonment of slavery would be considered, if offered, is not saying that nothing *else* or *less* would be considered." Lincoln concluded the letter with these words: "If Jefferson Davis wishes . . . to know what I would do if he were to offer peace and re-union, saying nothing about slavery, let him try me."[22]

In the same draft, however, and in an interview two days later with a pair of Wisconsin Republicans, the commander in chief explained forcefully and eloquently why he included abandonment of slavery as a necessary condition for a peace that restored the Union. "No human power can subdue this rebellion without using the emancipation lever as I have done," he insisted. Lincoln pointed out that one hundred thousand or more black soldiers and sailors were fighting for the Union. "If they stake their lives for us they must be prompted by the strongest motive — even the promise of freedom. And the promise being made, must be kept." To jettison emancipation as a condition, in such a public way, would "ruin the Union cause itself," Lincoln insisted. "All recruiting of colored men would instantly cease, and all colored men in our service would instantly desert us. And rightfully too. Why should they give their lives for us, with full notice of our purpose to betray them? . . . I should be damned in time and eternity for so doing. The world shall know that I will keep my faith to friends and enemies, come what will."[23]

Recognizing the inconsistency of these sentiments with his "let Jefferson Davis try me" challenge, Lincoln filed that letter away unsent. When he did so, he and everyone else expected that he would be defeated for reelection on the peace issue. "I am going to be beaten," he told a visitor, "and unless some great change takes place *badly* beaten." On August 23 Lincoln wrote his famous "blind memorandum" and asked cabinet members to sign it sight unseen (probably to prevent a leak): "This morning, as for some days past, it seems exceedingly probable that this Administration will not be re-elected. Then it will be my duty to so co-operate with the President elect, as to save the Union between the election and the inauguration; as he will have secured his election on such ground that he can not possibly save it afterwards."[24]

This memorandum may have been prompted by a letter the president received that day from Henry Raymond, who was both editor of the *New York Times* and chairman of the National Executive Committee managing Lincoln's reelection campaign. "The tide is setting strongly against us," wrote Raymond. "Two special causes are assigned to this great reaction in public sentiment, — the want of military success, and the impression . . . that we can have peace with Union if we would . . . [but] that we are not to have peace *in any event* under this Administration until Slavery is abandoned." To correct this impression, Raymond urged Lincoln to appoint a commissioner to *"make distinct proffers of peace to Davis . . . on the sole condition"* of reunion, leaving "all the other questions to be settled in a convention of all the people of all the States." Of course, Raymond added, Davis would reject such a proffer, and this rejection would "dispel all the delusions about peace that prevail in the North . . . [and] reconcile public sentiment to the War, the draft, & the tax as inevitable necessities."[25]

Once again Lincoln seemed to yield to such pressure. On August 24 he drafted instructions for Raymond to go to Richmond and "propose, on behalf [of] this government, that upon the restoration of the Union and national authority, the war shall cease at once, all remaining questions to be left for adjustment by peaceful modes." Lincoln's private secretaries and later biographers, John G. Nicolay and John Hay, maintained that Lincoln never had any intention of sending Raymond to Richmond. His purpose in drafting this document, they asserted, was to make Raymond "a witness of its absurdity."[26]

In any event Raymond and the rest of the National Executive Committee met with Lincoln and three cabinet members on August 25. The committeemen, according to Nicolay, were "laboring under a severe fit of despondency and discouragement . . . almost the condition of a disastrous panic." Lincoln convinced them that the proposed mission to Richmond "would be utter ruination . . . worse than losing the Presidential contest — it would be ignominiously surrendering it in advance."[27] To back away from emancipation would not only betray a promise; it would also give the impression of an administration floundering in impotence and would alienate the radical wing of the Republican Party.[28] Lincoln may have been aware of closed-door meetings among some Republicans to plan a maneuver to get both Lincoln and Frémont to withdraw their candidacies and to hold a new convention to name another candidate — Chase, Butler, or even Grant! Whether or not Lincoln knew anything of these desperate intrigues, he did know that he had been renominated on a platform calling for the "unconditional surrender" of the Rebels and pledging a constitutional amendment to abolish slavery. For weal or woe the president intended to stand on that platform.[29]

During all these complicated transactions about peace, Lincoln also had to continue managing the war. Republican politicians were not the only people pushing the panic button that August. With a new draft lottery imminent, General Halleck feared a repeat of the previous summer's riots. He suggested that Grant should send part of his army north to suppress these outbreaks. Grant responded that to do so would not only loosen his grip on the enemy at Petersburg but would also endanger Sherman in Georgia by enabling Lee to detach troops to reinforce the Confederate army defending Atlanta. Northern governors should call out the militia if necessary to enforce the draft, Grant told Halleck. "If we are to draw troops from the field to keep the loyal States in harness it will prove difficult to suppress the rebellion in the disloyal States."[30]

Lincoln read this exchange of telegrams and immediately wired Grant: "I have seen your despatch expressing your unwillingness to break your hold where you are. Neither am I willing. Hold on with a bulldog grip, and chew & choke, as much as possible." When Grant read this message "he broke into a hearty laugh" and told his aides: "The President has more nerve than any of his advisors."[31]

Grant's bulldog grip was just what the Democratic Party resolved could never restore the Union. That party remained divided between its peace and war wings, but the pessimistic mood of the North seemed to have catapulted the peace faction into the majority. Clement Vallandigham returned from his exile in Canada, in violation of Lincoln's order banishing him for the rest of the war. Not wanting to make him a martyr again, the president ignored his return — perhaps also hoping that if he gave Vallandigham enough rope he might hang his party as well as himself. That is just what happened — with an assist from William T. Sherman.

Meeting in Chicago at the end of August, the Democratic national convention adopted a platform plank written by Vallandigham: "After four years of failure to restore the Union by the experiment of war . . . [we] demand that immediate efforts be made for a cessation of hostilities, with a view to an ultimate convention of the states, or other peaceable means, to the end that, at the earliest practicable moment, peace may be restored on the basis of the Federal Union."[32]

This last phrase was little more than window dressing. Almost everyone recognized that an appeal by the United States for an armistice without agreement on any prior conditions would be tantamount to confessing defeat. In effect, "ultimate" and "the earliest practicable moment" meant never. The convention did give the presidential nomination to McClellan, who represented the prowar wing of the party. But the vice-presidential nomination went to Representative George Pendleton of Ohio, a Vallandigham ally, which reinforced the Copperhead image of the convention's work. McClellan tried to overcome that image with his letter accepting the nomination, in which he pledged to make peace negotiations dependent on Southern acceptance of reunion. His effort to shed the party's copper tinge, however, proved to be an uphill struggle. Nevertheless, if the election had been held two days after his nomination, McClellan would undoubtedly have won.

But three days after the nomination, on September 3, a telegram from General Sherman arrived in Washington: "Atlanta is ours, and fairly won."[33] The impact of this news was astounding. It turned around Northern opinion about the success or failure of the war by 180 degrees almost overnight. "Glorious news this morning — Atlanta taken at last!!!" wrote George Templeton Strong. "It is (coming at this political crisis) the greatest event of the war." A Republican newspaper captured the meaning of this event:

VICTORY
Is the War a Failure?
Old Abe's Reply to
the Chicago Convention[34]

The war was far from over, however. Atlanta had fallen, but the Confederate army defending it lived to fight another day. And so of course did the Army of Northern Virginia, including Jubal Early's corps, which still controlled the Shenandoah Valley a month after Phil Sheridan had been ordered to go after Early and follow him to the death. No longer able to say that the whole war was a failure, Democratic newspapers switched to criticizing Sheridan as a failure.

Lincoln was concerned. He telegraphed Grant on September 12 asking if something could be done to end the "dead lock" in the

Shenandoah Valley by getting Sheridan "to make a strike." This message brought Grant from his headquarters at City Point near Petersburg for the second time to prod Sheridan into action. He arrived at Sheridan's headquarters on September 15 to learn that the general planned an imminent attack on Early's army at Winchester. Grant had brought his own plan of campaign for Sheridan, but he left it in his pocket and simply told him: "Go in!"[35]

Once started, Sheridan proved to be one of the most energetic and aggressive Union commanders of the war. On September 19 he launched a two-pronged assault on Early's army east and north of Winchester. A misunderstood order tangled one Union infantry corps in its own wagon train and caused the attack to falter. But with superb (and profane) battlefield leadership, Sheridan straightened out the mess. While his infantry slogged forward in a savage firefight, two divisions of Union cavalry thundered down on the Confederate left in an old-fashioned mounted charge. The Confederate infantry broke and fled southward. "We have just sent them whirling through Winchester," wired Sheridan's chief of staff, "and we are after them tomorrow."[36]

Lincoln telegraphed his congratulations to

Sheridan for "your great victory. God bless you all, officers and men. Strongly inclined to come up and see you."[37] Whether Lincoln intended the final sentence seriously is impossible to say. He may have wondered if Sheridan would really go "after them tomorrow." With so many of his previous commanders in Virginia, "tomorrow" had meant maybe in a few days, maybe never. The commander in chief may have wanted to "come up" in order to hold Sheridan to his promise. He did not go, and he need not have worried. Sheridan did go after them without letup and attacked again at Fisher's Hill, twenty miles south of Winchester, on September 22. Once more the Federals — infantry this time — struck the Confederate left and sent the Rebels whirling south another sixty miles.

Sheridan then proceeded to carry out Grant's earlier orders to consume or destroy Confederate resources in the Shenandoah Valley so thoroughly "that crows flying over it for the balance of the season will have to carry their provender with them." By October 7, Sheridan reported, "I have destroyed over 2,000 barns filled with wheat, hay, and farming implements; over seventy mills filled with flour and wheat; have driven in front of the army over 4,000 head of stock, and have killed and issued to the troops no less than 3,000 sheep." This was just the beginning. By the time he was done, said Sheridan, "the Valley, from Winchester up to Staunton, ninety-two miles, will have little in it for man or beast."[38]

Before he could complete the task, however, Early struck back. In mid-October, Sheridan prepared to return the Sixth Corps to Grant and went personally to Washington to confer about future plans for his own army now that — as he thought — Early was no longer a threat. But even as Sheridan returned to Winchester on the evening of October 18, Early's troops were moving into position for a surprise dawn attack at Cedar Creek, fifteen miles south of Winchester. The assault was an initial success, wrecking two Union corps and winning what appeared to be a smashing victory by noon. But when Sheridan in Winchester heard the guns he jumped on his famous horse, Rienzi, and galloped to the battlefield. His extraordinary energy and charisma enabled him to reorganize and inspire his broken divisions and to lead them in a devastating counterattack that all but destroyed Early's army. An apparent Union defeat that might have neutralized Sheridan's earlier victories and even jeopardized Lincoln's reelection was turned into one of the most decisive victories of the war that virtually assured the president's political triumph three weeks later. No one appreciated Sheridan's achievements more than Lincoln himself, who again telegraphed the general "my own personal admiration and gratitude, for the month's operations in the Shenandoah Valley; and especially for the splendid work of October 19."[39]

Elections are never over until they are over, however. Despite the shot in the arm that Sherman's and Sheridan's victories gave Lincoln's prospects, some potential dangers remained. The Democrats played every race card they could think of, including the charge that the "Black Republicans" were the party of "miscegenation" (a new word they invented for this campaign). They illustrated this canard with crude cartoons portraying black men kissing white women in the "millennium of abolitionism" to be ushered in by Lincoln's reelection.

One race issue that directly involved Lincoln's functions as commander in chief was the prisoner exchange controversy. The Democratic platform denounced the administration's "shameful disregard" of "our fellow-citizens who now are, and long have been, prisoners of war in a suffering condition."[40] The breakdown in the prisoner exchange cartel had piled tens of thousands of captives into such prisons as Andersonville in Georgia, Elmira in New York, and dozens of others in almost every state. Overcrowding, disease, malnutrition, and mental depression caused the prisoner death toll to soar alarmingly, especially in Southern prisons.

The Lincoln administration came under tremendous pressure to resume exchanges despite the Confederacy's continued refusal to exchange black prisoners who had been slaves. Many Union prisoners at Andersonville and elsewhere signed petitions to Lincoln pleading for a renewal of exchanges. Sensing an opportunity for favorable propaganda, Confederate officials allowed delegations of prisoners to carry these petitions to Washington. Prisoner diaries at Andersonville included many entries expressing bitterness toward their own government: "What can the Government be thinking of to let soldiers die in this filthy place?" "We are losing all trust in old Abe." "It appears that the federal government thinks more of a few hundred niggers than of the thirty thousand whites here in bondage."[41] Local Republican leaders warned the administration that many Union men "will work and vote against the President, because they think sympathy with a few negroes, also captured, is the cause of a refusal" to exchange.[42]

Lincoln could have renewed the exchanges if he had been willing to accept Confederate conditions. But he was no more willing to do that than he was to drop emancipation as a condition of peace — for the same reason: "why should [black soldiers] give their lives for us, with full notice of our purpose to betray them?"[43] On August 27 the Union exchange commissioner wrote to his Confederate counterpart that the United States was prepared to renew exchanges if the Confederates agreed to make no discrimination. The sufferings of prisoners, he declared, "would move me to consent to anything to procure their exchange, except to barter away the honor and the faith of the United States, which has been so solemnly pledged to the colored soldiers in its ranks. Consistently with national faith and justice we cannot relinquish that position."[44]

The Confederate answer came from General Lee a few weeks later. He proposed to Grant an exchange of prisoners captured by each side in a Union attack and Confederate counterattack ten miles southeast of Richmond on September 28–30. Several black regiments participated, and some of their men were captured. Grant agreed to the exchange so long as the black soldiers were included. But Lee replied that "negroes belonging to our citizens are not considered subjects of exchange and were not included in my proposition." That was unfortunate, responded Grant, because the U.S. "Government is bound to secure to all persons received into her armies the rights due to soldiers." Lee's refusal to honor this obligation therefore "induces me to decline making the exchanges you ask."[45]

Union captives in Southern prison camps could not vote in the presidential election, of course, but most other soldiers could. By 1864 all Northern states except the three whose legislatures were controlled by Democrats — Illinois, Indiana, and New Jersey — had provided for soldiers to cast absentee ballots. Those three exceptions seemed to indicate that Democrats knew quite well which way most soldiers would vote. Nevertheless the nomination of McClellan encouraged many in the party to anticipate that his popularity might garner a majority of the soldier vote — at least in the Army of the Potomac. This turned out to be a false hope. By 1864, if not earlier, Lincoln was personally more popular with soldiers than McClellan — or indeed perhaps any general. The president's common touch, his frequent visits (often with his wife) to sick and wounded soldiers in Washington hospitals, his empathy with these citizens in uniform that manifested itself by mitigating the severity of regular-army punitive discipline and commuting many court-martial death sentences for desertion, and his image as a father figure to many soldiers who called him, affectionately, Father Abraham or Old Abe, won him widespread respect among soldiers.[46]

Even more important for many soldiers was what they thought the two parties stood for in 1864. The Republican policy was No Peace Without Victory. The War Failure plank of the Democratic platform seemed to mean peace at any price — even the price of a dishonorable peace. Were all their sacrifices to be in vain? asked many soldiers. "To ellect McClellan would be to undo all that we have don in the past four years," wrote a Michigan corporal. "Old Abe is slow but sure, he will accept nothing but an unconditional surrender." Another soldier insisted that "I can not vote for one thing and fight for another."[47] A New York officer could not see how "any soldier can vote for such a man, nominated on a platform which acknowledges that we are whipped." A Connecticut soldier thought "there are a good many soldiers who would vote for McClellan but they cannot go Vallandigham."[48] A lieutenant from New York who had been a lifelong Democrat repudiated his party. "I had rather stay out here a lifetime (much as I dislike it)," he wrote to one of McClellan's prominent supporters, "than consent to a division of our country. . . . We all want peace, but none *any* but an *honorable* one."[49]

When the votes were counted, Lincoln won 78 percent of the soldier votes in the states that tabulated them separately. The percentage was probably similar in states that lumped those votes with the civilian tally. The president's civilian-vote majority was about 53 percent. He would have been reelected without the soldier vote. But the most impressive thing about the 1864 election was that the men who would have to do the fighting and dying had voted overwhelmingly for their commander in chief to help him finish the job.

Lincoln interpreted his reelection as evidence that "the purpose of the people" to "maintain the integrity of the Union, was never more firm, nor more nearly unanimous, than now." Jefferson Davis had made it clear that no peace was possible without unconditional victory by one side or the other. "He does not attempt to deceive us. He affords us no excuse to deceive ourselves. He cannot voluntarily reaccept the Union; we cannot voluntarily yield it. Between him and us the issue is distinct, simple, and inflexible. It is an issue that can only be tried by war, and decided by victory."[50]

Davis accepted that challenge. He insisted that the Confederacy remained "as erect and defiant as ever. Nothing has changed in the purpose of its Government, in the indomitable valor of its troops, or in the unquenchable spirit of its people. . . . There is no military success of the enemy which can accomplish its destruction."[51] It was this last-ditch defiance that Gen. William T. Sherman set out to break in his famous march from Atlanta to the sea.

Sherman's first victory in that march was permission to make it. After losing Atlanta, Gen. John Bell Hood's Army of Tennessee moved north along the Union army's supply line, forcing Sherman to chase Hood with a large part of the army. The restless, voluble, impatient Union commander disliked this defensive role. He proposed a daring plan to cut loose from his supply line and march with sixty thousand veterans from Atlanta 285 miles to the coast, "smashing things to the sea." To Grant's objection that leaving Hood's army in his rear would open Tennessee to invasion by the Rebels, Sherman responded that he would send George Thomas with sixty thousand men to Tennessee, more than enough to deal with Hood. "If I turn back now, the whole effect of my campaign will be lost," Sherman wrote. "It will be a physical impossibility to protect the [rail]roads, now that Hood, Forrest, and Wheeler, and the whole batch of devils, are turned loose without home or habitation. By attempting to hold the roads, we will lose a thousand men monthly and will gain no result."

Sherman assured Grant that "I could cut a swath through Georgia to the sea, divide the Confederacy in two, and come up on the rear of Lee. . . . We cannot remain on the defensive. . . . I can make the march. . . . Instead of being on the defensive, I would be on the offensive." In addition to destroying Confederate railroads and resources and consuming Southern food that would otherwise feed Confederate armies, the march

418

would have a powerful psychological impact. "If we can march a well-appointed army right through [Jefferson Davis's] territory it is a demonstration to the world, foreign and domestic, that we have a power which Davis cannot resist. This may not be war, but rather statesmanship."[52]

Lincoln appreciated the value of an offensive operation that was as much "statesmanship" as war. But the president was reluctant to approve the march so long as Hood's army remained intact. And Lincoln also felt "much solicitude" about the potential danger to Sherman's troops deep in enemy territory with no possibility of coming to their aid if they ran into trouble. "A misstep by General Sherman," Lincoln feared, "might be fatal to his army." Sherman finally persuaded Grant to approve the march, however, and Grant in turn assured Lincoln that Sherman's veterans could handle anything the enemy could throw against them and that Thomas could handle Hood. Lincoln finally gave his approval, though still with misgivings. Grant then sent a brief message to Sherman: "Go as you propose."[53]

Sherman left Atlanta on November 15, and, as feared, Hood marched in the opposite direction into Tennessee. At the

Battle of Franklin on November 30, part of Thomas's army bloodied the invaders, killing or wounding no fewer than twelve Confederate generals and fifty-four regimental commanders. Hood kept right on going north, however, and arrived before Union defenses at Nashville on December 2. Six hundred miles away in Washington, the crippled condition of Hood's army was not apparent. Instead his movements looked like Jubal Early's raid to the outskirts of Washington the previous summer, which had had such a devastating effect on Northern opinion. Lincoln wondered why Thomas did not counterattack Hood. Stanton wired Grant that "the President feels solicitous about the disposition of General Thomas to [lie] in fortifications" instead of attacking. "This looks like the McClellan and Rosecrans strategy of do nothing and let the rebels raid the country."[54]

Grant reacted more emphatically than Lincoln expected. The general-in-chief had never fully appreciated Thomas's qualities. The tall, portly general, whose nickname in the prewar army had been "Old Slow-Trot," was a superb defensive commander — the Rock of Chickamauga. But Sherman had been critical of Thomas's alleged sluggishness on the offense in the Atlanta campaign, and Grant had picked up on that criticism. In response to Lincoln's expression of concern, Grant sent a series of increasingly urgent dispatches to Nashville ordering Thomas to attack. That general promised to do so as soon as his cavalry was remounted. Both Grant and Stanton expressed frustration. "Thomas seems unwilling to attack because it is 'hazardous,'" wrote Stanton on December 7, "as if all war was anything but hazardous. If he waits for Wilson [James Wilson, the cavalry commander] to get ready, Gabriel will be blowing his last horn."[55]

Grant suggested that Thomas be replaced by Gen. John Schofield, his senior corps commander.[56] Lincoln was taken aback. He had wanted Thomas to be energized, not relieved. The president admired Thomas for his steadfastness at Chickamauga and on other battlefields. He also appreciated the sacrifices that Thomas, a Virginian, had made to remain loyal to the Union — including ostracism by his family. Halleck conveyed to Grant the president's hesitancy about removing Thomas, and Grant backed off. But when two more days went by without an attack, and then an ice storm delayed it further, Grant completely lost patience. He sent Gen. John Logan to

Nashville to relieve Thomas unless he had launched his attack by the time Logan arrived. Upon further reflection Grant decided to follow Logan to Nashville himself. He stopped on the way in Washington to see Lincoln, who tried to talk him out of relieving Thomas. Grant insisted on going ahead, but before he could leave for Nashville a telegram arrived from Thomas stating that he had attacked and had the enemy on the run. Stanton rushed to the White House at midnight on December 15 with the news, which a "highly delighted" Lincoln, holding a candle, received in his nightshirt.[57]

The next morning the president wired Thomas congratulations "for a magnificent beginning" and urged him to finish the job.[58] Thomas did so with a crushing attack on December 16 that sent the enemy into headlong retreat. The Battle of Nashville was an even more decisive victory than Sheridan's at Cedar Creek two months earlier. Having started his invasion of Tennessee with forty thousand men, Hood counted fewer than fifteen thousand by the time his retreat fetched up at Tupelo, Mississippi, in January. As a fighting force the Army of Tennessee had virtually ceased to exist.

While the drama of General Thomas at Nashville was taking place, Sherman's sixty thousand soldiers were cutting a swath of destruction fifty miles wide through the heart of Georgia. Once he left Atlanta, Sherman was not in telegraphic contact with the North for more than a month. The only information that reached Washington came from fragmentary and partisan reports in Southern newspapers that found their way across the lines. Lincoln continued to worry about Sherman. He told the general's brother John that "I know what hole he went in at, but I can't tell what hole he will come out of." General Sherman emerged from his hole near Savannah in mid-December. The city's Confederate defenders evacuated it before Sherman could attack them. The general sent Lincoln a jaunty telegram on December 22 (carried by ship to Fort Monroe for transmittal to Washington): "I beg to present to you as a Christmas gift the city of Savannah with 150 heavy guns & plenty of ammunition & also about 25,000 bales of cotton."[59]

Lincoln received this message on Christmas Day. He sent Sherman a congratulatory letter similar to the one he had sent Grant after the capture of Vicksburg. "When you were about leaving Atlanta for the

Atlantic coast, I was anxious, if not fearful," the president confessed, "but feeling that you were the better judge, and remembering that 'nothing risked, nothing gained' I did not interfere. Now, the undertaking being a success, the honor is all yours; for I believe none of us went farther than to acquiesce." In conjunction with Thomas's victory at Nashville, Sherman's march "brings those who sat in darkness, to see a great light."[60]

Much of that light was shed by the destruction that Sherman's "bummers" wreaked in Georgia. The general estimated the damage "at $100,000,000; at least $20,000,000 of which has inured to our advantage, and the remainder is simple waste and destruction."[61] When Sherman's army marched north through South Carolina in February 1865, they destroyed even more property than in Georgia. Lincoln was a compassionate man, but like Sherman and Sheridan he had concluded that the devastation of Southern resources, even at the cost of civilian suffering, was necessary to overcome the rebellion. After all, he had warned Southerners back in July 1862 that he no longer intended to fight this war "with elder-stalk squirts charged with rose water." In another metaphor he had pointed out that the longer the Confederates fought, the more eggs would be broken. Now, in early 1865, he switched metaphors again, telling a visitor to the White House that "Grant has the bear by the hind leg while Sherman takes off the hide."[62]

By 1865 many of the essential supplies for the Army of Northern Virginia came through Wilmington, North Carolina, the last port of any significance still available to blockade-runners. Grant had been slow to perceive the value of capturing Fort Fisher, a huge earthwork that protected the entrance to the Cape Fear River below Wilmington and kept Union blockaders at bay. But in the fall of 1864 Grant planned a joint army-navy campaign to capture the fort. To Grant's annoyance, Benjamin Butler took personal command of the expedition by virtue of his seniority as head of the Department of Virginia and North Carolina. On Christmas Eve the largest naval fleet of the war began a two-day bombardment of the fort. Butler landed part of his troops the next day but decided that the shelling had not sufficiently damaged the fort and reembarked them again. For Grant this was the last straw. He asked for Butler's removal, and with the election over, Lincoln immediately complied.[63] The president told

Grant and Adm. David D. Porter, commander of the fleet, to renew the attack. Grant organized a new expedition with the army troops commanded by Brig. Gen. Alfred Terry. This time the fleet bombardment on January 13–15 did major damage, and the infantry assault captured the fort on January 15.

Confederate vice president Alexander Stephens considered the loss of Fort Fisher to be "one of the greatest disasters that had befallen our Cause from the beginning of the war."[64] The disaster brought to a head a growing peace movement in the Confederacy. Two weeks after the fall of Fort Fisher, Stephens participated in yet another effort for a negotiated peace. This one was set in motion by the venerable Francis Preston Blair, the old Jacksonian Democrat who became one of the founders of the Republican Party in the 1850s. Blair had maintained his ties across party lines, however, and even across the bloody chasm of war. With Lincoln's tacit consent, Blair traveled to Richmond under flag of truce in January 1865 to visit his former friend and political associate Jefferson Davis. Although the content of their conversations remained secret, Blair's presence in Richmond gave rise to endless speculation in the press in both the North and the South. Blair's purpose was to see whether there might be some way to reunite the country and put an end to this seemingly interminable war.

Signs abounded that the Southern people, if not Jefferson Davis, were ready to give up. Desertions from Confederate armies soared. The previously indefatigable chief of Confederate ordnance, Josiah Gorgas, made despairing entries in his diary during January: "Where is this to end? No money in the Treasury, no food to feed Gen. Lee's Army, no troops to oppose Gen. Sherman. There is a strong disposition among members of congress to come to terms with the enemy. . . . Wife & I sit talking of going to Mexico to live out the remnant of our days."[65]

Mexico was also on Blair's mind. He seemed obsessed with the idea that a joint campaign of Union and Confederate armies to throw the French and their puppet emperor Ferdinand Maximilian out of Mexico would pave the way to reunion. Davis returned a cool response to this notion, but he did give Blair a letter for Lincoln's eyes, offering to appoint commissioners to "enter into conference with a view to secure peace to the two countries." Lincoln wanted nothing to do with Blair's proposed Mexican adventure. But the president thought he saw an opportunity to end the war on his own terms without compromising his refusal to recognize the legitimacy of the Confederacy. He authorized Blair to return to Richmond with an offer to receive any commissioner whom Davis "may *informally* send to me with the view of securing peace to the people of our *one common country.*"[66]

Davis overlooked the discrepancy between "two countries" and "one common country." He appointed a commission composed of Vice President Stephens, President Pro Tem of the Senate Robert M. T. Hunter, and Assistant Secretary of War John A. Campbell, a former U.S. Supreme Court justice. Davis expected their efforts to fail because he knew that Lincoln would stick to his terms of Union and freedom. That was the outcome Davis wanted, for it would enable him to rouse flagging Southern spirits to keep up the fight as the only alternative to a humiliating defeat.[67]

This peace effort almost foundered before it could float. Lincoln sent word to military officers that the Confederate commissioners should not be allowed through the lines for an "informal conference" with Secretary of State Seward, whom he had sent to Virginia, unless they agreed in advance to Lincoln's "one common country" formula as the basis for talks. The commissioners instead showed to the army major whom Lincoln dispatched to meet them their "two countries" instructions from Davis. The major therefore barred them from crossing Union lines.[68]

That would seem to have ended the matter. But this affair had generated huge coverage in the press — more even than the peace flurries of the previous summer — and had raised hopes that this cruel war might soon be over. On the morning of February 2 Lincoln read a telegram from General Grant: "I am convinced, upon conversation with Messrs Stephens & Hunter that their intentions are good and their desire sincere to restore peace and union. . . . I am sorry however that Mr. Lincoln cannot have an interview with [them]. . . . I fear now their going back without any expression from anyone in authority will have a bad influence."[69]

Grant's intervention was decisive. On the spur of the moment, Lincoln decided to go to Virginia personally to join Seward for a meeting with the Confederate commissioners. This extraordinary "informal" four-hour meeting of the five men took place February 3 on the Union steamer *River Queen,* anchored in Hampton Roads. No aides were present and no formal record was kept, although Seward and Campbell wrote brief summaries and Stephens later penned a lengthy account, which must be used with caution.[70] Despite an underlying tension, the mood was relaxed. Lincoln and Stephens had been fellow Whigs in Congress nearly two decades earlier, providing the basis for a cordial atmosphere.

Lincoln nevertheless stuck to the terms he had written out for Seward before the president decided to join him: "1 The restoration of the National authority throughout all the States. 2 No receding by the Executive of the United States, on the Slavery question. . . . 3 No cessation of hostilities short of an end of the war, and the disbanding of all forces hostile to the government."[71] Stephens tried to change the subject by alluding to Blair's Mexican project; Lincoln promptly disavowed it. What about an armistice while peace negotiations took place? No armistice, replied Lincoln, reiterating his third condition. Well then, said Hunter, would it be possible to hold official negotiations while the war went on? After all, he noted, even King Charles I had entered into agreements with rebels in arms during the English civil war. "I do not profess to be posted in history," replied Lincoln — one imagines with a twinkle in his eye. "All I distinctly recollect about the case of Charles I is, that he lost his head."[72]

On questions of punishing Confederate leaders and confiscating Southern property, Lincoln promised generous treatment based on his power of pardon. With respect to slavery Lincoln even suggested that if Confederate states abolished it themselves as part of a peace settlement, he would ask Congress to appropriate funds for partial compensation (an unlikely prospect). In any event the U.S. House of Representatives had passed the Thirteenth Amendment three days earlier (the Senate had done so the previous year) and several states, including Lincoln's Illinois as the first, had already ratified it.[73] Slavery was dead, Lincoln made clear, and to avoid further bloodshed the Southern leaders should face the reality that the Confederacy would soon be in the same condition.

Whatever their personal convictions, the commissioners had no authority to concede the death of their nation. They returned sadly to Richmond and admitted their failure. Davis was neither surprised nor disappointed. He reported to the Confederate Congress that Lincoln's terms required "degrading submission" and "humiliating surrender." Davis addressed a large rally in Richmond and predicted that Seward and "His Majesty Abraham the First" would find "they had been speaking to their masters," for Southern armies would yet "compel the Yankees, in less than twelve months, to petition us for peace on our own terms."[74]

Confederate military leaders did not share Davis's fantasy. At a meeting under flag of truce between Gen. James Longstreet and Union general Edward Ord to arrange an exchange of civilian prisoners at the end of February, the two generals discussed "the possibility of arriving at a satisfactory adjustment of the present unhappy difficulties, by means of a military convention." They thought that Lee and Grant might be able to conclude some kind of agreement. So Lee wrote to Grant proposing a meeting. Grant properly forwarded this letter to Stanton, who took it to Lincoln. The president wrote out a response, which Stanton telegraphed to Grant: The commander in chief "wishes you to have no conference with General Lee unless it be for the capitulation of Gen. Lee's army, or on some minor, and purely military, matter. . . . You are not to decide, discuss, or confer upon any political question. Such questions the President holds in his own hands; and will submit them to no military conferences or conventions."[75]

The next day Lincoln was inaugurated for his second term. His inaugural address was the shortest and most eloquent in American history. It offered a meditation on God's purpose in bringing this terrible war upon America. Perhaps, Lincoln suggested, it was a punishment for the sin of slavery. "Fondly do we hope — fervently do we pray — that this mighty scourge of war may speedily pass away," said Lincoln. "Yet, if God wills that it continue, until all the wealth piled up by the bond-man's two hundred and fifty years of unrequited toil shall be sunk, and until every drop of blood drawn with the lash, shall be paid by another drawn with the sword, as was said three thousand years ago, so still it must be said 'the judgments of the Lord, are true and righteous altogether.' "[76]

Mercifully it did not take that long. A month later came the fall of Richmond, and a week after that came Appomattox. Perhaps appropriately the commander in chief was with the Army of the Potomac when it achieved the decisive breakthrough. Grant had invited the careworn president to get away from the stresses of Washington for a few days for a visit to the army. Lincoln took him up on it and arrived at Grant's headquarters on March 24. He wound up staying two weeks, visiting the troops every day in camp and hospital. He once grabbed an ax to help them cut timber, and earned the raucous cheers of the men. On his second day with the army the president witnessed the aftermath of Lee's desperate attempt to break through Grant's constricting hold by a surprise attack on Fort Stedman, which failed at the cost of almost five thousand Confederate casualties. Grant seized this opportunity on April 1 to launch a flank attack on the Confederate right at Five Forks. The assault succeeded, and Grant followed it with an attack all along the Petersburg lines on April 2, which forced Lee to evacuate both Petersburg and Richmond that night.

When the news of Richmond's fall reached the North, wild celebrations broke out. Lincoln felt the same way, but his response was more restrained. He met with Grant in Petersburg on April 3 and discussed the pursuit of Lee, which would bring him to bay at Appomattox six days later. Meanwhile Lincoln returned to Adm. David D. Porter's flagship USS *Malvern,* anchored in the

James River, and told Porter: "Thank God I have lived to see this! It seems to me that I have been dreaming a horrid dream for four years, and now the nightmare is gone. I want to see Richmond."[77]

Porter was dubious about taking the president to the still-burning enemy capital two days after it fell. But Lincoln insisted, so they went. With an escort of just ten sailors, he walked the streets while thousands of freed slaves crowded to see the Moses they believed had led them to freedom. "I know that I am free," shouted one woman, "for I have seen father Abraham and felt him." To one black man who fell on his knees before him, an embarrassed Lincoln said: "Don't kneel to me. That is not right. You must kneel to God only and thank him for the liberty you will hereafter enjoy." The president was profoundly moved by these encounters. But he may have experienced the most satisfaction from sitting in Jefferson Davis's chair in the Confederate White House only two days after Davis had vacated it.[78]

While in Richmond, Lincoln met with John A. Campbell, one of the Confederate commissioners at the Hampton Roads "peace conference" two months earlier. Campbell now acknowledged that the war was lost. He suggested that the general commanding the Union forces occupying Richmond allow the Virginia legislature to meet to repeal the ordinance of secession and withdraw all Virginia soldiers from Confederate armies. Such an action, said Campbell, would set off a chain reaction in other Confederate states and bring the war to an end without any more battles. Lincoln liked the idea and ordered Gen. Godfrey Weitzel to permit "the gentlemen who have acted as the Legislature of Virginia" to meet for this purpose.[79]

Lincoln made a rare political mistake here. He should have anticipated that Campbell might proceed in a manner that treated the Confederate Virginia legislature as a legitimate governing body (instead of as "the gentlemen who have *acted* as the Legislature," in Lincoln's words). When Lincoln learned that this was precisely what Campbell had done, he angrily repudiated that action on April 12. By then Lee's surrender at Appomattox had made the whole matter moot, since almost all Virginia soldiers were in the Army of Northern Virginia.[80]

Back in Washington on April 11, the president delivered a speech from a White House balcony to a crowd of serenaders celebrating Lee's surrender. Looking forward to the problem of bringing the defeated Confederate states back into the Union, he said that the victorious army would have to stay in the South for an indefinite period to oversee this process and to suppress "disorganized and discordant elements." In most of the South "there is no authorized organ for us to deal with" — thereby disposing of Confederate state legislatures and the fugitive Confederate government fleeing southward. "We must simply begin with, and mould from" those disorganized and discordant elements. Lincoln had already begun this process in Louisiana, Arkansas, and Tennessee, where he hoped that his newly "moulded" state governments would soon grant the right to vote to literate African Americans and black Union army veterans. In those states as well as in the others, Lincoln's war powers as commander in chief would remain as important for winning the peace as they had been for winning the war. Concluding his speech, the president promised a "new announcement to the people of the South."[81]

One of the listeners in the crowd turned to his companion. "That means nigger citizenship," snapped John Wilkes Booth. "Now, by God, I'll put him through. That is the last speech he will ever make."[82]

EPILOGUE

Booth carried out his ugly threat three days later. A native of Maryland who supported the Confederacy, he hated the Union commander in chief for his success in winning the war and abolishing slavery. Granting equal rights to freed slaves would add insult to injury. So Booth "put him through." If Lincoln had been a failure, he would have lived a longer life.

Failure had often seemed imminent. Several times during the war Union prospects were dark. Three times in particular stand out. After the Confederate victory at Second Manassas in August 1862, demoralization in the Eastern Union armies and among the Northern people reached dire levels. Lincoln made the difficult decision — opposed by his cabinet and by principal congressional leaders — to give McClellan command of the reconstituted Army of the Potomac. Victory at Antietam followed, though Lincoln was grievously disappointed with McClellan's failure to follow it up and "destroy the rebel army."

Again in the spring of 1863 the North seemed on the verge of defeat as Grant's army apparently floundered in the swamps near Vicksburg and Lee's army headed north after its spectacular victory at Chancellorsville. Lincoln once more made difficult decisions — to keep Grant in command and to replace Joe Hooker with George Gordon Meade. The capture of Vicksburg and victory at Gettysburg followed — but Lee got back to Virginia without further major damage, to Lincoln's distress.

A year later, in the summer of 1864, Union prospects seemed to sink almost out of sight. Lincoln resisted enormous pressure to seek a compromise peace and to back away from emancipation. He stayed the course despite universal expectations that it would cost his reelection. The capture of Atlanta, victories in the Shenandoah Valley, and reelection followed. So did Appomattox and assassination.

Lincoln's on-the-job training as commander in chief went through some rough patches. He made mistakes — but he also learned from those mistakes. He deferred too long to McClellan's supposedly superior professional qualifications. Perhaps he should have overruled that general's preference for the Peninsula strategy. He gave command responsibilities beyond their capacities to such political generals as Frémont, McClernand, Banks, and Butler.

In retrospect it appears that he also made several wrong appointments to command the Army of the Potomac. Yet in each case the general he named seemed to be the best man for the job when he was appointed. McClellan was everyone's choice when he took command in July 1861. Burnside had achieved success with an independent command in North Carolina and seemed the logical choice in December 1862. Hooker was a controversial choice, but he did everything right in his first three months of command and appeared to have vindicated Lincoln's decision until he stumbled at Chancellorsville. Meade was a consensus choice, and despite Lincoln's disappointment with him after Gettysburg he remained commander of the Army of the Potomac through its final triumph.

Likewise the choices of McClellan and then Halleck as general-in-chief looked like the right appointments at the right time. No one was more disappointed with their shortcomings than the president himself. Their failures put a greater burden on Lincoln to function as his own general-in-chief during much of the war, until he *did* make the right choice at the right time when he named Grant to this position in March 1864. The visibility of commanding generals who turned out to be disappointments — which would also include Buell and Rosecrans — should not distract us from Lincoln's key role in placing Grant, Sheridan, Thomas, and (indirectly through his support of Grant) Sherman in top commands and keeping them there until they won the war.

In all five functions as commander in chief — policy, national strategy, military strategy, operations, and tactics — Lincoln's conception and performance were dynamic rather than static. He oversaw the evolution of the war from one of limited ends with limited means to a full-scale effort that destroyed the old Union and built a new and better one on its ashes. His initial *policy* was restoration of the Union — the Union of 1860, with slavery in fifteen of the thirty-three states. By 1864, if not earlier, the abolition of slavery was added to preservation of the Union. This revolutionary policy stemmed in part from the evolution of *na-*

tional strategy from conciliation of the border states and supposed Southern Unionists into an all-out effort to destroy Confederate resources including slavery and to mobilize those resources for the Union — including black soldiers who had been slaves. By July 1862 Lincoln had decided that he would no longer wage this war with elder-stalk squirts charged with rose water.

"We want the Army to strike more vigorous blows," Lincoln told cabinet members also in July 1862. "The Administration must set an example, and strike at the heart of the rebellion." In other words the destruction of slavery as both a national strategy and as policy must be matched by a *military strategy* of destroying enemy armies. The initial limited military strategy of suppressing rebellious elements in the South evolved by 1862 into one of capturing large expanses of Confederate territory. Union forces did capture a great deal of territory in the first half of 1862, but Confederate armies bounced back stronger than ever. Lincoln understood better than perhaps anyone else that those armies must be destroyed or crippled if the war was to be won. "Destroy the rebel army," he urged McClellan in September 1862. "*Lee's* Army, and not *Richmond,* is your true objective point," he told

Hooker in June 1863. If Meade could accomplish "the literal or substantial destruction of Lee's army" after Gettysburg, said Lincoln on July 7, 1863, "the rebellion [would] be over."

None of these generals carried out Lincoln's mandate. The generals who won the war did so by capturing or destroying whole armies: Grant at Vicksburg; Sheridan in the Shenandoah Valley; Thomas at Nashville; and Grant at Appomattox. They accomplished this by aggressive *operations* and *tactics* of the sort that Lincoln had urged in vain on other generals. In two cases — Sheridan in the valley and Thomas at Nashville — victory was achieved by counteroffensives against Confederate raids or invasions. On five other occasions Lincoln also saw Confederate offensives not primarily as threats but rather as opportunities to trap and destroy the invaders far from home: Jackson's Shenandoah Valley campaign in the spring of 1862; Lee's invasion of Maryland in September 1862; Bragg's and Kirby Smith's simultaneous invasion of Kentucky; Lee's invasion of Pennsylvania in June 1863; and Jubal Early's raid to the suburbs of Washington in July 1864. Each time his generals failed him, and in most cases they soon found themselves relieved of command: John C. Frémont and James Shields after failing to intercept Jackson; McClellan after letting Lee get away; Buell after Bragg and Kirby Smith got safely back to Tennessee; and David Hunter after Early's raid. Meade retained his command despite Lincoln's disappointment but played second fiddle to Grant in the war's last year.

Another hallmark of Lincoln's conception of military strategy and operations remained unfulfilled until he had the team of Grant, Sherman, Thomas, and Sheridan in place by 1864: concentration in *time* by simultaneous advances of two or more Union armies on exterior lines to counter the Confederate advantage of concentration in *space* by the use of interior lines. Lincoln had succinctly outlined this strategy in letters to Halleck and Buell in January 1862. Union forces fitfully carried out such a strategy in uncoordinated fashion in 1862 and 1863. But in this as well as in other respects, it was the team of Grant and Sherman who put it into the most effective practice in 1864. Even then, however, the political and ethnic generals whom Lincoln had appointed as part of his national strategy — Banks, Butler, and Sigel — fumbled away their parts of Grant's strategy of coordinated offensives in 1864.

Lincoln maintained that "as commander-in-chief of the army and navy, in time of war . . . I have a right to take any measure which may best subdue the enemy." This right exceeded any powers of Congress. "I conceive that I may in an emergency do things on military grounds that cannot be done constitutionally by Congress."[1] Lincoln cited these sweeping powers to justify the Emancipation Proclamation. On other occasions he made similar statements in defense of his suspension of habeas corpus and authorization of military tribunals to try civilians.

These actions were contentious at the time; the suspension of habeas corpus and the creation of military courts, if not the Emancipation Proclamation, remain controversial among historians today. Lincoln's use of these war powers established precedents invoked by subsequent presidents in wartime. Whether they were constitutional or necessary in the 1860s or in later wars remains a matter of dispute. In the *Milligan* case of 1866 the U.S. Supreme Court declared unconstitutional the trial of civilians by military courts in areas where the civil courts are open.[2] And some of the Lincoln administration's actions, such as the arrest of Maryland legislators and other officials in September 1861, seemed excessive and unjustified by any reasonable military necessity.

Whether these violations of civil liberties constitute a negative legacy that offsets the positive legacy of the Union and emancipation is a question everyone must decide for himself or herself. The crisis of the 1860s represented a far greater threat to the survival of the United States than did World War I, World War II, Communism in the 1950s, or terrorism today. Yet compared with the draconian enforcement of espionage and sedition laws in World War I, the internment of more than one hundred thousand Japanese Americans in the 1940s, McCarthyism in the 1950s, or the National Security State of our own time, the infringement of civil liberties from 1861 to 1865 seems mild indeed. And the problem of Reconstruction after the Civil War was not that the federal government exercised too much power but that it did not exercise enough.

ACKNOWLEDGMENTS

Almost fifty years ago I turned in my first research paper as a graduate student at Johns Hopkins University. The topic of this paper was Lincoln's secretary of war Edwin M. Stanton, and my principal sources were the Stanton and Lincoln Papers at the Library of Congress. In the five decades since that introduction to the rewards as well as the eye-numbing fatigue of research in primary sources, I have spent countless hours in scores of libraries and archives from Maine to California and from Minnesota to Louisiana. The subjects of my research in these repositories ranged from Northern abolitionists to Confederate soldiers. Either directly or indirectly most of that research contributed to my knowledge and understanding of Abraham Lincoln and the Civil War, and therefore also contributed to the findings and insights in this book. The librarians and curators at these repositories who helped me are far too numerous to name, as are the institutions themselves. But in addition to the Library of Congress and the Firestone Library at my home base of Princeton University, I must single out the Huntington Library in San Marino, California, and the Illinois State Historical Library (now the Abraham Lincoln Presidential Library) in Springfield for special mention.

I have spent three sabbatical years at the Huntington Library, whose collections as well as my lunchtime conversations with other historians and the Q&A sessions after lectures I delivered there have enriched my knowledge of Lincoln. Dialogue with students during thousands of hours in the classroom in forty-two years of teaching at Princeton and with people of widely varied backgrounds at hundreds of public lectures I have delivered in many venues over the years has also honed my understanding of the issues discussed in this book. To all of them I owe thanks for the contributions they have made, sometimes unwittingly, to my knowledge.

The large community of Lincoln and Civil War scholars has also enriched my understanding. No single mortal could read all of the books and articles produced by these scholars, but I have read as many as possible and have learned from all of them. These historians and biographers are too numerous to name, but I am particularly indebted to one of them, Michael Burlingame, whose editions of the writings of Lincoln's secretaries John G. Nicolay and John Hay have been invaluable, and whose encyclopedic knowledge of Lincoln and willingness to share that knowledge have been of great help. Careful readings of drafts of *Tried by War* by historians Craig L. Symonds and Ronald C. White, and by Eamon Dolan of The Penguin Press, saved me from embarrassing errors and yielded fruitful suggestions for revisions.

My greatest personal as well as intellectual debt is owed to Patricia McPherson, to whom the book is dedicated. We celebrated our fiftieth wedding anniversary one day after I turned in the final revisions of *Tried by War*. During those five decades she was often quite literally by my side as a research assistant at many of the libraries and archives mentioned earlier, and we edited one book together. More important than any book — indeed, than all books — she has enabled us to make a home and family for more than half a century.

NOTES

EXPLANATION OF CITATIONS

The following abbreviated citation is used for *War of the Rebellion: A Compilation of the Official Records of the Union and Confederate Armies,* 70 volumes in 128 serials (Washington, D.C., 1880–1901): *O.R.*

These records were published in four series. The overwhelming majority of citations in this book are to series 1. Many of the "volumes" in series 1 have two or more "parts." A full citation of a document in this publication would be: "series 1, vol. 14, part 2, p. 479." In this book, citations to documents in series 1 will be: *O.R.* 14, ii:479. All citations to documents in series 2, 3, or 4 will be full citations; for example: *O.R., series 2, vol. 3, p. 284.*

PREFACE

1. Gabor S. Boritt, ed., *The Historian's Lincoln: Pseudohistory, Psychohistory, and History* (Urbana, Ill.: University of Illinois Press, 1988); Don E. Fehrenbacher, *Lincoln in Text and Context: Collected Essays* (Stanford, Calif.: Stanford University Press, 1987); Merrill D. Peterson, *Lincoln in American Memory* (New York: Oxford University Press, 1994).
2. Roy P. Basler, ed., *The Collected Works of Abraham Lincoln,* 9 vols. (New Brunswick, N.J.: Rutgers University Press, 1953–55), 8:332.

INTRODUCTION

1. Roy P. Basler, ed., *The Collected Works of Abraham Lincoln,* 9 vols. (New Brunswick, N.J.: Rutgers University Press, 1953–55), 1:509–10.
2. Ibid., 4:235–36.
3. Francis B. Carpenter, *Six Months at the White House with Abraham Lincoln* (New York: Hurd and Houghton, 1866), 312–14.
4. Harlan Hoyt Horner, *Lincoln and Greeley* (Urbana, Ill.: University of Illinois Press, 1953), 251–52; William H. Herndon and Jesse W. Weik, *Herndon's Lincoln,* ed. Doug-

las L. Wilson and Rodney O. Davis (Urbana, Ill.: University of Illinois Press, 2006), 210.

5. Herndon and Weik, *Herndon's Lincoln,* 208.

6. John G. Nicolay and John Hay, *Abraham Lincoln: A History,* 10 vols. (New York: The Century Co., 1890), 5:155–56; T. Harry Williams, *Lincoln and His Generals* (New York: Alfred A. Knopf, 1952), vii.

7. *Fleming v. Page,* 50 U.S. (9 *Howard*) 614 (1850).

8. Michael Burlingame and John R. Turner Ettlinger, eds., *Inside Lincoln's White House: The Complete Civil War Diary of John Hay* (Carbondale, Ill.: Southern Illinois University Press, 1997), 20, diary entry of May 7, 1861; Basler, *Collected Works,* 4:268.

9. Basler, *Collected Works,* 7:23, 8:151.

10. *On War,* trans. and ed. Michael Howard and Peter Paret (Princeton, N.J.: Princeton University Press, 1976), 87–88. Emphasis in original.

11. Halleck to John M. Schofield, Sept. 20, Nov. 28, 1862, *O.R.* 13:264, 22, i:793–94.

CHAPTER 1: THE QUEST FOR A STRATEGY, 1861

1. Nicolay memorandums dated Nov. 15 and Dec. 13, 1860, in Michael Burlingame, ed., *With Lincoln in the White House: Letters, Memoranda, and Other Writings of John G. Nicolay, 1860–1865* (Carbondale, Ill.: Southern Illinois University Press, 2000), 10, 16–17.

2. Lincoln to Francis P. Blair, Dec. 21, 1860, Lincoln to Elihu B. Washburne, Dec. 21, 1860, Lincoln to David Hunter, Dec. 22, 1860, Lincoln to Lyman Trumbull, Dec. 24, 1860, in Roy P. Basler, ed., *The Collected Works of Abraham Lincoln,* 9 vols. (New Brunswick, N.J.: Rutgers University Press, 1953–55), 4:157, 159, 162; Nicolay memorandum dated Dec. 22, 1860, in Burlingame, *With Lincoln in the White House,* 21.

3. *Illinois Daily State Journal,* Dec. 20, 1860, Jan. 21, 1861. The second editorial may have been written by John Hay, who had joined John Nicolay to become Lincoln's second private secretary. See Michael Burlingame, ed., *Lincoln's Journalist: John Hay's Anonymous Writing for the Press, 1860–1864* (Carbondale, Ill.: Southern Illinois University Press, 1998), 350–51.

See also Allan Nevins, *The Emergence of Lincoln,* vol. 2, *Prologue to Civil War 1859–1861* (New York: Charles Scribner's Sons, 1950), 356–57.

4. George W. Hazzard to Lincoln, Oct. 21, 1860, Abraham Lincoln Papers, Library of Congress.

5. Basler, *Collected Works,* 4:195, 241, 243–44.

6. Ibid., 245, 237.

7. Ibid., 254, 266.

8. Robert Anderson to Samuel Cooper, Feb. 28, 1861, enclosed with Joseph Holt to Lincoln, March 5, 1861, Lincoln Papers.

9. The evidence for these two meetings is clouded and contradictory; for the best discussions of the issue see David M. Potter, *Lincoln and His Party in the Secession Crisis* (New Haven, Conn.: Yale University Press, 1942), 353–58; James G. Randall, *Lincoln the President: Springfield to Gettysburg,* 2 vols. (New York: Dodd, Mead, and Company, 1946), 1:325–28; and William C. Harris, "The Southern Unionist Critique of the Civil War," *Civil War History* 31 (March 1985), 50–51. For Lincoln's recollection of the meetings, see Michael Burlingame and John R. Turner Ettlinger, eds., *Inside Lincoln's White*

House: The Complete Civil War Diary of John Hay (Carbondale, Ill.: Southern Illinois University Press, 1997), 28 and 285n.104, diary entry of Oct. 22, 1861.

10. Samuel Ward to Samuel L. M. Barlow, March 31, 1861, Samuel L. M. Barlow Papers, Huntington Library, San Marino, Calif.

11. Memorandum by John Nicolay of a meeting between Lincoln and Browning, dated July 3, 1861, in Burlingame, *With Lincoln in the White House,* 46–47; see also Theodore Calvin Pease and James G. Randall, eds., *The Diary of Orville Hickman Browning,* 2 vols. (Springfield, Ill.: Illinois State Historical Library, 1925), 1:47, entry of July 3, 1861.

12. Scott's endorsement on a letter from Joseph Holt to Lincoln, March 5, 1861, Lincoln Papers.

13. Burlingame, *Lincoln's Journalist,* 55–56, from the *New York World,* March 8, 1861.

14. Howard K. Beale, ed., *The Diary of Edward Bates, 1859–1866* (Washington, D.C.: U.S. Government Printing Office, 1933), 177, entry of March 9, 1861; Lincoln to Scott, March 9, 1861, Basler, *Collected Works,* 4:279; Scott to Lincoln, March 11, 1861, Lincoln Papers.

15. Scott to Anderson, March 11, 1861, Scott to Cameron, March 11, 1861, Lincoln Papers.

16. The written opinions of the cabinet officers are in the Lincoln Papers and are excerpted in Basler, *Collected Works,* 4:285n.

17. Ibid., 4:288–90.

18. Scott to Cameron, March 28, *O.R.* 1, 200–201; Erasmus Keyes, diary entry of March 29, 1861, in Keyes, *Fifty Years' Observation of Men and Events, Civil and Military* (New York: Charles Scribner's Sons, 1884), 378.

19. John G. Nicolay and John Hay, *Abraham Lincoln: A History,* 10 vols. (New York: The Century Co., 1890), 3:394–95, 429–34; Basler, *Collected Works,* 4:301–2, 424.

20. Lincoln Papers; reprinted in Basler, *Collected Works,* 4:317–18n.

21. Basler, *Collected Works,* 4:316–17.

22. The documentation on this contretemps can be found in entries in the diary of Montgomery Meigs of March 29, 31, April 1, 5, 6, in "General M. C. Meigs on the Conduct of the Civil War," *American Historical Review* 26 (1920–21), 299–302; Basler, *Collected Works,* 4:313–15; and Howard K. Beale, ed., *Diary of Gideon*

Welles, 3 vols. (New York: W. W. Norton & Co., 1960), 1:21–26.

23. Basler, *Collected Works,* 4:316.

24. Ibid., 323.

25. Ibid., 324.

26. Leroy P. Walker to Beauregard, April 8, 10, 1861, *O.R.* 1:289, 297.

27. Basler, *Collected Works,* 4:329–31.

28. Ibid., 331–32.

29. *Life, Letters, and Journals of George Ticknor,* 2 vols. (Boston: Osgood, 1876), 2:433–34; Jane Stuart Woolsey to a friend, May 10, 1861, in Henry Steele Commager, ed., *The Blue and the Gray,* 2 vols. (rev. and abridged ed., New York: New American Library, 1973), 1:48.

30. Basler, *Collected Works,* 4:353–54.

31. Ibid., 338–39.

32. Ibid., 426, 440.

33. Clinton Rossiter, *The American Presidency,* rev. ed. (New York: Harcourt, Brace, 1960), 99, makes the same point.

34. Basler, *Collected Works,* 5:241–42.

35. *U.S. Statutes at Large,* 12:326 (Aug. 6, 1861).

36. *Prize Cases,* 67 U.S. 635.

37. *O.R.,* series 3, vol. 1, pp. 70, 72, 76, 81, 83.

38. Ibid., 71.

39. Thomas H. Hicks to Lincoln, April 22,

1861, Lincoln Papers; Basler, *Collected Works,* 4:340–42.

40. Basler, *Collected Works,* 4:370.

41. Ibid., 347, 419, 554; 5:35, 436–37.

42. *Ex parte Merryman,* 17 Fed. Cas., 148–53.

43. "Opinion of Attorney General Bates," July 5, 1861, *O.R.,* series 2, vol. 2, pp. 20–30; Reverdy Johnson, *Power of the President to Suspend the Habeas Corpus Writ* (New York: privately printed, 1861); Horace Binney, *The Privilege of the Writ of Habeas Corpus Under the Constitution* (Philadelphia: C. Sherman and Sons, 1862). See also Edward Bates to Lincoln, July 5, 1861, Lincoln Papers.

44. Lincoln to Scott, April 25, 1861, Basler, *Collected Works,* 4:344; "Reply to Committee from Maryland Legislature," May 4, 1861, ibid., 356.

45. "Memorandum: Military Arrests," c. May 17, 1861, ibid., 372. Emphasis in original.

46. Ibid., 430–31.

47. Ibid., 430.

48. Lincoln to Albert G. Hodges, April 4, 1864, ibid., 7:281.

49. Michael Stokes Paulsen, "The Civil War as Constitutional Interpretation," *Univer-*

sity of Chicago Law Review 71 (Spring 2004), 721. Emphasis in original.

50. Lincoln to Reverdy Johnson, April 24, 1861, Basler, *Collected Works,* 4:343.

51. *Congressional Globe,* 37th Cong., 2nd sess., appendix, 82.

52. Nicolay and Hay, *Abraham Lincoln: A History,* 4:209–22; Simon Cameron to Lyon, April 30, 1861, *O.R.* 1:675; Lincoln to Frank Blair, May 18, 1862, Lorenzo Thomas to William Harney, May 27, 1862, Basler, *Collected Works,* 4:372–73, 387.

53. *O.R.* 52, i:146–48.

54. *O.R.,* series 3, vol. 1, p. 191; Lincoln to Robert Anderson, May 14, 1861, Basler, *Collected Works,* 4:368–69; Joshua Speed to Lincoln, May 26, 1861, Robert Anderson to Lincoln, May 19, 1861, Kentucky Unionist Committee Report, May 28, 1861, Lincoln Papers.

55. For a similar conclusion, see William E. Gienapp, "Abraham Lincoln and the Border States," *Journal of the Abraham Lincoln Association* 13 (1992), 13–46.

56. Charles Winslow Elliott, *Winfield Scott: The Soldier and the Man* (New York: Macmillan, 1937), 698; *O.R.* 51, i:369–70.

57. Edward Davis Townsend, *Anecdotes of*

the Civil War in the United States (New York: D. Appleton and Co., 1884), 55–56. Colonel Townsend was Scott's chief of staff and was present at this conversation with Lincoln.

58. Basler, *Collected Works,* 4:332.

59. *New York Herald,* May 25, 1861; Basler, *Collected Works,* 4:437.

60. Montgomery Blair to Lincoln, May 16, 1861, Lincoln Papers.

Chapter 2: The Bottom Is Out of the Tub

1. Alexander K. Randall to Lincoln, May 6, 1861, Abraham Lincoln Papers, Library of Congress.

2. Lincoln to Winfield Scott, June 5, 1861, in Roy P. Basler, ed., *The Collected Works of Abraham Lincoln,* 9 vols. (New Brunswick, N.J.: Rutgers University Press, 1953–55), 4:394–95.

3. Meigs's diary entry of June 29, 1861, transcript in John Nicolay Papers, Library of Congress, quoted in Russell F. Weigley, *Quartermaster General of the Union Army: A Biography of M. C. Meigs* (New York: Columbia University Press, 1959), 172.

4. Edward Davis Townsend, *Anecdotes of the Civil War in the United States* (New

York: D. Appleton and Co., 1884), 57; McDowell's testimony to the Joint Committee on the Conduct of the War, part 2, *Bull Run — Ball's Bluff* (37th Cong., Washington, D.C., 1863), 35–38.

5. John Nicolay to Therena Bates, July 21, 1861, in Michael Burlingame, ed., *With Lincoln in the White House: Letters, Memoranda, and Other Writings of John G. Nicolay, 1860–1865* (Carbondale, Ill.: Southern Illinois University Press, 2000), 51.

6. *O.R.* 2:747.

7. Thomas R. R. Cobb to his wife, July 24, 1861, in E. Merton Coulter, *The Confederate States of America 1861–1865* (Baton Rouge, La.: Louisiana State University Press, 1950), 345 (emphasis in original); *Mobile Register,* July 25, 1861, in J. Cutler Andrews, *The South Reports the Civil War* (Princeton, N.J.: Princeton University Press, 1970), 92.

8. Allan Nevins and Milton Halsey Thomas, eds., *The Diary of George Templeton Strong: The Civil War 1860–1865* (New York: Macmillan, 1952), 169, entry of July 22, 1861; Greeley to Lincoln, July 29, 1861, Lincoln Papers.

9. Lorenzo Thomas to McClellan, July 22, 1861, *O.R.* 2:753; "Memoranda of Military Policy Suggested by the Bull Run

Defeat," Basler, *Collected Works,* 4:457–58.

10. *O.R.,* series 3, vol. 1, pp. 380–83; Nicolay to Therena Bates, July 23, 1861, Burlingame, *With Lincoln in the White House,* 52.

11. Halleck to William T. Sherman, April 29, 1864, *O.R.* 34, iii:332–33.

12. *Chicago Tribune,* Sept. 16, 1861, quoted in Thomas J. Goss, *The War Within the Union High Command: Politics and Generalship During the Civil War* (Lawrence, Kans.: Kansas University Press, 2003), 42.

13. William Howard Russell, *My Diary North and South,* ed. Fletcher Pratt (New York: Harper and Brothers, 1954), 240, entry of July 27, 1861; Allan Nevins, *The War for the Union,* vol. 1, *The Improvised War 1861–1862* (New York: Charles Scribner's Sons, 1959), 269.

14. McClellan to Mary Ellen Marcy McClellan (hereafter Ellen), July 27, 30, Aug. 9, Oct. 31, 1861, in Stephen W. Sears, ed., *The Civil War Papers of George B. McClellan* (New York: Ticknor & Fields, 1989), 70, 71, 82; McClellan Papers, Library of Congress (for Oct. 31 letter).

15. *O.R.* 5:6–8.

16. Ibid., 11, iii:3–4.
17. McClellan to Ellen, Aug. 8, 1861, Sears, *Civil War Papers,* 81; Scott to Cameron, Aug. 9, 1861, *O.R.* 11, iii:4.
18. McClellan to Lincoln, Aug. 10, 1861, Lincoln Papers.
19. McClellan to Ellen, Aug. 8, 9, 14, 16, 19, Sears, *Civil War Papers,* 81, 84, 85–86, 87.
20. McClellan to Ellen, Oct. 10, 11, ibid., 106–7.
21. Joint Committee on the Conduct of the War, part 1, *The Army of the Potomac* (37th Cong., Washington, D.C., 1863), 241.
22. McClellan to Simon Cameron, Sept. 13, 1861, McClellan to Nathaniel P. Banks, Sept. 12, 1861, Sears, *Civil War Papers,* 99–100.
23. Dean Sprague, *Freedom Under Lincoln* (Boston: Houghton Mifflin, 1965), 180–212; "Statement Concerning Arrests in Maryland," c. Sept. 15, 1861, Basler, *Collected Works,* 4:523.
24. McClellan to Samuel S. Cox, Feb. 12, 1864, Sears, *Civil War Papers,* 565.
25. Wade to Chandler, Oct. 8, 1861, in Russell H. Beatie, *Army of the Potomac: McClellan Takes Command, September 1861–February 1862* (Cambridge, Mass.:

Da Capo Press, 2004), 25–26; McClellan to Ellen, Oct. 26, 1861, Sears, *Civil War Papers,* 112; Scott to Simon Cameron, Oct. 31, 1861, *O.R.,* series 2, vol. 1, 611–12.

26. McClellan to Ellen, Oct. 19, 1861, Sears, *Civil War Papers,* 109.

27. Michael Burlingame and John R. Turner Ettlinger, eds., *Inside Lincoln's White House: The Complete Civil War Diary of John Hay* (Carbondale, Ill.: Southern Illinois University Press, 1997), 30, entry dated "November 1861."

28. Ibid., 25, 29, entries of Oct. 10 and 26, 1861.

29. McClellan to Simon Cameron, undated but probably Oct. 31, 1861, *O.R.* 5:9–11.

30. McClellan to Ellen, Oct. 31, 1861, Sears, *Civil War Papers,* 113.

31. Burlingame and Ettlinger, *Inside Lincoln's White House,* 32, entry of Nov. 13, 1861; McClellan to Ellen, Nov. 17, 1861, Sears, *Civil War Papers,* 135.

32. "Memorandum to George B. McClellan on Potomac Campaign," c. Dec. 1, 1861, Basler, *Collected Works,* 5:34–35.

33. Johnston to Davis, Nov. 22, 1861, *O.R.* 51:1072–73.

34. McClellan to Lincoln, Dec. 10, 1861, Sears, *Civil War Papers,* 143.

35. Frank Blair, Jr., to Montgomery Blair, Sept. 1, 1861, Lincoln Papers.

36. See especially the report by Lorenzo Thomas, in *O.R.* 3:540–49.

37. Lincoln Papers.

38. Basler, *Collected Works,* 4:562–63; 5:1–2.

39. *O.R.* 3:466–67.

40. *Congressional Globe,* 37th Cong., 1st sess., 222–23.

41. The relevant correspondence can be found in Ira Berlin et al., eds., *Freedom: A Documentary History of Emancipation 1861–1867,* series 1, vol. 1 (Cambridge, U.K.: Cambridge University Press, 1985), 70–74; Lincoln's comment was quoted in Montgomery Blair to Benjamin Butler, May 29, 1861, in Jessie A. Marshall, ed., *Private and Official Correspondence of General Benjamin F. Butler During the Civil War,* 5 vols. (Norwood, Mass.: Plimpton Press, 1917), 1:116.

42. *U.S. Statutes at Large,* 12:319.

43. Theodore Calvin Pease and James G. Randall, eds., *The Diary of Orville Hickman Browning,* 2 vols. (Springfield, Ill.: Illinois State Historical Library, 1925), 1:477–78, entry of July 8, 1861.

44. Lincoln to Frémont, Sept. 2, 1861, Basler, *Collected Works,* 4:506.

45. Burlingame and Ettlinger, *Inside Lincoln's White House,* 123, diary entry of Dec. 9, 1863. See also Basler, *Collected Works,* 4:515, 519–20.

46. Browning to Lincoln, Sept. 17, 1861, Lincoln Papers; Lincoln to Browning, Sept. 22, 1861, Basler, *Collected Works,* 4:531–32.

47. "Memorandum of a Plan of Campaign," c. Oct. 1, 1861, Basler, *Collected Works,* 4:544–45.

48. Noel C. Fisher, *War at Every Door: Partisan Politics and Guerrilla Violence in East Tennessee, 1860–1869* (Chapel Hill, N.C.: University of North Carolina Press, 1997), chap. 3.

49. *O.R.* 4:342, 355–56, 358–59; 7:457–58, 530–31.

50. *O.R.* 7:531. Emphasis in original.

51. Lincoln to Buell, Jan. 6, 1862, Basler, *Collected Works,* 5:91.

52. Lincoln to Buell, Jan. 7, 1862, Lincoln to Halleck, Jan. 7, 1862, ibid., 91–92.

53. *O.R.* 7:532–33; Basler, *Collected Works,* 5:95; "General M. C. Meigs on the Conduct of the Civil War," *American Historical Review* 26 (1921), 292, 302, diary entry of Jan. 10, 1862.

CHAPTER 3: YOU MUST ACT

1. *O.R.,* series 3, vol. 1, p. 500; John G. Nicolay and John Hay, *Abraham Lincoln: A History,* 10 vols. (New York: The Century Co., 1890), 5:254–55); draft of an order to Butler, Sept. 10, 1861, in Roy P. Basler, ed., *The Collected Works of Abraham Lincoln,* 9 vols. (New Brunswick, N.J.: Rutgers University Press, 1953–55), 4:515.

2. Roy P. Basler, ed., *Collected Works: Supplement 2* (New Brunswick, N.J.: Rutgers University Press, 1990), 39.

3. "General M. C. Meigs on the Conduct of the Civil War," *American Historical Review* 26 (1921), 292, 302, diary entry of Jan. 10.

4. Howard K. Beale, ed., *The Diary of Edward Bates 1859–1866* (Washington, D.C.: U.S. Government Printing Office, 1933), 218, 220, entries of Dec. 31, 1861, and Jan. 3, 1862. See also ibid., 200, 224, 228, entries of Nov. 1, 1861, Jan. 10 and Feb. 3, 1862.

5. Virginia Woodbury Fox diary, entry of Jan. 26, 1862, quoted in David Herbert Donald, *Lincoln* (New York: Simon & Schuster, 1995), 331.

6. Minutes of the meeting written by McDowell, in William Swinton, *Campaigns of*

the *Army of the Potomac* (New York: Charles B. Richardson, 1866), 80.

7. Ibid., 79–85; "Meigs on the Conduct of the Civil War," 292–93, 303, diary entry of Jan. 11.

8. Stephen W. Sears, *George B. McClellan: The Young Napoleon* (New York: Ticknor & Fields, 1988), 142–44; Theodore Calvin Pease and James G. Randall, eds., *The Diary of Orville Hickman Browning,* 2 vols. (Springfield, Ill.: Illinois State Historical Library, 1925), 1:525, entry of Jan. 18, 1862.

9. Nicolay memorandum dated Oct. 2, 1861, in Michael Burlingame, ed., *With Lincoln in the White House: Letters, Memoranda, and Other Writings of John G. Nicolay, 1860–1865* (Carbondale, Ill.: Southern Illinois University Press, 2000), 59.

10. Basler, *Collected Works,* 5:96–97; Doris Kearns Goodwin, *Team of Rivals: The Political Genius of Abraham Lincoln* (New York: Simon & Schuster, 2005), 410–13.

11. McClellan to Samuel L. M. Barlow, Jan. 18, 1862, Barlow Papers, Huntington Library, San Marino, Calif.; Stanton to Charles A. Dana, Jan. 24, 1862, in A. Howard Meneely, *The War Department, 1861* (New York: Columbia University

Press, 1928), 318n. Emphasis in original.

12. Basler, *Collected Works,* 5:111–12, 115.

13. Pease and Randall, *Diary of Browning,* 1:523, entry of Jan. 12, 1862; Halleck to Lincoln, Jan. 6, 1862, *O.R.* 7:532–33.

14. Lincoln to Buell, copy to Halleck, Jan. 13, 1862, Basler, *Collected Works,* 5:98–99.

15. Henry A. Wise to Foote, Feb. 10, 1862, *Official Records of the Union and Confederate Navies,* 22:549.

16. Kenneth P. Williams, *Lincoln Finds a General: A Military Study of the Civil War,* 5 vols. (New York: Macmillan, 1949–59), 3:261; *O.R.* 7:627, 637.

17. *O.R.* 7:676, 679–80, 682; John Y. Simon, ed., *The Papers of Ulysses S. Grant,* 28 vols. to date (Carbondale, Ill.: Southern Illinois University Press, 1967–), 4:319n., 331, 353.

18. Jean Edward Smith, *Grant* (New York: Simon & Schuster, 2001), 176–79; Brooks D. Simpson, *Ulysses S. Grant: Triumph over Adversity, 1822–1865* (Boston: Houghton Mifflin, 2000), 122–27; Lorenzo Thomas to Halleck, March 10, 1862, Halleck to Thomas, March 15, 1862, *O.R.* 7:683–84; Halleck to Grant, March 13, 1862, Simon, *Papers of Grant,* 4:354–55.

19. The entire exchange between Lincoln and McClellan is in Basler, *Collected Works,* 5:118–25. See also Stephen W. Sears, ed., *The Civil War Papers of George B. McClellan: Selected Correspondence 1860–1865* (New York: Ticknor & Fields, 1989), 162–71.

20. Burlingame, *With Lincoln in the White House,* 72; Nicolay's journal entry of Feb. 27, 1862.

21. Ibid.

22. McClellan to Samuel L. M. Barlow, Nov. 8, 1861, Barlow Papers.

23. Several versions of this anecdote exist; this one is from Helen Nicolay, *Lincoln's Secretary: A Biography of John G. Nicolay* (New York: Longman's, Green, 1949), 149, evidently based on recollections by her father, who may have been present at the meeting. See also Bruce Tap, *Over Lincoln's Shoulder: The Committee on the Conduct of the War* (Lawrence, Kans.: Kansas University Press, 1998), 113.

24. Mark R. Wilson, *The Business of Civil War: Military Mobilization and the State, 1861–1865* (Baltimore: Johns Hopkins University Press, 2006), 60–61. See also Russell H. Beatie, *Army of the Potomac,* vol. 2, *McClellan Takes Command, Septem-*

ber 1861–February 1862 (Cambridge, Mass.: Da Capo Press, 2004), 206, 329; and William Skelton, "Officers and Politicians: The Origins of Army Politics in the United States before the Civil War," *Armed Forces and Society* 6 (1979), 22–48, esp. 48n.52.

25. James J. Campbell to his wife, March 4, 1862, in Don E. Fehrenbacher and Virginia Fehrenbacher, eds., *Recollected Words of Abraham Lincoln* (Stanford, Calif.: Stanford University Press, 1996), 76.

26. William A. Croffut, ed., *Fifty Years in Camp and Field: The Diary of Ethan Allen Hitchcock* (New York: G. P. Putnam's Sons, 1909), 438–40, diary entries of March 15, 17, 1862.

27. George B. McClellan, *McClellan's Own Story* (New York: Charles L. Webster and Co., 1887), 195; Stephen W. Sears, *To the Gates of Richmond: The Peninsula Campaign* (New York: Ticknor & Fields, 1992), 4–5. McClellan's account is the only source for the substance of Lincoln's remarks. The meeting on March 7 did take place, however.

28. T. Harry Williams, *Lincoln and His Generals* (New York: Alfred A. Knopf, 1952), 67.

29. Basler, *Collected Works,* 5:149–51, 155.

30. McClellan to Barlow, March 16, 1862, Barlow Papers.

31. Benjamin Franklin Cooling, *Symbol, Sword, and Shield: Defending Washington During the Civil War* (Hamden, Conn.: Archon Books, 1975), 109.

32. Basler, *Collected Works,* 5:157.

33. The letters and memorandums about this matter are in *O.R.* 11, iii:57–62.

34. Sumner to John A. Andrew, May 28, 1862, in Beverly Wilson Palmer, ed., *The Selected Letters of Charles Sumner,* 2 vols. (Boston: Northeastern University Press, 1990), 2:115; Lincoln to Edwin M. Stanton, April 3, 1862, Basler, *Collected Works,* 5:179.

35. McClellan to Ellen, April 6, 11, 27, Sears, *Civil War Papers,* 230, 235, 250; McClellan Papers, Library of Congress (for more of April 27 letter).

36. *O.R.* 11, iii:71; Lincoln to McClellan, April 9, 1862, Basler, *Collected Works,* 5:184.

37. Lincoln to McClellan, April 6, 1862, Basler, *Collected Works,* 5:182; McClellan to Ellen, April 8, 1862, Sears, *Civil War Papers,* 234.

38. Pease and Randall, *Diary of Browning,* 1:537, entry of April 2, 1862; Basler, *Col-*

lected *Works,* 5:185.

39. *O.R.* 11, i:364–67, 372–73; McClellan to Ellen, April 18, 1862, Sears, *Civil War Papers,* 240.

40. Johnston to Robert E. Lee, April 22, 1862, *O.R.* 11, iii:455–56.

41. Ibid., 10, i:98–100.

42. Brooks D. Simpson, "Alexander Mc-Clure on Lincoln and Grant: A Questionable Account," *Lincoln Herald* 95 (1993), 83–86.

43. Washburne to Grant, Jan. 22, 1864, Simon, *Papers of Grant,* 9:522n.

44. *Congressional Globe,* 37th Cong., 2nd sess., 15.

45. *U.S. Statutes at Large,* 12:354, 376–78.

46. Basler, *Collected Works,* 3:92, 2:255.

47. Ibid., 7:281.

48. Ibid., 5:48–49.

49. Ibid., 5:29–30; H. Clay Reed, "Lincoln's Compensated Emancipation Plan and Its Relation to Delaware," *Delaware Notes,* 7th series (1931), 27–78, quotation on p. 51.

50. Basler, *Collected Works,* 5:144–46, 152–53, 160–61.

51. Memorandum of the meeting written by Representative John W. Crisfield of Maryland, in Charles M. Segal, ed., *Conversations with Lincoln* (New York: G. P.

Putnam's Sons, 1961), 164–68.

52. Lincoln to Chase, May 17, 1862, Basler, *Collected Works,* 5:219.

53. Ibid., 5:222–24. The sentence about a tendency to a total disruption of society in the South was deleted from the final version of Lincoln's order.

54. *New York Herald,* April 30, 1862; *New York Times,* April 9, 1862.

55. Mary Jones to Charles C. Jones, Jr., Feb. 21, 1862; Charles C. Jones, Jr., to Mary Jones, March 18, 1862, in Robert Manson Mayers, ed., *Children of Pride: A True Story of Georgia and the Civil War* (New Haven, Conn.: Yale University Press, 1972), 852, 863; William Kauffman Scarborough, ed., *The Diary of Edmund Ruffin,* 3 vols. (Baton Rouge, La.: Louisiana State University Press, 1972–89), 3:291, entry of April 30, 1862.

56. Lincoln to Flag Officer Louis M. Goldsborough, May 7, 10, 1862, Basler, *Collected Works,* 5:207, 209; William Keeler to his wife, May 9, 1862, in Robert W. Daly, ed., *Aboard the* USS Monitor, *1862: The Letters of Acting Paymaster William Frederick Keeler* (Annapolis, Md.: Naval Institute Press, 1964), 113, 115.

57. Salmon P. Chase to Janet Chase, May

11, 1862, in John Niven, ed., *The Salmon P. Chase Papers,* vol. 3, *Correspondence, 1858–March 1863* (Kent, Ohio: Kent State University Press, 1996), 193–97, quotation from 197.

58. Pease and Randall, *Diary of Browning,* 1:545, entry of May 14, 1862.

59. Francis A. Donaldson to Jacob Donaldson, May 25, 1862, in J. Gregory Acken, ed., *Inside the Army of the Potomac: The Civil War Experience of Captain Francis Adams Donaldson* (Mechanicsburg, Pa.: Stackpole Books, 1998), 85; Kerry A. Trask, *Fire Within: A Civil War Narrative from Wisconsin* (Kent, Ohio: Kent State University Press, 1995), 111; Harold Earl Hammond, ed., *Diary of a Union Lady, 1861–1865* (New York: Funk & Wagnalls, 1962), 127; diary entry by Maria Lydig Daly, May 11, 1862, quoting Ellen McClellan.

60. Helen Keary to her mother, May 7, 1862, in Edward A. Pollard, *Southern History of the War,* 2 vols. (New York: Charles B. Richardson, 1866), 1:381–82n.

61. Charles Minor Blackford to his wife, April 30, 1862, in Charles M. Blackford III, ed., *Letters from Lee's Army* (New York: Charles Scribner's Sons, 1947), 83.

Chapter 4: A Question of Legs

1. McClellan to Lincoln, May 14, 1862, *O.R.* 11, i:26–27; Lincoln to McDowell, May 17, 1862, in Roy P. Basler, ed., *The Collected Works of Abraham Lincoln,* 9 vols. (New Brunswick, N.J.: Rutgers University Press, 1953–55), 5:219.

2. *O.R.,* series 3, vol. 2, pp. 69–70, 72, 85, 86.

3. McClellan to Lincoln, May 23, 1862, *O.R.* 11, iii:32; McClellan to Ellen, May 25, 1862, in Stephen W. Sears, ed., *The Civil War Papers of George B. McClellan* (New York: Ticknor & Fields, 1989), 275.

4. McClellan to Lincoln, May 21, 1862, *O.R.* 11, i:28.

5. Lincoln to Frémont, May 24, 1862 (two telegrams), Frémont to Lincoln, May 24, Basler, *Collected Works,* 5:230–31.

6. Lincoln to McDowell, May 24, 1862 (two telegrams), May 28, McDowell to Stanton, May 24, McDowell to Lincoln, May 24, Basler, *Collected Works,* 5:232–33, 246.

7. McDowell to Shields, May 29, 1862 (two telegrams), *O.R.* 12, iii:278–79.

8. Basler, *Collected Works,* 5:243, 247, 250, 251; *O.R.* 12, i:644.

9. *O.R.* 12, i:651.

10. Report dated June 13, 1862, ibid., 12, i:685.

11. Lincoln to Frémont, June 9, 12, 13, 15, 16, 1862, Basler, *Collected Works*, 5:264, 267–68, 269, 270–71, 273–74.

12. *O.R.* 12, iii:437–38.

13. Kevin Dougherty with J. Michael Moore, *The Peninsula Campaign of 1862: A Military Analysis* (Jackson, Miss.: University Press of Mississippi, 2005), 44–45.

14. Lincoln to Halleck, June 4, 1862, Basler, *Collected Works*, 5:259; Stanton to Halleck, June 2, 11, 1862, *O.R.* 10, ii:242; 16, ii:8.

15. McClellan to Ellen, June 2, 23, 1862, Sears, *Civil War Papers*, 288, 306.

16. McClellan to Stanton, June 25, 1862, *O.R.* 11, i:51; Lincoln to McClellan, June 26, 1862, Basler, *Collected Works*, 5:26; McClellan to Ellen, June 22, 1862, Sears, *Civil War Papers*, 305.

17. Basler, *Collected Works*, 5:284, 312–13. Scott's memorandum dated June 24 and supposedly summarizing the matters he discussed with Lincoln is vague and uninformative. It does not mention the possible appointments of Pope and Halleck. Ibid., 284n.

18. McClellan to Stanton, June 27, 1862, *O.R.* 11, iii:266.

19. McClellan to Stanton, June 28, 1862, *O.R.* 11, i:61; David Homer Bates, *Lincoln in the Telegraph Office* (New York: Century Co., 1907), 108–10.

20. *New York World,* July 7, 1862; *Chicago Tribune,* July 5, 1862; *Illinois State Register,* July 3, 1862.

21. Adam Gurowski, *Diary from March 4, 1861, to November 12, 1862* (Boston: Lee and Shepard, 1862), 235, entry of July 4, 1862; Lincoln quoted by Henry C. Deming, in Don E. Fehrenbacher and Virginia Fehrenbacher, eds., *Recollected Words of Abraham Lincoln* (Stanford, Calif.: Stanford University Press, 1996), 136–37.

22. Lincoln to McClellan, July 1, 2, 1862, Basler, *Collected Works,* 5:298, 301.

23. Ibid., 288, 303; *O.R.* 11, iii:290–91.

24. *O.R.* 11, iii:271; Basler, *Collected Works,* 5:295, 300–301, 305, 308.

25. Meigs diary, entries of July 4 and 5, 1862, quoted in T. Harry Williams, *Lincoln and His Generals* (New York: Alfred A. Knopf, 1952), 130; Michael Burlingame and John R. Turner Ettlinger, eds., *Inside Lincoln's White House: The Complete Civil War Diary of John Hay* (Carbondale, Ill.: Southern Illinois University Press, 1997), 191, entry of April 28, 1864.

26. Basler, *Collected Works,* 5:291–92, 293–94, 296–97.
27. Ibid., 309–12; John G. Nicolay to Therena Bates, July 13, 1862, in Michael Burlingame, ed., *With Lincoln in the White House: Letters, Memoranda, and Other Writings of John G. Nicolay, 1860–1865* (Carbondale, Ill.: Southern Illinois University Press, 2000), 85.
28. McClellan to Ellen, July 10, 17, 1862, Sears, *Civil War Papers,* 348, 362.
29. McClellan to Samuel L. M. Barlow, July 23, 1862; McClellan to Ellen, July 20, 1862, ibid., 368, 369.
30. McClellan to Barlow, July 23, 1862, ibid., 370.
31. McClellan to Ellen, July 13, 22, 1862, ibid., 354, 368.
32. *New York Herald,* July 7, 15, 1862.
33. Oliver W. Norton to family, July 9, 1862, in Oliver Willcox Norton, *Army Letters 1861–1865* (Chicago: O. L. Deming, 1903), 98; letter of Edward G. Abbott, July 12, in "Letters from the Harvard Regiments," ed. Anthony J. Milano, *Civil War: The Magazine of the Civil War Society* 13, p. 44, from the research notes of John Hennessy, used with permission.
34. Basler, *Collected Works,* 5:358–59. Emphasis in original.

35. John Sherman to William T. Sherman, Aug. 24, 1862, in George Winston Smith and Charles Judah, eds., *Life in the North During the Civil War* (Albuquerque, N.M.: University of New Mexico Press, 1966), 99.

36. John Beatty, *Memoirs of a Volunteer 1861–1863,* ed. Harvey S. Ford (New York: W. W. Norton & Co., 1946), 118, diary entry of July 18, 1862; Illinois officer quoted in Bruce Catton, *Grant Moves South* (Boston: Little, Brown and Company, 1960), 294.

37. Charles Brewster to Mary Brewster, May 18, June 21, 1862, in David W. Blight, ed., *When This Cruel War Is Over: The Civil War Letters of Charles Harvey Brewster* (Amherst, Mass.: University of Massachusetts Press, 1992), 133, 152; Halleck to Grant, Aug. 2, 1862, *O.R.* 17, ii:150.

38. Stephen O. Himoe to his wife, June 26, 1862, in Luther M. Kuhns, ed., "An Army Surgeon's Letters to His Wife," *Proceedings of the Mississippi Valley Historical Association* 7 (1914), 311–12; Lucius Hubbard to Mary Hubbard, Sept. 8, 1862, in N. B. Martin, ed., "Letters of a Union Officer: L. F. Hubbard and the Civil War,"

Minnesota History 35 (1957), 314–15.

39. *O.R.* 11, i:73–74.

40. Roy P. Basler, ed., *The Collected Works of Abraham Lincoln: Supplement 1* (New Brunswick, N.J.: Rutgers University Press, 1990), 141; "General Orders No. 109," Aug. 16, 1862, *O.R.,* series 3, vol. 2, p. 397. See also Daniel Sutherland, "Lincoln, Pope, and the Origins of Total War," *Journal of Military History* 56 (Oct. 1992), 567–86.

41. *New York Times,* July 27, 1862.

42. McClellan to Ellen, July 17, 1862, Sears, *Civil War Papers,* 362; McClellan to Halleck, Aug. 1, 1862, *O.R.* 11, iii:345–46.

43. McClellan to Ellen, Aug. 8, 1862, Sears, *Civil War Papers,* 388; "General Orders No. 154," Aug. 9, 1862, *O.R.* 11, iii:362–64.

44. McClellan to Lincoln, July 7, 1862, Abraham Lincoln Papers, Library of Congress.

45. Lincoln to Cuthbert Bullitt, July 28, 1862, Lincoln to August Belmont, July 31, 1862, Basler, *Collected Works,* 5:344–46, 350–51.

46. John Sherman to William T. Sherman, Aug. 24, 1862, in Rachel T. Thorndike, ed., *The Sherman Letters: Correspondence*

Between General and Senator Sherman from 1837 to 1891 (New York: Charles Scribner's Sons, 1894), 156–57; *Boston Advertiser,* Aug. 20, 1862.

47. Basler, *Collected Works,* 5:317–19.

48. William Whiting, *The War Powers of the President, and the Legislative Powers of Congress in Relation to Rebellion, Treason, and Slavery,* 7th ed. (Boston: J. L. Shorey, 1863), passim.

49. Gideon Welles, "The History of Emancipation," *Galaxy* 14 (Dec. 1872), 842–43. See also Howard K. Beale, ed., *Diary of Gideon Welles,* 3 vols. (New York: W. W. Norton & Co., 1960), 1:70–71.

50. Basler, *Collected Works,* 5:336–37; Francis B. Carpenter, *Six Months at the White House with Abraham Lincoln* (New York: Hurd and Houghton, 1866), 20–22; John Niven, ed., *The Salmon P. Chase Papers,* vol. 1, *Journals, 1829–1872* (Kent, Ohio: Kent State University Press, 1993), 351, journal entry of July 22, 1862.

51. Carpenter, *Six Months at the White House,* 22.

Chapter 5: Destroy the Rebel Army, If Possible

1. Roy P. Basler, ed., *The Collected Works of Abraham Lincoln,* 9 vols. (New Brunswick, N.J.: Rutgers University Press, 1953–55), 5:323; Theodore Calvin Pease and James G. Randall, eds., *The Diary of Orville Hickman Browning,* 2 vols. (Springfield, Ill.: Illinois State Historical Library, 1925), 1:559–60, entry of July 15, 1862.

2. The best account of this exchange is Stephen W. Sears, *George B. McClellan: The Young Napoleon* (New York: Ticknor & Fields, 1988), 238–42. For the correspondence on this and related matters, see Stephen W. Sears, ed., *The Civil War Papers of George B. McClellan: Selected Correspondence, 1860–1865* (New York: Ticknor & Fields, 1989), 369–93; Halleck to McClellan, Aug. 6, 1862, *O.R.* 12, ii:9–11. See also John F. Marszalek, *Commander of All Lincoln's Armies: A Life of General Henry W. Halleck* (Cambridge, Mass.: Harvard University Press, 2004), 135–39.

3. Meigs to Halleck, July 28, 1862, *O.R.* 11, iii:340–41.

4. Pease and Randall, *Diary of Browning,* 1:563, entry of July 25, 1862.

5. William Marvel, *Burnside* (Chapel Hill,

N.C.: University of North Carolina Press, 1991), 99–100; Burnside's testimony to the Committee on the Conduct of the War, *Report of the Joint Committee on the Conduct of the War,* 37th Cong., 4 vols. (Washington, D.C., 1863), 2:650.

6. *O.R.* 12, iii:473–74.
7. McClellan to Ellen, Aug. 10, 1862, Sears, *Civil War Papers,* 389–90.
8. Halleck to his wife, Aug. 9, 1862, in James Grant Wilson, "General Halleck: A Memoir," *Journal of the Military Service Institution of the United States* (Governor's Island, N.Y.: Military Service Institution, 1905), 557.
9. McClellan to Ellen, Aug. 10, 23, 24, Sears, *Civil War Papers,* 389, 400, 404.
10. Buell to McClellan, Dec. 10, 1862, Civil War Collection, Huntington Library, San Marino, Calif.
11. Halleck to Buell, July 8, 1862, Buell to Halleck, July 11, 1862, *O.R.* 16, ii:104.
12. Halleck to Buell, Aug. 12, 18, 1862; Halleck to Gen. Horatio Wright, Aug. 25, 1862, ibid., ii:314–15, 360, 421.
13. For some examples, see Basler, *Collected Works,* 5:408, 409, 410, 416, 419.
14. *O.R.* 16, ii:530.
15. Ibid., 538–39, 549, 554–55.
16. Charles Francis Adams, Jr., to Charles

Francis Adams, Aug. 27, 1862, in Worthington Chauncey Ford, ed., *A Cycle of Adams Letters 1861–1865,* 2 vols. (Boston: Houghton Mifflin, 1920), 1:177–78.

17. Porter to Manton Marble, Aug. 10, 1862, Marble Papers, Library of Congress, quoted in T. Harry Williams, *Lincoln and His Generals* (New York: Alfred A. Knopf, 1952), 148.

18. This remarkable series of telegrams and events is conveniently reprinted and chronicled in Sears, *Civil War Papers,* 410–19.

19. Michael Burlingame and John R. Turner Ettlinger, eds., *Inside Lincoln's White House: The Complete Civil War Diary of John Hay* (Carbondale, Ill.: Southern Illinois University Press, 1997), 191–92, entry of April 28, 1864.

20. Marszalek, *Commander of All Lincoln's Armies,* 146–53.

21. McClellan to Lincoln, Aug. 29, 1862, Sears, *Civil War Papers,* 416; Burlingame and Ettlinger, *Inside Lincoln's White House,* 37, diary entry of Sept. 1, 1862.

22. *Report of the Joint Committee on the Conduct of the War,* 37th Cong., 2:363; *The Reminiscences of Carl Schurz,* 3 vols. (New York: McClure Co., 1907–8), 2:382.

23. Adams Hill to Sydney Howard Gay, Sept. 1, 1862, quoted in Stephen W. Sears, *Landscape Turned Red: The Battle of Antietam* (New Haven, Conn.: Ticknor & Fields, 1983), 13.

24. *New York Tribune,* Sept. 4, 1862; *New York Times,* Sept. 5, 1862.

25. *New York Times,* Sept. 7, 1862.

26. Henry Pearson to "friend," Sept. 5, 1862, in Annette Tapert, ed., *The Brothers' War: Civil War Letters to Their Loved Ones from the Blue and Gray* (New York: Times Books, 1988), 85; Washington Roebling to his father, early September 1862, in Paul M. Angle and Earl Schenck Miers, eds., *Tragic Years 1860–1865,* 2 vols. (New York: Simon & Schuster, 1960), 1:344–45; Davis S. Sparks, ed., *Inside Lincoln's Army: The Diary of General Marsena Rudolph Patrick* (New York: Thomas Yoseloff, 1964), 140, entry of Sept. 6, 1862.

27. Adams Hill to Sydney Howard Gay, Aug. 31, 1862, quoted in Burlingame and Ettlinger, *Inside Lincoln's White House,* 293n.; John Hay's diary entry of Sept. 1, 1862, ibid., 36–37.

28. Howard K. Beale, ed., *Diary of Gideon Welles,* 3 vols. (New York: W. W. Norton & Co., 1960), 1:93–102, entries of Aug. 31

and Sept. 1, 1862; John Niven, ed., *The Salmon P. Chase Papers,* vol. 1, *Journals, 1829–1872* (Kent, Ohio: Kent State University Press, 1993), 366–68, diary entries of Aug. 29, 30, 31, Sept. 1, 1862.

29. McClellan to Ellen, Sept. 5, 7, 8, 1862, Sears, *Civil War Papers,* 435, 438, 440.

30. Beale, *Diary of Gideon Welles,* 1:104–13, entries of Sept. 2 and 7, 1862; Burlingame and Ettlinger, *Inside Lincoln's White House,* 38–39, entry of Sept. 5, 1862; Basler, *Collected Works,* 5:486n., quoting a notation on the Sept. 2 cabinet meeting written by Attorney General Edward Bates. See also Doris Kearns Goodwin, *Team of Rivals: The Political Genius of Abraham Lincoln* (New York: Simon & Schuster, 2005), 475–80.

31. William H. Powell and George Kimball quoted in Clarence C. Buel and Robert U. Johnson, eds., *Battles and Leaders of the Civil War,* 4 vols. (New York: The Century Co., 1888), 2:490n. and 550–51n.; Stephen M. Weld to his father, Sept. 4, 1862, *War Diary and Letters of Stephen Minot Weld 1861–1865* (Boston: Riverside Press, 1912), 136.

32. *Chicago Tribune,* Sept. 9, 1862.

33. *O.R.* 19, ii:281.

34. McClellan to Halleck, Sept. 15, 1862 (two telegrams), ibid., ii:294–95.

35. Lincoln to McClellan, Sept. 15, 1862; Lincoln to Jesse K. DuBois, Sept. 15, 1862, Basler, *Collected Works,* 5:425–26.

36. *O.R.* 19, ii:322. Of the many books on the Battle of Antietam, the best are Sears, *Landscape Turned Red,* and James V. Murfin, *The Gleam of Bayonets: The Battle of Antietam and Robert E. Lee's Maryland Campaign, September 1862* (Baton Rouge, La.: Louisiana State University Press, 1965).

37. McClellan to Halleck, Sept. 19, 1862 (two telegrams), *O.R.* 19, ii:330; Beale, *Diary of Gideon Welles,* 1:140, entry of Sept. 19, 1862.

38. McClellan to Ellen, Sept. 18, 20 (two letters), Sears, *Civil War Papers,* 469, 473, 476.

39. Pinkerton to McClellan, Sept. 22, 1862, in James D. Horan and Howard Swiggett, *The Pinkerton Story* (New York: G. P. Putnam's Sons, 1951), 111–14.

40. *New York Times,* Sept. 18, 21, 1862.

41. Arthur B. Carpenter to parents, Dec. 5, 1861, quoted in Thomas R. Bright, "Yankees in Arms: The Civil War as a Personal Experience," *Civil War History* 19 (Sept. 1973), 202.

42. Frank L. Klement, *The Copperheads in the Middle West* (Chicago: University of Chicago Press, 1960), 14; V. Jacque Voegeli, *Free but Not Equal: The Midwest and the Negro During the Civil War* (Chicago: University of Chicago Press, 1967), 18.

43. Bell Irvin Wiley, *The Life of Billy Yank: The Common Soldier of the Union* (Indianapolis: Bobbs-Merrill Company, 1952), 112.

44. Basler, *Collected Works,* 5:370–75.

45. Niven, *Chase Papers, Journals,* 362; entry of Aug. 15, 1862.

46. Lincoln to Greeley, Aug. 22, 1862, Basler, *Collected Works,* 5:388–89.

47. John G. Nicolay and John Hay, *Abraham Lincoln: A History* (New York: The Century Co., 1890), 6:157; Basler, *Collected Works,* 6:419–25.

48. Beale, *Diary of Gideon Welles,* 1:142–45; Niven, *Chase Papers, Journals,* 393–95, entries of Sept. 22, 1862; Basler, *Collected Works,* 5:433–36.

49. Niven, *Chase Papers, Journals,* 395; Beale, *Diary of Gideon Welles,* 143–44; Gideon Welles, "The History of Emancipation," *The Galaxy* 14 (1872), 842–43.

50. *New York Tribune,* Sept. 23, 24, 1862.

51. T. J. Barnett to Samuel L. M. Barlow, Sept. 25, 1862, Barlow Papers, Huntington Library, San Marino, Calif.; Halleck to Grant, March 31, 1863, *O.R.* 24, iii:157.

52. Basler, *Collected Works,* 5:436–37.

53. Porter to Manton Marble, Sept. 30, 1862, Sears, *George B. McClellan,* 325; McClellan to Ellen, Sept. 25, 1862, Sears, *Civil War Papers,* 481.

54. McClellan to Aspinwall, Sept. 26, 1862, McClellan to Ellen, Oct. 5, 1862, Sears, *Civil War Papers,* 482, 490.

55. Basler, *Collected Works,* 5:442–43, 508–9; Burlingame and Ettlinger, *Inside Lincoln's White House,* 232, entry of Sept. 25, 1864.

56. *O.R.* 19, ii:395; original in Abraham Lincoln Papers, Library of Congress; also in Sears, *Civil War Papers,* 493–94.

57. *O.R.* 19, i:272.

CHAPTER 6: THE PROMISE MUST NOW BE KEPT

1. Halleck to Buell, Oct. 19, 23, *O.R.* 16, ii:627, 638.

2. Lincoln to McClellan, Oct. 13, 1862, in Roy P. Basler, ed., *The Collected Works of Abraham Lincoln,* 9 vols. (New Brunswick,

N.J.: Rutgers University Press, 1953–55), 5:460–61.

3. Shelby Foote, *The Civil War: A Narrative. Fort Sumter to Perryville* (New York: Random House, 1958), 430.

4. Rufus Ingalls to Montgomery Meigs, Oct. 26, 1862, *O.R.* 19, ii:492–93.

5. *Report of the Joint Committee on the Conduct of the War,* 37th Cong., 4 vols. (Washington, D.C., 1863), 2:135; Edward Hagerman, *The American Civil War and the Origins of Modern Warfare* (Bloomington, Ind.: Indiana University Press, 1988), xiii, xv.

6. Lincoln to Nathaniel P. Banks, Nov. 22, 1862, Basler, *Collected Works,* 5:505–6.

7. Oliver P. Morton to Lincoln, Oct. 21, 1862, Morton and Richard Yates to Lincoln, Oct. 25, 1862, Halleck to Rosecrans, Oct. 23, 24, 1862, *O.R.* 19, ii:634, 639, 640–42.

8. William C. Davis, *Lincoln's Men: How President Lincoln Became Father to an Army and a Nation* (New York: The Free Press, 1999), esp. chap. 3.

9. Michael Burlingame, ed., *An Oral History of Abraham Lincoln: John G. Nicolay's Interviews and Essays* (Carbondale, Ill.: Southern Illinois University Press, 1996),

16, from an interview by Nicolay with Ozias Hatch in 1875.

10. *New York Times,* Oct. 16, 19, 1862; Joseph Medill to Ozias M. Hatch, Oct. 13, 1862, in James V. Murfin, *The Gleam of Bayonets: The Battle of Antietam and Robert E. Lee's Maryland Campaign, September 1862* (Baton Rouge, La.: Louisiana State University Press, 1965), 300.

11. Halleck to Hamilton R. Gamble, Oct. 30, 1862, *O.R.,* series 3, vol. 2, pp. 703–4.

12. *Missouri Republican,* Oct. 5, 1862, in Michael Burlingame, ed., *Lincoln's Journalist: John Hay's Anonymous Writings for the Press, 1860–1864* (Carbondale, Ill.: Southern Illinois University Press, 1998), 314–16; David Davis to Leonard Swett, Nov. 26, 1862, quoted in Don E. Fehrenbacher and Virginia Fehrenbacher, eds., *Recollected Words of Abraham Lincoln* (Stanford, Calif.: Stanford University Press, 1996), 132.

13. Lincoln to McClellan, Oct. 13, 1862, Basler, *Collected Works,* 5:460–61.

14. Halleck to McClellan, Oct. 14, 1862, *O.R.* 19, ii:421; Meigs to Edwin M. Stanton, Oct. 25, 1862, ibid., i:21–22.

15. Ibid., 19, ii:485–86; Lincoln to McClellan, Oct. 25, 1862, Basler, *Collected Works,* 5:474; McClellan to Ellen, Oct. 29, 1862,

in Stephen W. Sears, ed., *The Civil War Papers of George B. McClellan* (New York: Ticknor & Fields, 1989), 515.

16. McClellan to Lincoln, Oct. 25, 1862, *O.R.* 19, ii:485; Lincoln to McClellan, Oct. 26, 1862, Basler, *Collected Works,* 5:477.

17. Lincoln to McClellan, Oct. 26, 1862, Basler, *Collected Works,* 5:477.

18. Francis P. Blair to Montgomery Blair, Nov. 7, 1862, in William E. Smith, *The Francis Preston Blair Family in Politics,* 2 vols. (New York: Macmillan, 1933), 2:144.

19. Basler, *Collected Works,* 5:485; *O.R.* 19, ii:549; McClellan to Ellen, Nov. 7, 1862, Sears, *Civil War Papers,* 520.

20. Bruce Catton, *Mr. Lincoln's Army* (Garden City, N.Y.: Doubleday, 1951), 334–36; William F. Keeler to Anna Keeler, Nov. 9, 1864, in Robert W. Daly, ed., *Aboard the* USS Florida, *1863–1865: The Letters of Paymaster William F. Keeler* (Annapolis, Md.: Naval Institute Press, 1968), 200.

21. Basler, *Collected Works,* 5:484.

22. Mary A. Livermore, *My Story of the War* (Hartford, Conn.: A. D. Worthington and Co., 1890), 556. Although these words were written from memory nearly thirty years later by a woman who heard them,

this quotation is remarkably similar to a memorandum that Lincoln wrote in November 1862, which included the words "hard desperate fighting." Basler, *Collected Works,* 5:484.

23. J. C. Wylie, *Military Strategy: A General Theory of Power Control* (New Brunswick, N.J.: Rutgers University Press, 1967), 52.

24. *O.R.* 19, ii:552–54.

25. Halleck to Burnside, Nov. 14, 1862, ibid., ii:579.

26. Burnside to Halleck, Dec. 17, 1862; Halleck to Burnside, Jan. 7, 1863, ibid., 21, 66–67, 953–54; Halleck's Report, Nov. 15, 1863, ibid., 46–47; Halleck's and Meigs's testimony to the Committee on the Conduct of the War, *Report of the Joint Committee,* 2:675, 680.

27. Basler, *Collected Works,* 5:514–15.

28. William Henry Wadsworth to Samuel L. M. Barlow, Dec. 16, 1862, Barlow Papers, Huntington Library, San Marino, Calif.; Basler, *Collected Works,* 6:13.

29. Samuel Wilkeson to Sydney Howard Gay, Dec. 19, 1862, Gay Papers, Columbia University Library; Theodore C. Pease and James G. Randall, eds., *The Diary of Orville Hickman Browning,* 2 vols. (Springfield, Ill.: Illinois State Historical

Library, 1927), 1:600–601, entry of Dec. 18, 1862.

30. The best contemporary accounts of this affair are Howard K. Beale, ed., *Diary of Gideon Welles,* 3 vols. (New York: W. W. Norton & Co., 1960), 1:194–204; and Pease and Randall, *Diary of Browning,* 1:596–604. The best secondary accounts are Allan Nevins, *The War for the Union,* vol. 2, *War Becomes Revolution* (New York: Charles Scribner's Sons, 1960), 350–65; Phillip Shaw Paludan, *The Presidency of Abraham Lincoln* (Lawrence, Kans.: Kansas University Press, 1994), 170–77; David Herbert Donald, *Lincoln* (New York: Simon & Schuster, 1995), 398–406; and Doris Kearns Goodwin, *Team of Rivals: The Political Genius of Abraham Lincoln* (New York: Simon & Schuster, 2005), 486–95.

31. Franklin and Smith to Lincoln, Dec. 20, 1862, *O.R.* 21, 868–70; Lincoln to Franklin and Smith, Dec. 22, 1862, Basler, *Collected Works,* 6:15.

32. Burnside's, Newton's, and Cochrane's testimony to the Committee on the Conduct of the War, *Report of the Joint Committee,* 37th Cong., 2:717–21, 730–46; Lincoln to Burnside, Dec. 30, 1862,

Basler, *Collected Works,* 6:22; Burnside to Lincoln, Dec. 30, 1862, Abraham Lincoln Papers, Library of Congress.

33. Burnside to Lincoln, Jan. 1, 1863, *O.R.* 21, 940–41.

34. Lincoln to Halleck, Jan. 1, 1863, Basler, *Collected Works,* 6:31.

35. Halleck to Stanton, Jan. 1, 1863, *O.R.* 21, 940–41; Basler, *Collected Works,* 6:31.

36. Halleck to Gen. Horatio Wright, Nov. 18, 1862, *O.R.* 20, ii:67.

37. Gasparin to Lincoln, July 18, 1862, Lincoln Papers; Lincoln to Gasparin, Aug. 4, 1862, Basler, *Collected Works,* 5:355–56.

38. Lincoln to Samuel Treat, Nov. 19, 1862, Basler, *Collected Works,* 5:501–2.

39. Halleck to Banks, Nov. 9, 1862, *O.R.* 15, 590–91.

40. Ibid.

41. In August 1862 Lincoln told the managing editor of the *New York Tribune* that "I regard General Banks as one of the best men in the army. He makes me no trouble; but, with a large force or a small force, he always knows his duty and does it." *New York Tribune,* Aug. 13, 1862.

42. Lincoln to McClernand, Nov. 10, 1861, Basler, *Collected Works,* 5:20.

43. McClernand to Lincoln, March 31, June 20, Sept. 28, 1862, Lincoln Papers;

Steven E. Woodworth, *Nothing but Victory: The Army of the Tennessee, 1861–1865* (New York: Alfred A. Knopf, 2005), 249–50.

44. McClernand to Edwin M. Stanton, Nov. 10, 1862, *O.R.* 17, ii:332–34; John Niven, ed., *The Salmon P. Chase Papers,* vol. 1, *Journals, 1829–1872* (Kent, Ohio: Kent State University Press, 1993), 417, entry of Oct. 7, 1862.

45. *O.R.* 17, ii:282; Basler, *Collected Works,* 5:468–69.

46. Col. William S. Hillyer to William T. Sherman, Oct. 29, 1862, *O.R.* 17, ii:307–308; Grant to Halleck, Nov. 10, 1862, Halleck to Grant, Nov. 11, 1862, Grant to Sherman, Nov. 14, 1862, Grant to Halleck, Dec. 9, 1862, in John Y. Simon et al., eds., *Papers of Ulysses S. Grant,* 28 vols. to date (Carbondale, Ill.: Southern Illinois University Press, 1967–), 6:288, 288n., 310; 7:6.

47. McClernand to Lincoln, Dec. 29, 1862, Jan. 7, 16, 1863, Lincoln Papers; Lincoln to McClernand, Jan. 22, 1863, Basler, *Collected Works,* 6:70.

48. Halleck to Rosecrans, Nov. 27, Dec. 4, 1862, *O.R.* 20, ii:102, 117–18.

49. Bragg to Samuel Cooper, Dec. 31, 1862, *O.R.* 20, i:662.

50. Lincoln to Rosecrans, Jan. 5, Aug. 31, 1863, Basler, *Collected Works,* 6:39, 425.

51. Ibid., 5:530; *Boston Commonwealth,* Dec. 6, 1862.

52. Basler, *Collected Works,* 5:530, 537.

53. Sumner to Samuel Gridley Howe, Dec. 28, 1862, Sumner Papers, Houghton Library, Harvard University.

54. Several contemporaries described this historic occasion. This account and Lincoln's words are from Frederick W. Seward, *Seward at Washington, as Senator and Secretary of State: A Memoir of His Life, with Selections from His Letters, 1861–1872* (New York: Derby and Miller, 1891), 151, and from Francis B. Carpenter, *Six Months at the White House with Abraham Lincoln* (New York: Hurd and Houghton, 1866), 87, 269–70.

55. Basler, *Collected Works,* 6:29–30.

56. Pease and Randall, *Diary of Browning,* 1:155, entry of July 1, 1862; Basler, *Collected Works,* 5:356–57.

57. Roy P. Basler, ed., *The Collected Works of Abraham Lincoln: Supplement 1* (New Brunswick, N.J.: Rutgers University Press, 1990), 173; Lincoln to Nathaniel Banks, Jan. 23, March 29, 1863, Lincoln to Andrew Johnson, March 26, 1863, Basler,

Collected Works, 6:73, 154, 149–50.

58. Richard Cobden to Charles Sumner, Feb. 13, 1863, in Belle Becker Sideman and Lillian Friedman, eds., *Europe Looks at the Civil War* (New York: The Orion Press, 1960), 222; Henry Adams to Charles Francis Adams, Jr., Jan. 23, 1863, in J. C. Levenson, ed., *The Letters of Henry Adams,* vol. 1, *1858–1868* (Cambridge, Mass.: Harvard University Press, 1982), 327.

59. James Shepherd Pike to William H. Seward, Dec. 31, 1862, quoted in Dean B. Mahin, *One War at a Time: The International Dimensions of the American Civil War* (Washington, D.C.: Brassey's, 1999), 139.

CHAPTER 7: LEE'S ARMY, AND NOT RICHMOND, IS YOUR TRUE OBJECTIVE POINT

1. Meigs to Ambrose Burnside, Dec. 30, 1862, *O.R.* 21, 916–18.

2. Stephen W. Sears, "The Revolt of the Generals," in *Controversies and Commanders: Dispatches from the Army of the Potomac* (Boston: Houghton Mifflin, 1999), 133–36.

3. M. P. Larry to his sister, Dec. 23, 1862, in Bell Irvin Wiley, *The Life of Billy Yank*

(Indianapolis: Bobbs-Merrill Company, 1952), 280.

4. Charles S. Wainwright, *A Diary of Battle,* ed. Allan Nevins (New York: Harcourt, Brace and World, 1962), 157–58, entry of Jan. 19, 1863; Hooker quoted in Sears, "Revolt of the Generals," 152.

5. Halleck to William B. Franklin, May 29, 1863, *O.R.* 21, 1008–9.

6. Don E. Fehrenbacher and Virginia Fehrenbacher, eds., *Recollected Words of Abraham Lincoln* (Stanford, Calif.: Stanford University Press, 1996), 375.

7. Lincoln to Hooker, Jan. 26, 1863, in Roy P. Basler, ed., *The Collected Works of Abraham Lincoln,* 9 vols. (New Brunswick, N.J.: Rutgers University Press, 1953–55), 6:78–79.

8. Ibid., 132–33.

9. Darius N. Couch, "Sumner's 'Right Grand Division,' " in Clarence C. Buel and Robert U. Johnson, eds., *Battles and Leaders of the Civil War,* 4 vols. (New York: The Century Co., 1888), 3:119.

10. Bruce Catton, *Glory Road: The Bloody Route from Fredericksburg to Gettysburg* (Garden City, N.Y.: Doubleday, 1952), 162; T. Harry Williams, *Lincoln and His Generals* (New York: Alfred A. Knopf,

1952), 232–34; Noah Brooks, *Washington in Lincoln's Time* (New York: The Century Co., 1895), 56.

11. Madeline Vinton Dahlgren, *Memoir of John A. Dahlgren* (Boston: J. R. Osgood and Co., 1892), 387, diary entry of Feb. 6, 1863; Benjamin B. French, *Witness to the Young Republic: A Yankee's Journal, 1828–1870,* ed. Donald B. Cole and John J. McDonough (Hanover, N.H.: University Press of New England, 1989), 417, entry of Feb. 18, 1863.

12. Howard K. Beale, ed., *Diary of Gideon Welles,* 3 vols. (New York: W. W. Norton & Co., 1960), 1:265, entry of April 9, 1863; Lincoln's telegram to Du Pont is quoted by *New York Tribune* reporter Albert Richardson in a letter to his managing editor, Sydney Howard Gay, March 20, 1863, in Fehrenbacher and Fehrenbacher, *Recollected Words,* 380. Richardson was present when Lincoln told one of Du Pont's officers who was in Washington to convey the same message to the admiral.

13. Beale, *Welles Diary,* 1:259, entry of April 2, 1863.

14. The best account of these events is Kevin J. Weddle, *Lincoln's Tragic Admiral: The Life of Samuel Francis Du Pont*

(Charlottesville, Va.: University of Virginia Press, 2005), 154–207.

15. William M. Strong to Samuel R. Curtis, Dec. 23, 1862, in Fehrenbacher and Fehrenbacher, *Recollected Words,* 431; Halleck to Grant, March 25, 1863, *O.R.* 24, i:22.

16. McClernand to Lincoln, March 15, 1863, Lincoln Papers, Library of Congress.

17. John Y. Simon, ed., *The Papers of Ulysses S. Grant,* 28 vols. to date (Carbondale, Ill.: Southern Illinois University Press, 1967–), 7:317–18n. for letter from Medill to Washburne, Feb. 19, 1863.

18. Chase to Lincoln, April 4, 1863, enclosing Halstead to Chase, April 1, 1863, Lincoln Papers; Cadwalader Washburn to Elihu Washburne (the brothers spelled their last name differently), March 28, 1863, in Jean Edward Smith, *Grant* (New York: Simon & Schuster, 2001), 230.

19. Fehrenbacher and Fehrenbacher, *Recollected Words,* 11, 292.

20. Albert D. Richardson to Sydney Howard Gay, March 20, 1863, ibid., 381; Halleck's dispatch in *O.R.* 24, i:25.

21. Charles Bracelen Flood, *Grant and Sherman: The Friendship That Won the Civil War* (New York: Farrar, Straus and Giroux, 2005), 154–55; Brooks D. Simpson,

Ulysses S. Grant: Triumph over Adversity, 1822–1865 (Boston: Houghton Mifflin, 2000), 184–85.

22. Halleck to Grant, April 2, May 11, 16, 1863, Halleck to Banks, May 23, 1863, *O.R.* 24, i:25, 36; ibid., 26, i:500–501.

23. Washburne to Lincoln, May 1, 1863, Lincoln Papers; Lincoln to Isaac Arnold, May 26, 1863, Basler, *Collected Works,* 6:230.

24. Sumner to Francis Lieber, Jan. 17, 1863, in Edward L. Pierce, *Memoir and Letters of Charles Sumner,* 4 vols. (Boston: Roberts Brothers, 1877–93), 4:114.

25. Clement L. Vallandigham, *The Great Civil War in America* (New York, 1863), a pamphlet publication of his January speech in the House, reprinted in Frank Freidel, ed., *Union Pamphlets of the Civil War,* 2 vols. (Cambridge, Mass.: Harvard University Press, 1967), 2:697–738, quotations from 706, 711, 719, 732.

26. *Dubuque Herald,* n.d., *Canton (Ill.) Weekly Register,* April 20, 1863, quoted in Wood Gray, *The Hidden Civil War: The Story of the Copperheads* (New York: The Viking Press, 1942), 12, 133. For draft resistance, encouragement of desertion, and other acts of resistance, see Jennifer

L. Weber, *Copperheads: The Rise and Fall of Lincoln's Opponents in the North* (New York: Oxford University Press, 2006), esp. chaps. 3–4.

27. Lincoln to Burnside, May 29, 1863, Basler, *Collected Works,* 6:237.

28. Erastus Corning et al. to the President, in Frank Freidel, ed., *Union Pamphlets of the Civil War,* 2:740–43; Matthew Birchard et al., "Resolutions Presented to Lincoln," in Basler, *Collected Works,* 6:300–301n.

29. The two letters are in Basler, *Collected Works,* 6:260–69, 300–306.

30. John G. Nicolay and John Hay, *Abraham Lincoln: A History,* 10 vols. (New York: The Century Co., 1890), 7:336–37. The quotation is a close paraphrase of the judge's opinion. In 1866, after the passions of the war had partly cooled, the Supreme Court overturned a similar conviction by a military court in 1864 of an Indiana Copperhead, Lambdin P. Milligan, on the grounds that a civilian cannot be tried by a military tribunal in an area where the civil courts are functioning. This principle would have voided Vallandigham's conviction. *Ex parte Milligan,* 4 Wallace 2.

31. Basler, *Collected Works,* 6:164–65.

32. Hooker to Lincoln, April 11, 1862, Lin-

coln Papers.

33. Darius N. Couch, "The Chancellorsville Campaign," in Buel and Johnson, *Battles and Leaders,* 3:155.

34. In Hooker's defense it should be noted that on the morning of May 3 he suffered a concussion when a pillar of the Chancellor house, on which he was leaning, was hit by an enemy cannonball and fell on his head. He did not fully recover his faculties for several hours and was not able thereafter to do much to shape the course of events. Stephen W. Sears, "In Defense of Fighting Joe," in *Controversies and Commanders,* 169–89. But even before his concussion Hooker seemed to have lost control of events, so it is not clear how much difference the concussion made.

35. Brooks wrote several versions of this incident that vary only in minor details. This account is from his dispatch to the *Sacramento Union* dated May 8 and published in that newspaper on June 5, in Michael Burlingame, ed., *Lincoln Observed: Civil War Dispatches of Noah Brooks* (Baltimore: Johns Hopkins University Press, 1998), 50; and from Brooks, *Washington in Lincoln's Time,* 57–58.

36. Meade to his wife, May 8, 1863, George G. Meade III, ed., *The Life and Letters of*

George Gordon Meade, 2 vols. (New York: Charles Scribner's Sons, 1913), 1:372–73; Lincoln to Hooker, May 7, 1863, Basler, *Collected Works,* 6:201.

37. Lincoln to Hooker, May 14, 1863, Basler, *Collected Works,* 6:217.

38. George G. Meade to his wife, June 13, 1863, *Life and Letters of Meade,* 1:385.

39. James Dixon to Lincoln, June 28, 1863, Alexander McClure to Lincoln, July 1, 1863, Lincoln Papers; Allan Nevins and Milton Halsey Thomas, eds., *The Diary of George Templeton Strong,* vol. 3, *The Civil War 1860–1865* (New York: Macmillan, 1952), 324, entry of June 24, 1863.

40. Adam Gurowski, *Diary, 1863* (Boston: Lee and Shepard, 1866), 241, entry of June 5, 1863; William A. Croffut, ed., *Fifty Years in Camp and Field: The Diary of Ethan Allen Hitchcock* (New York: G. P. Putnam's Sons, 1909), 447, entry of May 24, 1863.

41. Halleck to Hooker, June 5, 1863, *O.R.* 27, i:31–32; Lincoln to Hooker, June 5, 1863, Basler, *Collected Works,* 6:249.

42. Hooker to Lincoln, June 10, 1863, *O.R.* 27, i:35; Lincoln to Hooker, June 10, 14, 1863, Basler, *Collected Works,* 6:257, 273.

43. Lincoln to Hooker, June 16 (three telegrams), Lincoln to Joel Parker, June

30, 1863, Basler, *Collected Works,* 6:280–82, 311.

44. Beale, *Welles Diary,* 1:334, 348, entries of June 26 and 28, 1863; *O.R.* 27, i:58–60.

45. Freeman Cleaves, *Meade of Gettysburg* (Norman, Okla.: University of Oklahoma Press, 1960), 171; Nevins and Thomas, *Diary of George Templeton Strong,* 330, entry of July 6, 1863.

46. Basler, *Collected Works,* 6:319–20; French, *Witness to the Young Republic,* 426, entry of July 8, 1863.

47. *O.R.* 27, iii:567.

48. James B. Fry, in Allen Thorndike Rice, ed., *Reminiscences of Abraham Lincoln by Distinguished Men of His Time* (New York: North American Publishing Co., 1885), 402; Michael Burlingame and John R. Turner Ettlinger, eds., *Inside Lincoln's White House: The Complete Civil War Diary of John Hay* (Carbondale, Ill.: Southern Illinois University Press, 1997), 62, entry of July 14, 1863.

49. Lincoln to Halleck, July 6, 1863, Basler, *Collected Works,* 6:318; Halleck to Meade, July 7 (two dispatches), July 8, 1863, *O.R.* 27, i:82–83, 84–85.

50. Beale, *Diary of Welles,* 1:364–65, entry of July 7, 1863; Lincoln to Halleck, July

7, 1863, Basler, *Collected Works*, 6:319. The original of this note from Lincoln to Halleck was recently found in the National Archives.

51. Meade to Halleck, July 8, 1863, *O.R.* 27, i:84; Burlingame and Ettlinger, *Diary of Hay*, 61, entry of July 11, 1863.

52. David Homer Bates, *Lincoln in the Telegraph Office* (New York: The Century Co., 1907), 157; Meade to Halleck, July 13, 1863, Halleck to Meade, July 13, 1863, *O.R.* 27, i:91, 92.

53. Beale, *Diary of Welles*, 370–71, entry of July 14, 1863; Chase to William Sprague, July 15, 1863, in John Niven, ed., *The Salmon P. Chase Papers*, vol. 4, *Correspondence, April 1863–1864* (Kent, Ohio: Kent State University Press, 1997), 81–82; Burlingame and Ettlinger, *Diary of Hay*, 63, entry of July 15, 1863.

54. Halleck to Meade, July 14, 1863 (two dispatches), Meade to Halleck, July 14, 1863, *O.R.* 27, i:92–94.

55. Basler, *Collected Works*, 6:327–28.

56. Beale, *Diary of Welles*, 1:374, entry of July 17, 1863; Lincoln to Oliver O. Howard, July 21, 1863, Basler, *Collected Works*, 6:341.

57. Lincoln to Grant, July 13, 1863, Basler,

CHAPTER 8: THE HEAVIEST BLOW YET DEALT TO THE REBELLION

1. Michael Burlingame and John R. Turner Ettlinger, eds., *Inside Lincoln's White House: The Complete Civil War Diary of John Hay* (Carbondale, Ill.: Southern Illinois University Press, 1997), 63, entry of July 15, 1863; Hay to Nicolay, Aug. 7, 1863, in Tyler Dennett, ed., *Lincoln and the Civil War in the Diaries and Letters of John Hay* (New York: Dodd, Mead & Company, 1939), 76.

2. Lincoln to Seymour, Aug. 7, 11, 15, 16, in Roy P. Basler, ed., *The Collected Works of Abraham Lincoln,* 9 vols. (New Brunswick, N.J.: Rutgers University Press, 1953–55), 6:369–70, 381–82, 389–92.

3. Lynn M. Case and Warren F. Spencer, *The United States and France: Civil War Diplomacy* (Philadelphia: University of Pennsylvania Press, 1970), esp. chaps. 15–16.

4. Lincoln to Grant, Aug. 9, 1863, Basler, *Collected Works,* 6:374. See also Lincoln to Edwin M. Stanton, July 29, 1863, Lincoln to Francis P. Blair, July 30, 1863, Lincoln to Nathaniel P. Banks, Aug. 5,

Sept. 19, 1863, ibid., 354–55, 356, 364, 465–66; Henry W. Halleck to Banks, July 24, Aug. 6, 10, 12, 20, *O.R.* 26, i:652–53, 673, 675, 682–83; Halleck to Grant, Aug. 6, 1863, *O.R.* 24, iii:578.

5. Lincoln to Rosecrans, Feb. 17, 1863, Basler, *Collected Works,* 6:108–9.

6. Halleck to Rosecrans, June 11, 16, 1863, Rosecrans to Halleck, June 16, 1863, *O.R.* 23, i:8, 10.

7. Basler, *Collected Works,* 2:32–36.

8. Robert V. Bruce, *Lincoln and the Tools of War* (Indianapolis: Bobbs-Merrill Company, 1956). Basler, *Collected Works,* contains dozens of communications and orders by Lincoln concerning weapons, gunpowder, and other aspects of ordnance and naval technology.

9. *O.R.* 23, ii:518.

10. Ibid., ii:552, 554–56, 592, 594; Rosecrans to Halleck, Aug. 1, 1863, Civil War Collection, Huntington Library, San Marino, Calif.

11. Rosecrans to Lincoln, Aug. 1, 1863, Lincoln Papers, Library of Congress; Lincoln to Rosecrans, Aug. 10, 1863, Basler, *Collected Works,* 6:377–78.

12. Daniel Harvey Hill, "Chickamauga — The Great Battle of the West," Clarence C. Buel and Robert U. Johnson, eds.,

Battles and Leaders of the Civil War, 4 vols. (New York: The Century Co., 1888), 3:644.

13. Burlingame and Ettlinger, *Inside Lincoln's White House,* 85, entry of Sept. 27, 1863.

14. David Homer Bates, *Lincoln in the Telegraph Office* (New York: The Century Co., 1907), 202; Lincoln to Rosecrans, Sept. 21, 1863 (two dispatches), Lincoln to Burnside, Sept. 21, 25, 1863, Basler, *Collected Works,* 6:469, 470, 472, 480–81.

15. Lincoln to Burnside, Sept. 27 (two telegrams), 28, Oct. 12, 1863, Basler, *Collected Works,* 6:483, 484, 510–11.

16. Burlingame and Ettlinger, *Inside Lincoln's White House,* 85–86, entry of Sept. 27, 1863.

17. John E. Clark, Jr., *Railroads in the Civil War: The Impact of Management on Victory and Defeat* (Baton Rouge, La.: Louisiana State University Press, 2001), 141–212; John Niven, ed., *The Salmon P. Chase Papers,* vol. 1, *Journals, 1829–1872* (Kent, Ohio: Kent State University Press, 1993), 450–54, entry of Sept. 24, 1863.

18. Burlingame and Ettlinger, *Inside Lincoln's White House,* 99, entry of Oct. 24, 1863.

19. Howard K. Beale, ed., *Diary of Gideon Welles,* 3 vols. (New York: W. W. Norton & Co., 1960), 1:470, entry of Oct. 14, 1863.

20. Halleck to Grant, Oct. 16, 1863, Thomas to Grant, Oct. 19, 1863, *O.R.* 30, iv:404, 479.

21. Lincoln to Stanton, Dec. 18, 21, 1863, Basler, *Collected Works,* 7:78–79, 84–85.

22. Lincoln to Grant, Dec. 8, 1863, ibid., 7:53.

23. Beale, *Diary of Welles,* 1:383, entry of July 26, 1863; Kenneth P. Williams, *Lincoln Finds a General: A Military Study of the Civil War,* 5 vols. (New York: Macmillan, 1949–59), 5:99–101; Grant to Dana, Aug. 5, 1863, in John Y. Simon, ed., *The Papers of Ulysses S. Grant,* 28 vols. to date (Carbondale, Ill.: Southern Illinois University Press, 1967–), 9:145–47.

24. Beale, *Diary of Welles,* 1:439–40, entry of Sept. 21, 1863.

25. Lincoln to Halleck, Sept. 19, 1863, Basler, *Collected Works,* 6:466–67.

26. Lincoln to Halleck, Oct. 16, 1863, ibid., 6:518; Meade to his wife, Oct. 23, 1864, in George Gordon Meade III, ed., *Life and Letters of George Gordon Meade,* 2 vols. (New York: Charles Scribner's Sons, 1913), 2:154.

27. Meade to Hancock, Nov. 6, 1863, in Jeffry D. Wert, *The Sword of Lincoln: The Army of the Potomac* (New York: Simon & Schuster, 2005), 318.

28. Banks to Lincoln, Aug. 17, 1863, Lincoln Papers.

29. Charles A. Dana, *Recollections of the Civil War* (New York: D. Appleton and Co., 1898), 86.

30. Lincoln to Grant, Aug. 9, 1863, Basler, *Collected Works,* 6:374; Grant to Lincoln, Aug. 23, 1863, Lincoln Papers.

31. Lincoln to James Conkling, Aug. 26, 1863, Basler, *Collected Works,* 6:408–10.

32. Frederick Douglass, *Life and Times of Frederick Douglass* (Hartford, Conn.: Park Publishing Co., 1882), 386–87; the final sentence is from Douglass's article in Allen Thorndike Rice, ed., *Reminiscences of Abraham Lincoln by Distinguished Men of His Time* (New York: North American Publishing Co., 1886), 188.

33. Dunbar Rowland, ed., *Jefferson Davis, Constitutionalist: His Letters, Papers, and Speeches,* 10 vols. (Jackson, Miss.: Mississippi Department of Archives and History, 1923), 5:409; *O.R.,* series 2, vol. 5, pp. 797, 808, 940–41.

34. *O.R.,* series 2, vol. 5, pp. 128, 286.

35. Basler, *Collected Works,* 6:357; Douglass, *Life and Times,* 387.

36. *O.R.,* series 2, vol. 6, pp. 441–42, 528, 556–57, 647–49, 226; Michael Burlingame, ed., *Lincoln Observed: Civil War Dispatches of Noah Brooks* (Baltimore: Johns Hopkins University Press, 1998), 90, dispatch dated Nov. 11, 1863, in *Sacramento Union,* Dec. 12.

37. Basler, *Collected Works,* 7:23.

38. Ibid., 49–50; *Illinois Daily State Journal,* Dec. 1, 1863, quoted in V. Jacque Voegeli, *Free but Not Equal: The Midwest and the Negro During the Civil War* (Chicago: University of Chicago Press, 1967), 131.

39. Basler, *Collected Works,* 7:53–56.

40. Lincoln to Banks, Nov. 5, 1863, ibid., 1; "Proclamation About Amnesty," March 24, 1864, ibid., 269–70.

41. Lincoln to Frederick Steele, June 29, 1864, ibid., 418; "Proclamation Concerning Reconstruction," ibid., 433–34.

CHAPTER 9: IF IT TAKES THREE YEARS MORE

1. Halleck to Grant, Jan. 18, 1864, *O.R.* 32, ii:40–42.

2. Grant to Halleck, Jan. 15, 1864, Halleck

to Grant, Jan. 18, 1864, ibid., 90–91, 126–27.

3. Grant to Halleck, Jan. 19, 1864, Halleck to Grant, Feb. 17, 1864, Halleck to Sherman, Feb. 16, 1864, ibid., 407–8, 411–13; ibid., 33, 394–95.

4. Brooks D. Simpson, *Ulysses S. Grant: Triumph over Adversity, 1822–1865* (Boston: Houghton Mifflin, 2000), 254–57.

5. Halleck to Edwin M. Stanton, March 9, 1864, Abraham Lincoln Papers, Library of Congress; *O.R.* 32, iii:58, 33; ibid., 663.

6. Memorandum by John G. Nicolay dated March 8, 1864, in Michael Burlingame, ed., *With Lincoln in the White House: Letters, Memoranda, and Other Writings of John G. Nicolay, 1860–1865* (Carbondale, Ill.: Southern Illinois University Press, 2000), 130.

7. *The Personal Memoirs of U.S. Grant,* 2 vols. (New York: Charles L. Webster and Company, 1885–86), 2:122–23.

8. *O.R.* 46, i:11.

9. Grant to Meade, April 9, 1864, *O.R.* 33, 827–28; Grant to Sherman, April 4, 1864, *O.R.* 32, iii:246.

10. Michael Burlingame and John R. Turner Ettlinger, eds., *Inside Lincoln's White House: The Complete Civil War Diary of*

John Hay (Carbondale, Ill.: Southern Illinois University Press, 1997), 193–94, entry of April 30, 1864; *O.R.* 32, iii:245–46.

11. For some of the extensive documentation of these massacres, see Noah Andre Trudeau, *Like Men of War: Black Troops in the Civil War 1862–1865* (Boston: Little, Brown and Company, 1998), chaps. 5–7; Ira Berlin, ed., *Freedom: A Documentary History of Emancipation 1861–1867,* series 2: *The Black Military Experience* (Cambridge, U.K.: Cambridge University Press, 1982), 539–48, 588–89; Richard L. Fuchs, *An Unerring Fire: The Massacre at Fort Pillow* (Mechanicsburg, Pa.: Stackpole Books, 2002); John Cimprich, *Fort Pillow, a Civil War Massacre, and Public Memory* (Baton Rouge, La.: Louisiana State University Press, 2005); and Andrew Ward, *River Run Red: The Fort Pillow Massacre in the American Civil War* (New York: Viking, 2005).

12. Speech in Baltimore on April 18, 1864, in Roy P. Basler, ed., *The Collected Works of Abraham Lincoln,* 9 vols. (New Brunswick, N.J.: Rutgers University Press, 1953–55), 7:302.

13. Howard K. Beale, ed., *Diary of Gideon*

Welles, 3 vols. (New York: W. W. Norton and Co., 1960), 2:24–25, entries of May 5 and 6, 1864; Lincoln "To Cabinet Members," May 3, 1864, and Lincoln to Edwin M. Stanton, May 17, 1864, Basler, *Collected Works,* 7:328–29, 345–46; John G. Nicolay and John Hay, *Abraham Lincoln: A History,* 10 vols. (New York: The Century Co., 1890), 6:478–84.

14. *O.R.,* series 2, vol. 6, p. 171.

15. Ludwell H. Johnson, *Red River Campaign: Politics and Cotton in the Civil War* (Baltimore: Johns Hopkins University Press, 1958); Gary Dillard Joiner, *One Damn Blunder from Beginning to End: The Red River Campaign of 1864* (Lanham, Md.: SR Books, 2003).

16. Grant to Halleck, April 22, 25, 29, 30, 1864, Halleck to Grant, April 23, 26, 29, May 3, 1864, Halleck to Canby, May 7, 1864, *O.R.* 34, iii: 252–53, 331, 357, 293, 331–32, 409–10.

17. Allan Nevins and Milton Halsey Thomas, eds., *The Diary of George Templeton Strong: The Civil War 1860–1865* (New York: Macmillan, 1952), 449, entry of May 20, 1864.

18. Beale, *Diary of Welles,* 2:33, 25, entries of May 17 and 7; Francis B. Carpenter,

Six Months at the White House with Abraham Lincoln (New York: Hurd and Houghton, 1866), 30.

19. Doris Kearns Goodwin, *Team of Rivals: The Political Genius of Abraham Lincoln* (New York: Simon & Schuster, 2005), 620; Grant to Halleck, May 11, 1864, *O.R.* 36, ii:627.

20. Burlingame and Ettlinger, *Inside Lincoln's White House,* diary entry of May 9, 1864; Carpenter, *Six Months at the White House,* 283.

21. *New York Times,* May 9, 1864; *New York Herald,* May 14, 1864; *New York Tribune,* May 14, 1864.

22. Michael Burlingame, ed., *Lincoln Observed: Civil War Dispatches of Noah Brooks* (Baltimore: Johns Hopkins University Press, 1998), 113, dispatch of June 14, 1864, in *Sacramento Union,* July 9.

23. *O.R.* 46, i:20.

24. Howard K. Beale, ed., *The Diary of Edward Bates, 1859–1866* (Washington, D.C.: U.S. Government Printing Office, 1933), 366, entry of May 15, 1864; Elizabeth Blair Lee to Samuel P. Lee, May 20, 1864, in Virginia Jeans Laas, ed., *Wartime Washington: The Civil War Letters of Elizabeth Blair Lee* (Urbana, Ill.: University of

Illinois Press, 1991), 386.

25. Nevins and Thomas, *Diary of George Templeton Strong,* 447, entry of May 17, 1864.

26. Basler, *Collected Works,* 7:395.

27. These paragraphs are based on the voluminous correspondence in *Private and Official Correspondence of General Benjamin F. Butler During the Period of the Civil War,* 5 vols. (Norwood, Mass.: Plimpton Press, 1917), vols. 2, 3, and 4; and on Hans L. Trefousse, *Ben Butler: The South Called Him Beast!* (New York: Twayne Publishers, 1957).

28. Thaddeus Lyman to his wife, July 20, 1864, in George R. Agassiz, ed., *Meade's Headquarters, 1863–1865* (Boston: Atlantic Monthly Press, 1922), 192–93. The sources on which these paragraphs are based include many letters and telegrams in *O.R.* 40, ii and iii; vol. 4 of the *Private and Official Correspondence of Butler;* Edward G. Longacre, *Army of Amateurs: General Benjamin F. Butler and the Army of the James, 1863–1865* (Mechanicsburg, Pa.: Stackpole Books, 1997); William D. Mallam, "The Grant-Butler Relationship," *Mississippi Valley Historical Review* 41 (1954), 259–76; and Lewis Taylor Merrill,

"General Benjamin F. Butler in the Presidential Campaign of 1864," ibid., 33 (1947), 537–70. Much of the evidence about this contretemps is ambiguous or contradictory, and Lincoln's precise role in the whole matter is obscure.

29. Halleck to Grant, July 6, 1864, *O.R.* 40, iii:31–32; Lincoln to Grant, July 10, 1864, Basler, *Collected Works,* 7:437.

30. Burlingame and Ettlinger, *Inside Lincoln's White House,* 221, diary entry of July 11, 1864.

31. For summaries of the evidence and legends connected with this incident, see Frederick C. Hicks, "Lincoln, Wright, and Holmes at Fort Stevens," *Journal of the Illinois State Historical Society* 39 (1946), 323–32; and John H. Cramer, *Lincoln Under Enemy Fire* (Baton Rouge, La.: Louisiana State University Press, 1948).

32. Burlingame and Ettlinger, *Inside Lincoln's White House,* 221–23, diary entries of July 11, 13, 14, 1864.

33. Ibid., 222, entry of July 13, 1864; Beale, *Diary of Bates,* 384–85, entries of July 14 and 15, 1864.

34. Grant to Halleck, July 18, 1864, Halleck to Grant, July 21, 1864, Grant to Lincoln, July 25, 1864, Stanton to Halleck, July

27, 1864, *O.R.* 37, ii:374, 408, 433–34; Meade to his wife, July 29, Aug. 3, 1864, in George Gordon Meade III, ed., *Life and Letters of George Gordon Meade,* 2 vols. (New York: Charles Scribner's Sons, 1913), 2:216, 218–19; Lincoln to Grant, July 28, 29, 1864, Basler, *Collected Works,* 7:469–70.

35. Grant to Halleck, Aug. 1, 1864, *O.R.* 40, i:17.

36. The leading Grant scholar, John Y. Simon, editor of *The Papers of Ulysses S. Grant,* suggests that Lincoln may have rebuked Grant. The general's foremost biographer, however, rejects this interpretation. Simon, "Grant, Lincoln, and Unconditional Surrender," in Gabor Boritt, ed., *Lincoln's Generals* (New York: Alfred A. Knopf, 1994), 178–83; Simpson, *Ulysses S. Grant,* 367, 510–11n.52.

37. *O.R.* 37, ii:558.

38. Lincoln to Grant, Aug. 3, 1864, Basler, *Collected Works,* 7:476.

CHAPTER 10: NO PEACE WITHOUT VICTORY

1. *New York World,* July 12, 30, Aug. 6, 1864.

2. Roy P. Basler, ed., *The Collected Works of Abraham Lincoln,* 9 vols. (New Brunswick,

N.J.: Rutgers University Press, 1953–55), 7:448–49; *New York World,* July 19, 1864.

3. Howard K. Beale, ed., *Diary of Gideon Welles,* 3 vols. (New York: W. W. Norton & Co., 1960), 2:44, 73, entries of June 2 and July 11, 1864; Adam Gurowski, *Diary,* 3 vols. (Boston, 1862–66), 3:254, entry of Aug. 19, 1864.

4. Allan Nevins and Milton Halsey Thomas, eds., *The Diary of George Templeton Strong,* vol. 3, *The Civil War 1860–1865* (New York: Macmillan, 1952), 474, entry of Aug. 19, 1864; Sarah Butler to Benjamin Butler, June 19, 1864, in Jesse A. Marshall, ed., *Private and Official Correspondence of General Benjamin F. Butler during the Period of the Civil War,* 5 vols. (Norwood, Mass.: Plimpton Press, 1917), 4:418.

5. *Columbus Crisis,* Aug. 24, 1864, in Wood Gray, *The Hidden Civil War: The Story of the Copperheads* (New York: The Viking Press, 1942), 174; *Boston Pilot,* quoted in Jennifer Weber, *Copperheads: The Rise and Fall of Lincoln's Opponents in the North* (New York: Oxford University Press, 2006), 144.

6. Clement C. Clay to Judah P. Benjamin, Aug. 11, 1864, *O.R.,* series 4, vol. 3, p. 585. For the activities of Confederate agents in Canada, see Oscar A. Kinchen,

Confederate Operations in Canada and the North (North Quincy, Mass.: Christopher Pub. House, 1970), esp. 35–103.

7. Henry Swiggett, ed., *A Rebel War Clerk's Diary at the Confederate States Capital* (John B. Jones), 2 vols. (New York: Old Hickory Bookshop, 1935), 2:229, entry of June 11, 1864; Longstreet to Alexander R. Lawton, March 5, 1864, *O.R.* 32, iii:588.

8. *Richmond Dispatch,* July 23, 1864; Nevins and Thomas, *Diary of George Templeton Strong,* 470, entry of Aug. 6, 1864; Weed to Seward, Aug. 22, 1864, Abraham Lincoln Papers, Library of Congress.

9. Greeley to Lincoln, July 7, 1864, Lincoln Papers.

10. Lincoln to Greeley, July 9, 1864, Basler, *Collected Works,* 7:435.

11. Lincoln to Greeley (two telegrams), July 15, 1864; "Order for John Hay," July 15, 1864; "To Whom It May Concern," July 18, 1864, Basler, *Collected Works,* 7:440–42, 451.

12. Clement C. Clay and James Holcombe to Greeley, July 21, 1864, in *New York Times,* July 22. This letter was published in many Northern newspapers on July 22 or 23 and appeared in Southern newspapers soon after, with extensive editorial

commentary.

13. *New York Times,* July 23, 1864; Clay to Benjamin, Aug. 11, 1864, *O.R.,* series 4, vol. 3, pp. 585–86.

14. *Independent,* July 26, 1864; *New York Tribune,* Aug. 5, 1864; Greeley to Lincoln, Aug. 9, 1864, Lincoln Papers.

15. *New York Times,* July 25, 1864; Greeley to Lincoln, Aug. 9, 1864, Lincoln Papers.

16. No official record of this meeting was kept. This account and the quotation are taken from Gilmore's article in the *Atlantic Monthly* 8 (Sept. 1864), 372–83. Gilmore wrote a briefer version describing the meeting in the *Boston Transcript,* July 22, 1864, and a longer one in his memoirs many years later. These versions vary slightly in detail but agree in substance, as does Judah Benjamin's account in a circular sent to Confederate envoys abroad after Gilmore's article was published in the *Atlantic Monthly.* Benjamin to James M. Mason, Aug. 25, 1864, in *Official Records of the Union and Confederate Navies,* 30 vols. (Washington, D.C., 1894–1922), series 2, vol. 3, pp. 1190–94.

17. *New York Times,* Aug. 20, 1864.

18. *New York World,* Aug. 15, 1864; *Columbus Crisis,* Aug. 3, 1864; *New York News,* quoted in *Washington Daily Intelligencer,*

July 25, 1864.

19. *New York World,* July 25, 1864; *New York Herald,* Aug. 7, 1864.

20. *Newark Daily Advertiser* and *Ann Arbor Journal,* quoted in *Washington Daily Intelligencer,* Aug. 8, 1864.

21. *New York Tribune,* July 28, 1864; Nevins and Thomas, *Diary of George Templeton Strong,* 474, entry of Aug. 19, 1864.

22. Lincoln to Charles Robinson, Aug. 17, 1864, Basler, *Collected Works,* 7:499–501.

23. Ibid., 500, 506–7.

24. William Frank Zornow, *Lincoln and the Party Divided* (Norman, Okla.: University of Oklahoma Press, 1954), 112; Basler, *Collected Works,* 7:514.

25. Raymond to Lincoln, Aug. 22, 1864, Lincoln Papers. Emphasis in original.

26. Basler, *Collected Works,* 7:517; John G. Nicolay and John Hay, *Abraham Lincoln: A History,* 10 vols. (New York: The Century Co., 1890), 9:220.

27. Nicolay to Hay, Aug. 25, 1864, Nicolay to Therena Bates, Aug. 28, 1864, in Michael Burlingame, ed., *With Lincoln in the White House: Letters, Memoranda, and Other Writings of John G. Nicolay, 1860–1865* (Carbondale, Ill.: Southern Illinois University Press, 2000), 152–53.

28. On this matter see Michael Burlingame and John R. Turner Ettlinger, eds., *Inside Lincoln's White House: The Complete Civil War Diary of John Hay* (Carbondale, Ill.: Southern Illinois University Press, 1997), 238, entry of Oct. 11, 1864; and Charles A. Dana to Henry J. Raymond, n.d., in Francis Brown, *Raymond of the Times* (New York: Norton, 1951), 260n.

29. Zornow, *Lincoln and the Party Divided,* 108–16; for the platform, see Edward McPherson, *The Political History of the United States during the Great Rebellion,* 2nd ed. (Washington, D.C.: Philip and Salomans, 1865), 406–7.

30. Halleck to Grant, Aug. 11, 1864, Grant to Halleck, Aug. 15, 1864, *O.R.* 42:111–12, 193–94.

31. Lincoln to Grant, Aug. 17, 1864, Basler, *Collected Works,* 7:499; Horace Porter, *Campaigning with Grant* (New York: The Century Co., 1897), 279.

32. McPherson, *Political History of the United States,* 419–20.

33. Sherman to Halleck, Sept. 3, 1864, *O.R.* 38, v:77.

34. Nevins and Thomas, *Diary of George Templeton Strong,* 480–81, entry of Sept. 3, 1864; *St. Paul Press,* Sept. 4, 1864,

quoted in Gray, *Hidden Civil War,* 189.

35. Lincoln to Grant, Sept. 12, 1864, Basler, *Collected Works,* 7:548; Grant to Lincoln, Sept. 13, 1864, Lincoln Papers; *Personal Memoirs of U.S. Grant,* 2 vols. (New York: Charles L. Webster & Company, 1885–86), 2:583.

36. James W. Forsyth to John D. Stevenson, Sept. 19, 1864, *O.R.* 43, ii:124.

37. Lincoln to Sheridan, Sept. 20, 1864, Basler, *Collected Works,* 8:13.

38. Grant to Halleck, July 14, 1864, *O.R.* 40, iii:223; Sheridan to Grant, Oct. 7, 1864, *O.R.* 43, i:30–31.

39. Lincoln to Sheridan, Oct. 22, 1864, Basler, *Collected Works,* 8:73–74.

40. McPherson, *Political History of the United States,* 420.

41. Ovid L. Futch, *History of Andersonville Prison* (Gainesville, Fla.: University of Florida Press, 1968), 43; William Marvel, *Andersonville: The Last Depot* (Chapel Hill, N.C.: University of North Carolina Press, 1994), 147–49.

42. H. Brewster to Edwin M. Stanton, Sept. 8, 1864, Samuel White to Lincoln, Sept. 12, 1864, *O.R.,* series 2, vol. 7, pp. 787, 816.

43. Basler, *Collected Works,* 7:500.

44. Benjamin Butler to Robert Ould, Aug.

27, 1864, *O.R.,* series 2, vol. 7, p. 691. This letter was published in the *New York Times,* Sept. 6, 1864, and also printed as a leaflet by the government for general circulation.

45. Lee to Grant, Oct. 1, 1864, Grant to Lee, Oct. 2, Lee to Grant, Oct. 3, Grant to Lee, Oct. 3, *O.R.,* series 2, vol. 7, pp. 906–7, 909, 914.

46. William C. Davis, *Lincoln's Men: How President Lincoln Became Father to an Army and a Nation* (New York: The Free Press, 1999); Thomas P. Lowry, *Don't Shoot That Boy: Abraham Lincoln and Military Justice* (Mason City, Iowa: Savas Publishing, 1999).

47. Delos Lake to his mother, July 12, Nov. 1, 1864, Lake Papers, Huntington Library, San Marino, Calif.; Henry Kauffman to Katherine Kreitzer, Oct. 15, 1864, in David McCordick, ed., *The Civil War Letters (1861–1865) of Private Henry Kauffman* (Lewiston, N.Y.: E. Mellen Press, 1991), 89.

48. Henry Crydenwise to his parents, Oct. 25, 1864, Crydenwise Papers, Woodruff Library, Emory University; Connecticut soldier quoted in Bruce Catton, *A Stillness at Appomattox* (Garden City, N.Y.:

Doubleday, 1957), 303.

49. John Berry to Samuel L. M. Barlow, Aug. 24, 1864, Barlow Papers, Huntington Library.

50. Basler, *Collected Works,* 8:149, 151.

51. Dunbar Rowland, ed., *Jefferson Davis, Constitutionalist: His Letters, Papers, and Speeches,* 10 vols. (Jackson, Miss.: Mississippi Department of Archives and History, 1923), 6:386.

52. These quotations are from Sherman's letters and telegrams to Grant (with citations also to Grant's replies), in *O.R.* 39, iii:3, 63–64, 161, 202, 576, 594–95, 660.

53. Stanton to Grant, Oct. 12, 13, 1864, Grant to Sherman, Nov. 2, 1864, ibid., iii:222, 239, 595.

54. Stanton to Grant, Dec. 2, 1864, ibid., 45, ii:15–16.

55. Grant to Thomas, Dec. 2, 6, 8, Thomas to Grant, Dec. 2, 6, Stanton to Grant, Dec. 7, 1864, ibid., 45, ii:17–18, 70, 97.

56. Grant to Stanton, Dec. 7, 1864, ibid., 97.

57. Grant to Halleck, Dec. 8, 9, 1864, Halleck to Grant, Dec. 8, 9, Thomas to Halleck, Dec. 9, 11, 12, 14, Halleck to Thomas, Dec. 14, Grant to Thomas, Dec. 9, 11, ibid., 45, ii:96, 115–16, 143, 168, 180; David Homer Bates, *Lincoln in the*

Telegraph Office (New York: The Century Co., 1907), 312–18.

58. Lincoln to Thomas, Dec. 16, 1864, Basler, *Collected Works,* 8:169.

59. John Sherman to Alexander McClure, Jan. 29, 1892, in McClure, *Lincoln and Men of War Times* (Philadelphia: Times Publishing Co., 1892), 238n.; Sherman to Lincoln, Dec. 22 (dated Dec. 25 from Fort Monroe), Lincoln Papers.

60. Lincoln to Sherman, Dec. 26, 1864, Basler, *Collected Works,* 8:181–82.

61. Sherman's campaign report, Jan. 1, 1865, *O.R.* 44, p. 13.

62. Lincoln to Cuthbert Bullitt, July 28, 1862, Lincoln to August Belmont, July 31, 1862, Basler, *Collected Works,* 5:346, 350; the remark about Sherman taking off the bear's hide is quoted by several authors, most notably Shelby Foote, *The Civil War: A Narrative. Red River to Appomattox* (New York: Random House, 1974), 864. I have not been able to trace it back to the original source.

63. Lincoln to Grant, Dec. 28, 1864, Basler, *Collected Works,* 8:187; Grant to Lincoln, Dec. 28, 1864, *O.R.* 42, iii:1087; Grant to Stanton, Jan. 4, 1865, Halleck to Grant, Jan. 7, 1865, *O.R.* 46, ii:29, 60.

64. Alexander H. Stephens, *A Constitutional*

View of the Late War Between the States, 2 vols. (Philadelphia: National Publishing Co., 1868–70), 2:619.

65. Sarah Woolfolk Wiggins, ed., *The Journals of Josiah Gorgas, 1857–1878* (Tuscaloosa, Ala.: University of Alabama Press, 1995), 147–49, entries of Jan. 6 and 18, 1865.

66. Davis to Blair, Jan. 12, 1865, Lincoln to Blair, Jan. 18, 1865, Basler, *Collected Works,* 8:275–76. Emphasis added.

67. William C. Cooper, Jr., *Jefferson Davis, American* (New York: Alfred A. Knopf, 2000), 510–11.

68. Basler, *Collected Works,* 8:277–81.

69. Grant to Stanton, Feb. 2, 1865, ibid., 282.

70. "Memorandum of the Conversation at the Conference in Hampton Roads," in John A. Campbell, *Reminiscences and Documents Relating to the Civil War During the Year 1865* (Baltimore: John Murphy, 1877), 11–17; Seward to Charles Francis Adams, Feb. 7, 1865, *O.R.* 46, ii:471–73; Stephens, *Constitutional View of the Late War Between the States,* 1:598–619. The best study of the Hampton Roads Conference is William C. Harris, "The Hampton Roads Peace Conference: A Final Test of

Lincoln's Presidential Leadership," *Journal of the Abraham Lincoln Association* 21 (2000), 31–61.

71. Basler, *Collected Works,* 8:279.

72. Stephens, *Constitutional View of the Late War Between the States,* 2:613.

73. In his account Stephens maintained that Lincoln had urged him to persuade the Georgia legislature to take the state out of the war and to ratify the Thirteenth Amendment prospectively, to take effect in five years. Stephens either misunderstood or deliberately distorted Lincoln's words. The president was too good a lawyer to suggest any such absurdity as a "prospective" ratification of a constitutional amendment. Lincoln had just played a leading part in getting Congress to pass the Thirteenth Amendment, and he was using his influence to get every Republican state legislature as well as those of Maryland, Missouri, and Tennessee to ratify it. Stephens, *Constitutional View of the Late War Between the States,* 2:611–12. See also Harris, "Hampton Roads Peace Conference," 51.

74. *Richmond Examiner,* Feb. 6, 1865; Rowland, *Jefferson Davis, Constitutionalist,* 6:465–67.

75. Basler, *Collected Works,* 8:330–31.

76. Ibid., 332–33.

77. David Dixon Porter, *Incidents and Anecdotes of the Civil War* (New York: D. Appleton and Co., 1885), 294.

78. Ibid., 295; T. Morris Chester's dispatches to the *Philadelphia Press,* in that newspaper, April 11 and 12, 1865.

79. Lincoln to Weitzel, April 6, 1865, Basler, *Collected Works,* 8:389.

80. For documentation of this matter, see ibid., 386–89, 405–8.

81. Ibid., 399–405.

82. "Impeachment of the President," 40th Cong., 1st sess., 1867, H. Rep. 7, 674, quoted in William Hanchett, *The Lincoln Murder Conspiracies* (Urbana, Ill.: University of Illinois Press, 1983). A similar version is quoted in Michael W. Kauffman, *American Brutus: John Wilkes Booth and the Lincoln Conspiracies* (New York: Random House, 2004), 210.

EPILOGUE

1. Roy P. Basler, ed., *The Collected Works of Abraham Lincoln,* 9 vols. (New Brunswick, N.J.: Rutgers University Press, 1953–55), 5:421; Michael Burlingame and John R. Turner Ettlinger, eds., *Inside Lincoln's White House: The Complete Civil War Diary*

of John Hay (Carbondale, Ill.: Southern Illinois University Press, 1997), 217–18, entry of July 4, 1864.

2. *Ex parte Milligan,* 4 Wallace 2.

ABOUT THE AUTHOR

James M. McPherson is the George Henry Davis '86 Professor of History Emeritus at Princeton University. He is the bestselling author of numerous books on the Civil War, including *Battle Cry of Freedom,* which won the Pulitzer Prize; *For Cause and Comrades,* which won the prestigious Lincoln Prize; and *Crossroads of Freedom.*

The employees of Thorndike Press hope you have enjoyed this Large Print book. All our Thorndike, Wheeler, and Kennebec Large Print titles are designed for easy reading, and all our books are made to last. Other Thorndike Press Large Print books are available at your library, through selected bookstores, or directly from us.

For information about titles, please call:
    (800) 223-1244

or visit our Web site at:
    http://gale.cengage.com/thorndike

To share your comments, please write:
    Publisher
    Thorndike Press
    295 Kennedy Memorial Drive
    Waterville, ME 04901